I0815900

TRI-STATE
JIM THOMPSON
RoD ShoP
Dodge
RISLONE
CRAGAR
Hays
CRANE CAMS
B&M

DRAG RACING IN THE 1970s
AA 712
Revell
Wynn's
DON Snake PRUDHOMME
ARMY
PENNZOIL
VHT
SUZUKI
CarTech®

Dodge
MOTOWN MISSILE
DON CARLTON
DIAMOND
FENTON
BOB GLIDDEN
PRO 1
Winston
Plymouth
Valvoline
McLeod
MOROSO
DieHard
MSD
CRAGAR
GOODYEAR
Winston
INE
DR
BELL

Doug Boyce

CarTech®

CarTech®, Inc.
6118 Main Street
North Branch, MN 55056
Phone: 651-277-1200 or 800-551-4754
Fax: 651-277-1203
www.cartechbooks.com

Edit by Bob Wilson
Layout by Connie DeFlorin

ISBN 978-1-61325-842-2
Item No. CT699

Library of Congress Cataloging-in-Publication Data Available

Written, edited, and designed in the U.S.A.
Printed in China
10 9 8 7 6 5 4 3 2 1

PUBLISHER'S NOTE: In reporting history, the images required to tell the tale will vary greatly in quality, especially by modern photographic standards. While some images in this volume are not up to those digital standards, we have included them, as we feel they are an important element in telling the story.

Parting shot: *Engine builder Keith Black raises his arm to guide the Fueler back in its tracks. (Photo Courtesy J. R. Bloom)*

DISTRIBUTION BY:

Europe
PGUK
63 Hatton Garden
London EC1N 8LE, England
Phone: 020 7061 1980 • Fax: 020 7242 3725
www.pguk.co.uk

Australia
Renniks Publications Ltd.
3/37-39 Green Street
Banksmeadow, NSW 2109, Australia
Phone: 2 9695 7055 • Fax: 2 9695 7355
www.renniks.com

Canada
Login Canada
300 Saulteaux Crescent
Winnipeg, MB, R3J 3T2 Canada
Phone: 800 665 1148 • Fax: 800 665 0103
www.lb.ca

TABLE OF CONTENTS

ACKNOWLEDGMENTS

A project of this magnitude takes many hands to complete, so I want to give a big thank-you to the following people: Ed Aigner, Gary L. Anderson, Steve Bagwell, Grant Bittner, John Bloom, Bob Boudreau, Darren Boyce, William Bozgan, Rich Carlson, Mike Cochran, Ariel Cordero, Yoland Cormier, Bubba Corzine, Fabian Dewar, Mike Dimery, Terry Earwood, John Eichinger, Bob Frey, Derk Frizzell, Jim Glenn, Steve Goddard, Terry Gray, Ed Hamburger, James Handy, Terry Hardy, Lou Hart, Doug Hilak, Wayne Tonia Holland, Buddy Houts, Keith Hudak, Tommy Ivo, Steve Jackson, Stephen Justice, Tom Kasch, Bill Kelso, Brian Kennedy, Howard Koby, Dave Kommel, Tom Kosiara, Mike Lacelle, Roger Leister, Daniel Levesque, Bob Martin, Raymond Maurel, Don McElroy, James Morgan, Jack Muller, Bruce Nelson, Gary Parham, Allan Patterson, John Pattison, Larry Pfister, Roger Phillips, Rob Potter, Michael Pottie, Bill Pratt, Don Prieto, Ed Racis, Ken Rappaport, Steve Reyes, Robbie Robertson, Roger Rodgers, Carl Rubrecht, Robert Runne, Dale Schafer, the Schley Brothers, Bob Shaw, Tommy Shaw, Bob Sitre, F. J. Smith, Bob Snyder, Mike Sopko Sr., Jerry Stein, Arvid Svendsen, Bob Swaim, Ruth Tice, Allen Tracy, Bill Truby, Rex Turner, Todd Veney, Rick Voegelin, Todd Webber, Dan Williams, Todd Wingerter, Charlene Wood, and Bob Wytosky.

Acknowledgments must be given to the many publications and websites that I visited while researching this project: *National Dragster*, *Drag News*, *Hot Rod*, *Super Stock & Drag Illustrated*, *Car Craft*, *Popular Hot Rodding*, *Drag Racing USA*, and *Hi-Performance Cars*. In the 1970s, we flocked to the newsstands for the latest issue of these magazines. Sadly, aside from *National Dragster*, they are no longer in print.

Websites that were a big help included: Bill Pratt's draglist.com, nhra.com, competitionplus.com, hemmings.com, motortrend.com, and various social media sites.

INTRODUCTION

The 1960s was a turbulent decade. As the calendar was flipped, the 1970s were welcomed with a renewed sense of optimism. The all-consuming battle that was raging in southeast Asia seemed to be winding down, the music on the airwaves couldn't be better, and the cars never looked or performed better. Cruising the main drag on Friday nights and street racing on desolate back roads resulted in good times. They were times that some of us wished would never end.

Drag racing was in great shape with its record attendance and three sanctioning bodies to start the decade. An air of professionalism had taken ahold of the sport. The 1970s was the decade when drag racing became big business with big sponsors, big pay-outs, and big rigs.

Ingenuity, a proven strength of Americans, was alive and well. The Pro Stock class was born, and rear-engine dragsters (or "mid-engine dragsters," as some prefer) emerged. Let the difference of opinion rage. Ongoing efforts spurred improvements in safety, elapsed times (ETs), and top speeds.

This book covers every facet of drag racing in the 1970s, including how the categories evolved, advancements, and racing highlights.

CHAPTER ONE

1971: WHAT'S HAPPENING

In 1971, Gil Kirk and Jim Thompson's Rod Shop teamed up with Dodge to bring a new level of professionalism to drag racing. Jim's C/Gas Hemi Challenger competed in what was generally considered Chevy territory and won. (Photo Courtesy Bob Martin)

As the decade began, singer Marvin Gaye asked the poignant question, "What's going on?" Plenty of things were going on—some were good and some were not so good. Concerning drag racing, the sport was doing well.

In 1971, Larry Carrier created the International Hot Rod Association (IHRA). In doing so, he joined the National Hot Rod Association (NHRA) and the American Hot Rod Association (AHRA) as one of drag racing's key sanctioning bodies. Carrier got his start under NHRA President Wally Parks.

In 1965, Carrier, along with partners Carl Moore and Hal Hamrick, opened Bristol Dragway in Tennessee. After Carrier had a falling out with Wally Parks, the track switched from being sanctioned by the NHRA to being sanctioned by the AHRA in 1968. Carrier's relationship with AHRA President Jim Tice was no better than it had been with Parks, which led Carrier to part ways with Tice and form the IHRA.

Carrier adopted AHRA rules, class structure, and the AHRA's practice of "buying" seeded racers. Under the format, the top eight drivers in each pro category were guaranteed money if they competed. In 1971, the IHRA had 5 national events, the AHRA had 10, and the NHRA had 8. So, drag racing fans got their fill.

Top Fuel

The NHRA category name AA/Fuel Dragster was changed to Top Fuel in 1971, and the Gas Dragster category became Top Gas. Top Fuel was considered to be the leading category in the sport, but it had been losing ground since the mid-1960s with the advent of the Funny Car. A change was needed if the Fueler was to retain its place at the top of the sport. That change came as the new decade began and was instigated by concerns for driver safety.

Looking Back

In the early to mid-1950s, when the sport was still in its infancy, the design of Top Eliminator cars varied. Generally speaking, most dragsters were built using

Bill Hopper's Cadillac-powered rail epitomizes the appearance of the sport's first dragsters. This photo was taken in September 1954 on the last day of the Gilbert Drags in Arizona. (Photo Courtesy J. R. Bloom)

original equipment manufacturer (OEM) frame rails—hence, the nickname "rail jobs." The average car had a front-mounted, overhead-valve V-8 or flathead, and the driver was positioned over the top of the rear axle. The slingshot-style dragster that placed the driver behind the rear axle took hold of the sport in 1955. Mickey Thompson was credited with the design. With the driver behind the rear axle, it placed a greater amount of weight on the rear to help the primitive slicks of the day grip the equally primitive tracks.

The slingshot went through several changes through 1970. A few areas that wreaked havoc with the front-engine dragster included an increasing number of clutch and blower explosions that helped expedite its demise. By design, clutches would slip to aid in getting the power to the ground. Due to the excessive amount of heat generated by the slippage, clutches disintegrated and caused grave bodily injury. Likewise, blowers were overloaded and overworked, which led to explosions that sprayed flaming fuel onto the driver. It was time for change.

Looking Forward

Although racers had toyed with rear- and or mid-engine designs from when the sport began, it wasn't until guys (such as Bernie Schacker) had success with the configuration that others began to take a more serious look. Although Schacker's self-made rear-engine car found success and

New York's Bernie Schacker rarely receives credit for his part in advancing Top Fuel. In 1970, Bernie fabricated the 215-inch-wheelbase chassis, which supported a 392 Hemi. (Photo Courtesy Ken Rappaport)

Clint Brown in the Brown and Stigsell *Fueler (seen here in 1964) is indicative of the general appearance of a Fueler through the 1960s. The lack of a quality clutch and the lack of quality tires generated lots of smoke and little traction. (Photo Courtesy J. R. Bloom)*

Early passes on Swamp Rat 14 were made without the full body. In April, a rear wing was added to plant the car and allow "Big Daddy" Don Garlits to pick up a few tenths of a second. Garlits held the class record at the end of the 1971 season with a 6.26 ET. (Photo Courtesy Michael Pottie)

Dwane Ong and his Pawnbroker went down in history as the first rear-engine Top Fueler to win a national event after it won class at the 1970 AHRA Summer Nationals. (Photo Courtesy Bob Snyder)

has been recognized as being the first into the 6s, Woody Gilmore and Pat Foster can take credit for building the first modern rear-engine Fuel Dragster to win a national event.

In 1969, after watching John Mulligan's fatal clutch explosion at the NHRA Nationals, Gilmore and Foster were determined to not see it happen again. In December 1969, they tested their first rear-engine car. The dragster crashed during initial testing at Lions Bay, taking flight at approximately 200 mph. Undeterred, the pair worked on a second car while driver Pat Foster recovered from injuries that he suffered from the crash. Gilmore and Foster determined that the cause of the accident was quick steering, and a lower ratio cured the issue.

Their new car featured a 223-inch wheelbase and was raced by Dwane Ong. In February 1970, Ong debuted the car at Orange County, where he posted a best ET of 6.93 at 214 mph. In August, Ong won the AHRA Summer Nationals in Long Island, New York, and became the first racer to win a national event in a modern, rear-engine Fueler. In the final round, Ong defeated Fred Ahrberg's conventional dragster with a 6.82 ET at 217.39 mph to a 6.85 at 221.21.

Garlits Solidifies the Future

After Don Garlits experienced a violent transmission explosion at Lions Drag Strip on March 8, 1970, which literally blew his *Swamp Rat 13* in half and annihilated

Top Gas

Despite an assurance from the NHRA in 1970 that Top Gas would be around for years to come, the sanctioning body dropped the class at the end of 1971 and merged it with Comp Eliminator.

Top Gas was born in 1963, when the NHRA welcomed back nitromethane-powered dragsters. According to the NHRA, the reason for the category's demise was a lack of participation. By 1971, diversity in the class was all but gone, as everyone who was anyone campaigned a twin-engine car. The final world champion was Austin Myers in his twin Hemi car.

John Peters campaigned his twin-engine **Freight Train** *rails (three in total) from 1959 through 1971. The* **Freight Train** *cars had been powered by small-block Chevy engines until 1970, when Peters joined forces with Walt Rhodes and they switched to twin Hemis. Rhodes drove the car to a Gatornationals win in 1971. When Top Gas was dropped, Peters retired the winningest car in class history. (Photo Courtesy Michael Pottie)*

You couldn't tell Bill Schultz, owner of the **Schultz & Glenn** *Top Fuel dragster, that the front-engine design was dead. Driver Gerry Glenn defeated Don Garlits at the NHRA World Finals in 1971. (Photo Courtesy Rich Carlson/Grant Bittner Collection)*

part of his right foot, he began to design his own rear-engine car.

The build took months of planning and four weeks of construction. On December 27, 1970, Garlits made the first trial runs in the rear-engine dragster at the Sunshine Drag Strip in St. Petersburg, Florida. The *Swamp Rat 14* was built with a 215-inch wheelbase and weighed 1,250 pounds, and Garlits rectified the initial handling issues by slowing down the steering. By the end of the day, Garlits held the new track record with a 6.81 ET at 220.04 mph. Garlits's first national event with the new

Ed Donovan based his aluminum Hemi block on the early Chrysler 392 block (as opposed to the 426) because it was better suited for the rigors of drag racing. This resulted in a weight reduction of 100 pounds.

cars was on January 10, 1971, at Lions Drag Strip, where he was runner-up to Gary Cochran at the AHRA Grand American race. In February 1971, Garlits headed to Pomona, where he won the NHRA Winternationals. Then, in March 1971, he won the U.S. Fuel and Gas Championship.

Holding Out

While Garlits's success had all but spelled the end of the front-engine Top Fuel dragster, several holdouts remained. One of the holdouts was the team of Bill Schultz and Gerry "the Hunter" Glenn. Their front-engine dragster differed drastically from any front-engine car that came before it. Don Tuttle's California Chassis Engineering fabricated the Bill Schultz–designed, 230-inch-wheelbase chassis that placed the engine significantly ahead of where it was usually placed. When the car debuted in 1971 at Lions Drag Strip, Glenn stunned the spectators by running back-to-back record-setting 6.41 ETs.

At the season-ending 1971 World Finals, Garlits was ready to take his place as a dual world champion, having already been crowned the AHRA Top Fuel champ. Glenn had other ideas. Garlits was able to choose his lane due to his previous-round low ET of 6.60. If it wasn't for that nasty red-light, history may have recorded different results. Glenn took the win and the last NHRA Top Fuel Championship for a front-engine dragster with a 6.59 ET.

John Wiebe was the first to make use of the aluminum Donovan block, which was mounted in a Woody Gilmore chassis. Wiebe was the AHRA Top Fuel World Champion in 1970, 1975, and 1976. (Photo Courtesy Michael Pottie)

Chassis builder Roy Fjastad took the wedge shape to the extreme. Bill Tidwell set the national speed record in the car in July 1972 at Lions Drag Strip at 239.64 mph. (Photo Courtesy Don Prieto)

New Block

Ed Donovan can take credit for producing the first aftermarket engine block for the Top Fuel and Funny Car categories. The time was right, as increasing power levels due to increased fuel and blower boost showed the fragility of the OEM blocks.

The Donovan block was a godsend. To ease costs, the design was close to Chrysler's early 392 Hemi and shared many parts, including the crank and valvetrain. The block weighed 125 pounds and featured chromoly cylinder sleeves, improved oiling, and a beefed-up valley and bottom end. The engine was 417 ci and featured a 4.125-inch bore. Unlike the 392 or 426 Hemis (or any other engine used in Fuel cars up to this point), the Donovan block could be maintained on the road. There was no reason why a racer needed access to a machine shop to make repairs.

On November 19, the Donovan block, nestled in the engine bay of John Wiebe's Top Fueler, debuted at the NHRA Supernationals. The engine proved its worth by covering the 32-car field with a best ET of 6.53. A red-light in the final against Hank Johnson marred the engine's debut.

The success of the Donovan block opened the door to other aftermarket blocks. The aluminum Keith Black 426 block and Milodon's (Milo Franklin and Don

The Burn Down

A memorable front-engine versus rear-engine Top Fuel showdown occurred in 1971 during the final round at Indy. It was a starting-line duel between Steve Carbone's front-engine car and Don Garlits's rear-engine car. Each racer refused to stage his car before the other.

Commonly referred to as a "burn down," this one is still discussed today. The burn down is usually instigated by the slower car hoping to gain an advantage, as it has nothing to lose. Such was the case here, as Carbone's best ET of 6.39 lagged behind Garlits's string of 6.20s. The waiting game can lead to the engines overheating and frayed nerves. However, the spectators loved it and were usually on their feet cheering.

In Garlits's book *Big Daddy*, he described Carbone winning the coin toss to be able to choose his lane, and how he (Garlits) offered to toss a coin to see who stages first. Carbone refused and stated that they didn't need to do so because Garlits was going to stage first. Of course, no one was going to tell Garlits what to do. After each car completed its burnouts, they each pre-staged, and there they sat for 2 minutes–each one waiting for the other to stage. Finally, Garlits's crew chief, T. C. Lemons waved Garlits forward, and Carbone followed immediately.

Carbone's ploy worked, as Garlits, having built up too much heat, smoked the tires off the line. Carbone was gone and won the race with a 6.48 to Garlits's 6.65. Carbone stated afterward that Garlits played right into his hands. Carbone kept his cool by adding extra water to his block prior to the run.

Steve Carbone continued racing his front-engine dragster through 1971. He didn't have a reason to switch because the 426-ci Don Long-chassis car kept winning. (Photo Courtesy Michael Pottie)

Alderson) aluminum VII Liter Hemi block followed. Rodeck and Arias gave Chevy racers hope when each company introduced aluminum Hemi-headed Chevy blocks later in the decade. Although these aftermarket blocks were not cheap (prices were up to $2,500), they proved to be well worth the investment.

The Shape of Things to Come

As with the earliest days of the sport, racers in the 1970s looked for ways to use the wind to their advantage. Although changes were made well into the 2000s (wheel size, driver canopies, and spoiler angle and height) in the name of aerodynamics as safety, the 1970s would be the final decade before imagination was stymied under ever-tightening rules.

One of the more unusual aerodynamic designs was Roy Fjastad's Speed Process Engineering (SPE) hexagon-shaped wedge. Looking more like a doorstop than a conventional dragster, the car featured a Tom Hanna–formed aluminum body over a 180-inch chassis that housed a Keith Black 470-ci Hemi.

Vince Rossi and Tommy Lisa purchased the car, and Bill Tidwell, Danny Ongais, and Jack Martin each spent time in the driver's seat. According to Rossi's son Jim, the wedge was the first Top Fueler with ETs in the 5s. In 1972, Bill Tidwell reportedly posted a 5.99 ET at Lions Drag Strip, but Track Manager Steve Evans refused to recognize the time. At the 1972 Supernationals, the wedge made the record books when Ongais ran a top speed of 243.24 mph.

Rossi and Lisa ran the wedge into 1974 before turning their attention to a conventional rear-engine dragster. The wedge was sold to Harry Nunn in Texas, and it passed through a few more hands before it disappeared. As history showed, this was not the shape of things to come.

Twig Zeigler is a Northwest drag-racing legend. His rags-to-riches story began in the 1960s with racing and assisting numerous other teams. In 1970, he took the chassis of the burnt-up Whipple and McCulloch car and competed with it in the Funny Car category. (Photo Courtesy J. R. Bloom)

Funny Car

The Funny Car class evolved from the match-race Stockers of the early 1960s. These cars, when compared to dragsters, were relatable for fans, which made them an instant favorite. Mercury was given credit for introducing the first flip-up, full-tube-chassis Funny Car in 1966, when it unveiled four single overhead cam–powered fiberglass Comets.

Although the basic layout has remained constant, the chassis design evolved in the following years, wheelbases grew, and bodies became more aerodynamic. Entering 1970, the narrow, almost dragster-style chassis was introduced. In 1971, the NHRA rules set the minimum body width at 66 inches and allowed a top chop of 2 inches. The wheelbase had to fall between 100 and 125 inches, and the body length could be no more than 10 percent of the stock, Detroit-produced car that was being mimicked.

Additional rules revisions required fire-suppression systems on all cars after Gas Ronda nearly lost his life in a Funny Car fire at the 1970 AHRA Winter Nationals. A redesign of the latch that held the flip-up bodies in place was required. This may have stemmed from when the *Ramchargers* Dodge Challenger burned to the ground in 1970 after crews were unable to reach the latch located

The Lenco 2-Speed

By the early 1970s, the Fuel guys had caught on to Leonard Abbott's Lenco Shur-Shift planetary transmission. The Lenco, initially an underdrive transmission, made its debut in 1969 at the US Nationals and helped Don Prudhomme win Top Fuel.

The Lenco is a semi-automatic transmission. It uses a clutch only to engage first gear or the optional reverse gear. Once the car is in motion, gear changes are made without engaging the clutch. As used by the Fuel cars, the Lenco has two separate housings. When the shift is made, the lever moves the clutch pack together to engage the gear in each housing. This transmission, which cost about $2,000 (at the time), was said to reduce ETs by 2/10 of a second.

on the underside of the body. Little else changed as the decade began, but the racers always put forth the effort to make advancements.

Mickey Thompson was never short on ideas or sponsors. This is proven by his titanium Pinto. Pat Foster welded the lighter-than-steel chassis, and Dale Pulde drove the car. (Photo Courtesy J. R. Bloom)

Thompson's Idea

You could always count on the innovative Mickey Thompson to come up with something different. After his experimental monocoque Mustang in 1970 that went nowhere, Thompson had Woody Gilmore weld up a titanium chassis for his 1971 Pinto Funny Car. Welding titanium is tricky and expensive. The chassis was said to have cost more than $6,000. This was a massive amount of money when compared to a conventional chromoly chassis, which cost less than half the amount (at the time). The total weight of Thompson's Pinto was said to be more than 1,700 pounds—68 pounds of which were comprised of the chassis.

Initially, the Pinto was powered by a Boss 429 (Ford's answer to the Chrysler Hemi) and backed by a Crowerglide clutch and a titanium 2-speed rear differential. Whether the rear end survived is unknown. In 1971, driver Dale Pulde won the AHRA World Finals with that combination and defeated Ron O'Donnell in his *Damn Yankee* Plymouth with a 6.84 ET. After switching from the 429 to a Chrysler Hemi at the end of the season, Pulde won class at the 1972 AHRA Winter Nationals with a solo 6.88 ET at 205 mph. With Ford support gone, Thompson retired the Pinto in the summer of 1972.

Engine Experimenting

Thompson, in conjunction with Keane Engineering, wanted to do away with the horsepower-robbing GMC blower by developing a compressed-air Boss 429. This was an idea that Thompson began experimenting with in 1968 and 1969 with a small-block Chevy-powered dragster.

Thompson's setup forced air into the engine from four self-contained underwater breathing apparatus (SCUBA) tanks that were pressurized to 2,000 psi. By the time that it reached the engine, the pressure dropped to 35 psi for a cooler and more dense air charge. The setup was said to produce 2,700 hp at a time when conventional blown cars produced about 1,800 hp. However, due to ongoing development issues and the NHRA shunning the compressed-air tanks, the project was shelved.

One of Mickey Thompson's many ideas was this compressed-air, Hemi-powered Funny Car. The experiment made the power but was doomed from the beginning because the NHRA didn't allow the use of compressed-air tanks. (Photo Courtesy Rich Carlson/Grant Bittner Collection)

Turbo Test

Gene Snow, with a hand from Hilborn, also experimented with various induction systems, as did Romeo Palamides. Palamides's career dates back to the mid-1950s, when he began building dragster chassis. Although Snow's turbo car never made it beyond trial runs, Palamides ran his twin-turbo Dodge Challenger at several events. Driver Raymond Maurel stated that they saw no success with the setup before Palamides switched to a GMC blower.

"The car had a Crower-glide, and you couldn't spool up," Maurel said. "If you gave it any throttle, the clutch would engage automatically. We couldn't get the car to ET, but from the eighth mile onward, it was just a beast. It would run near 200 mph with the turbos."

Driver Raymond Maurel recalled racing this twin-turbocharged Challenger four times. He hit a guardrail while racing in Kentucky and broke the front end, and that was the end of the Challenger. (Photo Courtesy Raymond Maurel)

The Romeo Palamides-built car featured twin Switzer turbos. Palamides was involved with many endeavors—from dragsters, Funny Cars, and jet chassis to forming American Racing. (Photo Courtesy Raymond Maurel)

Gene Snow toyed with the idea of ditching the Roots blower. The injected twin-turbo setup was designed and built by Hilborn. Mounted on an alcohol-fed Keith Black Hemi, the Charger recorded 7-second ETs before it was retired. (Photo Courtesy Lou Hart)

Popular Funny Car pilot Dick Harrell tragically lost his life in September 1971 while racing up in Canada. Harrell was well known for his Chevy Funny Cars, doorslammers, and line of production super cars. To some, the sport was never the same after his passing. (Photo Courtesy J. R. Bloom)

The Ramchargers team consisted of several Chrysler engineers. They, along with the Mopar Missile team, were at the forefront of parts development, including 16-plug cylinder heads, high-volume oil pumps, and improvements in fuel delivery. (Photo Courtesy Michael Pottie)

One of the most successful Funny Cars of the early 1970s was the Richard Tharp-driven Blue Max *of Harry Schmidt. The pair drove the wheels off the Ramchargers Hemi-powered Mustang and won several national events and match races. (Photo Courtesy Ed Aigner)*

Don Prudhomme's cars carried only the best equipment. His 'Cuda featured a 118-inch John Buttera chassis and a stroked Keith Black Hemi. A new type of fuel pump overdrive helped produce record mid-6-second ETs. A spectacular top-end fire at Seattle in April destroyed this body. (Photo Courtesy J. R. Bloom)

Convention Wins Out

At the end of the 1971 season, convention won out. Gene Snow accumulated enough points with his Dodge Charger to win the AHRA world title. Phil Castronovo, in his Dodge Charger, won the NHRA crown when Jake Johnston in Gene Snow's number-two car broke. Although the IHRA didn't crown world champions until 1974, the 1971 World Finals saw Richard Tharp in the *Blue Max* Mustang defeat Kelly Chadwick's Chevy-powered Camaro in the category final.

The Cost to Play

By the time that the 1970s rolled around, the cost of racing the pro classes had become prohibitive. Those without deep pockets or sponsorship were fading fast. Serious sponsor money entered the sport of drag racing for the first time when Tom McEwen and Don Prudhomme signed a deal with Hot Wheels. This opened the floodgates, as racers went hunting for big sponsorship deals.

The McEwen-Prudhomme Hot Wheels deal ran from 1970 through 1972 and initially featured the pair campaigning a Top Fuel dragster and a Funny Car. The deal

Prudhomme Makes History

In May 1970, when Don Prudhomme won Funny Car at the AHRA Grand American race at Frontier Dragway in Oklahoma, he became the first person to win a national event in Top Fuel and Funny Car. Prudhomme had previously won Top Fuel in 1966 and 1968 at AHRA national events and in 1966, 1969, and 1970 at NHRA events.

came together partially due to leg work by McEwen. It helped that his mother worked as a secretary for Mattel (the parent company of Hot Wheels) and his stepfather was an attorney for the company. This, no doubt, gained him an audience with Art Spear, the company's vice president. In the end, the deal reportedly pocketed the pair a quarter million dollars, which was an unheard of sum of money at the time in the world of drag racing.

Pro Stock

The United Drag Racer's Association (UDRA) and AHRA had been running a heads-up, no breakout Super Stock class since 1967 and 1968, respectively, and fans loved it. The NHRA finally got with the program in 1970, when it introduced the Pro Super Stock category, which was renamed Pro Stock in 1971. The rules were simple. Entries were required to be American-made vehicles (1967 and newer), have a minimum wheelbase of 97 inches and a minimum weight of 2,700 pounds, and use any engine produced by the same manufacturer of the chosen car. The rulebook did not list a maximum allowable engine displacement, but dating to the early 1960s, the Stock (Stock, Top Stock, and Factory Experimental) category of cars could run no more than 430 ci.

Small-Block Pro Stocks

In 1971, the first of the soon-to-be-feared 351 Cleveland-powered Pro Stocks appeared. Ed Terry and Dick Loehr of the Ford Drag Team each campaigned factory-backed Cleveland-powered Mavericks.

Bob Swaim, the director of Ford's Drag Team, saw the possibilities when the NHRA reduced its minimum weight rule of the 7-pounds-per-cubic-inch class from 2,700 pounds to 2,400 pounds. With horsepower in the high 500s for the Cleveland, Swaim felt that the combination could battle head-to-head with an approximately 3,000-pound Hemi Mopar that produced about 700 hp. Although expectations fell short, the high-9-second/low-10-second ETs showed that he was on the right track.

Despite no longer being a factory-supported racer, Bill Ireland competed in Pro Stock with this 351-powered Maverick. Times were changing, and drag racing was no longer a priority for Ford, which curtailed its racing activities by April 1971. (Photo Courtesy Rich Carlson/Grant Bittner)

Grumpy's Toy VIII ***debuted in mid-1970 and carried Cragar's first set of spun aluminum wheels. This style of wheel became standard through the 1970s for all categories of racing. (Photo Courtesy Carl Rubrecht)***

Pro Stock quickly took on more of a "Pro" than "Stock" flavor, as those with funding or factory support built cars with acid-dipped bodies and one-off parts. Chevy supplied Bill "Grumpy" Jenkins with parts, cars, and the 430-ci Can-Am engine that he used to win the first two national events of the 1970 season. Ford had its drag team, and "Dyno" Don received parts. Chrysler couldn't lose, as the Ramchargers and Motown Missile teams were staffed by its own employees, who designed and tested one-off parts specifically for its racers.

Sox & Martin

The team of Sox & Martin (the sweethearts of Chrysler Corporation) dominated the 1970 and 1971 seasons. With Ronnie Sox (arguably the best 4-speed racer of the day) driving the team's Plymouth 'Cuda, Jake King building the engines, and Buddy Martin spearheading the operation, the competition didn't stand a chance. The twin-plug Hemi mounted first a "rat's nest" intake manifold and then an independent-runner intake. The newly developed Weiand tunnel ram and Holley's recently released 4500-series Dominator carburetors increased the Hemi's power. ETs quickly dropped from 9.90s during the 1970 season to 9.60s in 1971. Sox & Martin won the NHRA and AHRA world championships in 1970, while Mike Fons and his Dodge Challenger won the NHRA title in 1971.

A poor decision by Chrysler cost itself the AHRA world title in 1971, which was won by the Camaro of Jim Hayter. When the sanctioning body introduced weight breaks in April (7 pounds per cubic inch for the Hemi cars versus 6.75 pounds per cubic inch for everyone else), the

As the decade began, the team of Sox & Martin fielded two cars and placed Herb "Mr. 4-Speed" McCandless at the wheel of the second car. Here, at the 1971 NHRA World Finals, Ronnie Sox (near lane) competes against Butch "the California Flash" Leal. (Photo Courtesy Rich Carlson/ Grant Bittner Collection)

A Ted Spehar-built, twin-plug Hemi engine powered the Motown Missile, *and it initially used a Clutchflite transmission. The* Motown Missile *set NHRA's first Pro Stock ET record at 9.95 seconds. (Photo Courtesy Michael Pottie)*

manufacturer made the decision to boycott AHRA races. In total, Chrysler cars won four AHRA-series events. Chrysler would have won many more if it hadn't backed out.

Battling Chrysler

The Chevys, Fords, and American Motors Corporation (AMC) products never stood a chance against the Mopar onslaught. Chevy had its diehards, including Bill "Grumpy" Jenkins, Dave Strickler, Wally Booth, etc., running punched-out 427s of cast-iron or aluminum that measured 430 ci. However, those canted-valve big-block Chevys didn't breathe as well as the Hemis. After Jenkins won the 1970 NHRA Winternationals and Gatornationals, the well ran dry. In legal class competition, the Chevys lagged at least a tenth of a second behind the Chryslers through 1971.

For a while, Booth had the quickest Pro Stock Chevy in the nation, when his second-generation Camaro ran a 9.53 ET at 143.78 mph at Milan Dragway. It took the help of a stout Chrysler A-833 transmission, a Dana 60 rear end, and Chrysler Super Stock springs to do the job. Booth's Camaro lasted about six months before he was wooed by AMC to run a Pro Stock Gremlin in 1972.

Ford was in a similar situation as Chevy. Its SOHC 427 was capable of creating power alongside the Hemi but not as consistently. The 1969 Boss 429 was underdeveloped, and it took until 1980 before it proved to be a winner. "Dyno" Don Nicholson was one of the few bright

When it came to building winning Chevys, Bill "Grumpy" Jenkins (near lane) was considered to be one of the best. Here, at Indy, he faces Dave Strickler, who is driving Grumpy's Toy VIII. *The 1970 and 1971 seasons were uphill battles for Jenkins and Strickler. (Photo Courtesy Brian Kennedy)*

In 1971, Wally Booth debuted his second-generation Camaro at Indy, and it survived until the third round of eliminations. Booth campaigned the Camaro through the end of the season before he signed on with AMC to lead its emerging Pro Stock program. (Photo Courtesy Michael Pottie)

"Dyno" Don Nicholson began the new decade in an SOHC 427–powered Maverick. He won the AHRA Pro Stock Championship in 1972, the IHRA Championship in 1975, and the NHRA Championship in 1977. (Photo Courtesy Rich Carlson/Grant Bittner Collection)

In 1971, AMC Pro Stock was represented by H. L. and Shirley Shahan, who campaigned a Gremlin and a pair of Hornets. Shirley managed a best ET of 9.89 from her 366-ci Hornet, which is seen here at Ontario. Unable to get the factory AMC support that they desired, the pair retired at the end of 1971. (Photo Courtesy Rich Carlson/Grant Bittner)

lights in the Ford camp. For a while in 1970, Nicholson held both ends of the NHRA class record with a 9.81 ET at 139.31 mph. Nicholson broke Sox & Martin's hold on the category when he won the 1971 NHRA Summernationals. Nicholson defeated the Dodge Challenger of Mike Fons in the final round with a 9.63 ET. By the end of the season, the class ET record of 9.52 was held by Sox & Martin. Butch Leal held the top-speed record at 144.92 mph.

Comp Eliminator

To start the new decade, NHRA Comp Eliminator encompassed the following classes: A/Fuel Dragster; BB and A/Gas Dragster; AA and A/Competition; AA and A/Fuel Altered; A/Funny Car; AA and A/Altered; and AA, BB, and CC/Gas Supercharged. As with other categories, Comp ran off a handicap system to equal the field. Just like other categories, classes came and went as the decade progressed.

Illinois resident Tom Trisch, driving his Hemi-powered AA/A Bantam, was the Comp world champion in 1971. Coming off a category win at Indy, Trisch's record holder (8.15 ET) defeated the C/Dragster of Bob Amos with an 8.43 ET to earn the world title. Patience paid off for Trisch, who returned to

Grand Touring: The Poor Man's Pro Stock

The AHRA had a great idea in 1970, when it introduced the Grand Touring category. It was meant to be a category that consisted of three heads-up, no breakout classes. The rules were simple: no cars older than 1967, an OEM interior, and a steel body (with the exception of a fiberglass hood). First-year rules dictated the use of a single 4-barrel carburetor. Any intake manifold could be used, except for tunnel rams. Engine blocks could be bored 0.060 over, head work was allowed, and any camshaft was allowed. Harnessing the power were any tires that fit the stock wheel wells.

Fans and racers loved the racing, but it became a one-car show, as Chevy's Camaro quickly dominated action in all three classes. In 1971, the AHRA reduced the category to two classes. In 1972, the category disappeared altogether.

An exception to a category that was dominated by Camaros was this G-D Hemi Challenger, which is sponsored by Bill Breck Dodge in Colorado Springs. (Photo Courtesy J. R. Bloom)

Tom Trisch was the 1971 NHRA Comp Eliminator World Champion in his AA/A Bantam. Here, Trisch faces Dallas Schneider at the 1971 NHRA Division 5 World Championship Series (WCS) meet in Omaha, Nebraska. (Photo Courtesy Tommy Shaw)

Indy in 1981 to win Comp once again in the Barlow, Trisch, & Watson AA/Altered.

Modified Eliminator

The NHRA's Modified Eliminator category debuted in 1970. The category initially consisted of 30 classes: Gas Dragsters (B/D through E/D), Altereds (B/A through F/A), Gassers (A/G through J/G), Street Roadsters (A/SR through C/SR), and Modified Production (A/MP through H/MP). With such a variety of classes, handicap starts (based on national records) could range up to 5 seconds.

The first Modified world champion was Division 4 Points Champion Car-

Carroll Caudle raced his '55 Chevy in the C/MP through G/MP classes with small-blocks that he built by boring, stroking, and de-stroking. In 1970, his world title went along with a Division 4 championship, which he won numerous times through his career.

roll Caudle and his 310-ci F/MP (12 to 12.99 pounds per cubic inch) '55 Chevy. Caudle toyed with several small-blocks of various bores and strokes and de-stroked displacements to fit a number of classes. In a pounds-per-cubic-inch category, the fewer cubic inches, the less weight that a car had to carry. Years of experimentation has shown that the small-block Chevy loses little horsepower when it is de-stroked within reason. At the World Finals, Caudle defeated the red-lighting B/Dragster of Dave Armbruster with a record-setting 11.83 ET.

Class Standouts

As the decade began, the Modified Production and Gas classes were categories loved by those who had a thing for high-revving small-blocks, wheels-up launches, and banging 4-speeds. Chevys and Chevy-powered cars were dominant. One car that drew the attention of the masses was the Chevy-powered Ford Maverick of Bobby Cross, David Reher, and Buddy Morrison.

Reher and Morrison, the terrors of 1980s Pro Stock, first joined forces in 1971, when they formed Reher-Morrison Racing Engines in Mansfield, Texas. The team made use of various displacement small-blocks in the Maverick (down to 292 ci). A tremendous off-the-line start was made possible by a 2.56-first-gear Muncie and a 6.17-gear Chevy 12-bolt rear end.

The guys ran the Maverick in multiple Gas and Modified Production classes until the hybrid engine body combinations were banned from Modified Production in 1974. It forced a permanent move to Gas. Lee Shepherd, who had been driving a Modified Production Chevy II station wagon for Morrison, hopped in the Maverick when Bobby Cross took a hiatus in 1972.

Head Games

Slicing V-8 cylinder heads to use on 6-cylinder engines was an idea that first brought racing teams success in the late 1960s. In late 1967, the team of Wes Rydell, Ralph Hope, and Wayne Lang was one of the first to do so on its Chevy 6-cylinder-powered *Mr. Crude Anglia*. By 1971, the better-breathing, fabricated heads were all the rage in the lower Modified classes. Rydell, Hope, and Lang; Kay Sissell; and AHRA World Champion Joe Williamson also earned record results running fabricated heads.

The first step to fabricate these heads was to cut the end chamber from each head. The remaining six chambers were heated in a furnace, removed, wrapped in an asbestos blanket (to retain the heat), and welded together. It was a time-consuming process, but it was worth the effort.

For the Chevys, this worked because the bore spacing on the 6-cylinder and V-8 engines was nearly identical. Wrapping up the package was modified Crower injection or

Wheels-in-the-air launches for the Cross, Reher, & Morrison Maverick were possible due to the engine revving at 9,000-plus rpm, a 40-pound flywheel, and 6.17 rear gears. The Cross, Reher, & Morrison Maverick's best ETs were in the 10.30s. (Photo Courtesy Tommy Shaw)

A lower-class standout was the Preparation H *Maverick of Bruce Sizemore, which was built specifically for the H/MP class. The class was reserved for cars powered by a flathead V-8, a straight-8, or a 6-cylinder engine. In 1971, Bruce ran a reworked 300-ci 6-cylinder that was capable of high-11-second ETs. Bruce fabricated his own intake manifold and used three Weber 48-mm carburetors for induction. (Photo Courtesy Bob Martin)*

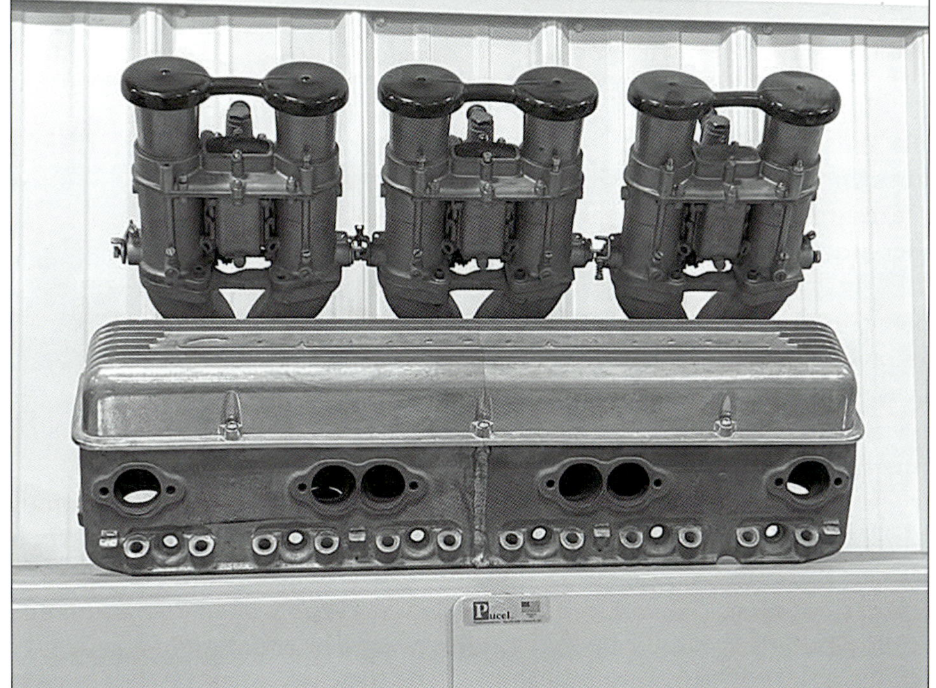

Slicing V-8 cylinder heads to fit a 6-cylinder engine proved that if there's a will, there's a way. This fabricated Chevy head has Weber carburetors.

Hilborn injection, fabricated side covers, and fabricated rocker covers. Some Ford racers did the same with Cleveland heads, but more finessing was required to make it work because of the greater difference in the bore spacing.

Super Stock

The no-breakout rule showed the masses how fast an SS/A car could run. Supernationals winner Ron Mancini and his Hemi Dart could have qualified as a Pro Stocker after he recorded a 10.09 ET. Since class records weren't recognized at the invitation-only Supernationals, Mancini had to be content with his class record, a 10.21 ET that he held well into 1972.

Fabricating a head for the Ford 6-cylinder engine was more difficult than it was for the Chevy 6-cylinder engine. Joe Williamson proved that the result was worth the effort, as he recorded numerous category wins and set the E/A class record with 9.60 ETs. (Photo Courtesy Michael Pottie)

In 1970, Ray Allen and the Truppi-Kling LS-6 Chevelle walked into Mopar's stomping ground of SS/EA and won. In 1971, Allen paid the price, as Chrysler ringers knocked him out of contention. (Photo Courtesy Michael Pottie)

Chrysler Hemi cars held their own in the upper S/S classes. Albert Branham came a long way from his home in Winnipeg, Canada, to compete in the World Finals. In 1971, his SS/DA Old Trapper *Hemi 'Cuda was a 125.93-mph record holder that was capable of 10.80 ETs. (Photo Courtesy Rich Carlson/Grant Bittner Collection)*

Cobra Stomp

The 1968 Cobra Jet Mustangs, with their underrated horsepower rating, proved to be winners from Day 1. They owned Super Stock's middle classes (F, G, and H) in the stick and automatic categories through the decade. Ken McLellan, based in Friona, Texas, propelled his *Cobrastang* Mustang to the 1971 Super Stock World Championship.

The season began with Barrie Poole winning the Winternationals in an SS/H Mustang coupe that everyone said couldn't win due to having no weight on the back end. Unlike Poole's Mustang, which was built at the Sandy Elliott dealership in Chatham, Ontario, Canada, Ken's CJ was one of a half dozen factory race cars prepared by Holman-Moody-Stroppe. These initial cars were readied for a Winternationals debut in 1968. However, Ford sold the Mustangs directly to its contacted racers for $1 due to liability concerns. Ken and his brother Joe

Ken McLellan's 1969 Mustang was one of the $1 cars that Ford sold to its team members. The Cobrastang won the Super Stock World Championship in 1971. (Photo Courtesy Dale Schafer)

performed additional modifications of their own. Local painter Bob Fulks applied the multi-hued paint. The brothers put the farm equipment to use by running the Cobra Jet on their irrigation pump to break it in before tearing it down for a rebuild.

While Joe tended the 1,000-acre farm, Ken headed to regional tracks with the Mustang. In 1970, they won the Division 4 title. At the World Finals in 1971, Ken defeated Canadian Dick Panter's SS/DA Hemi 'Cuda with an 11.75 ET at 117.95 mph.

Stock

The final year for the Stock category as we knew it was 1971. In 1972, the NHRA implemented a Pure Stock format and rejected cars that were older than 1963 models. No doubt, this made Detroit's manufacturers happy, as it eliminated those bothersome Tri-Five Chevys that had dominated class action for the past decade.

Boertman Repeats

The 1971 Stock World Champion was Michigan's Dave Boertman in his Rod Shop–sponsored J/SA 1971 Dodge. In 1971, Boertman, who previously campaigned nothing but Chevys and used one to win the world championship in 1969, was convinced to join Gil Kirk's Rod Shop race team after he was made an offer that he couldn't refuse. According to Boertman, the only way that the Rod Shop was going to land a deal with Chrysler was for Kirk to sign him. Boertman learned this after the fact.

"I guess I had been a big enough pain in their butts that it was a way of eliminating me, " Boertman said.

The Michigan native made the move to Super Stock in 1972 and added three more NHRA world titles to the two that he previously won in the Stock category.

Dave Boertman said that if he hadn't joined the Rod Shop team, the Rod Shop deal with Dodge may never have happened. Here, the 1971 NHRA World Champion is shown at the Supernationals. (Photo Courtesy Rich Carlson/Grant Bittner Collection)

CHAPTER TWO

1972:

CHALLENGING TIMES

The Pratte and Burkitt Beehemoth *Charger was supplied by Chrysler. Bob Burkitt said that the car didn't meet expectations, as the acid dip made it too flimsy. (Photo Courtesy Bob Martin)*

The first time that the three sanctioning bodies ran a full schedule of national events was the 1972 season. Many independent shows also took place, including circuit races, Bakersfield, the Super Stock Nationals, and the Popular Hot Rodding meet. Finally, there was the Professional Racers Association (PRA) National Challenge, which was organized by Don Garlits and hosted by the AHRA. It was scheduled at the same time as the NHRA Nationals and threatened to set drag racing on its ear. The times were challenging, as the sport of drag racing fumbled through growing pains.

Top Fuel

In 1972, the number of front-engine cars that were still in contention dwindled dramatically. The final Top Fuel national event win by a front-engine dragster went to 23-year-old Art Marshall. Marshall earned the win at the 1972 NHRA Grandnationals driving Don Prudhomme's old *Hot Wheels* dragster. A young Jeb Allen, looking for his second national event victory in a row, faced Marshall in the final. Allen made it an easy race for Marshall when he smoked the tires and had to watch Marshall win with a 6.57 ET at 220.58 mph.

Knocking On the Door

For years, breaking into the 5s was a barrier that seemed unobtainable. The naysayers said that there was no way that a man or machine was capable of achieving that feat. However, as the 1972 season began, the Fuelers were knocking on the door, due to advancements with the rear-engine dragster and aftermarket blocks in 1971.

In January, John Wiebe and Don Prudhomme kicked off the year by recording 6.17 ETs at the AHRA Grand American race at Lions Drag Strip. Wiebe drove his Donovan front-engine car, and Prudhomme drove his Kent Fuller–built *Yellow Feather*. A few more 6.13 to 6.19 ETs were run before Jerry Ruth, the self-proclaimed king of

The ex-Don Prudhomme Hot Wheels *dragster found a home in the Northeast, as Art Marshall drove it for Van Iderstine Speed Shop. The car was the last front-engine dragster to win Top Fuel at a national event when Marshall won the 1972 Grandnationals. (Photo Courtesy Michael Pottie)*

the Northwest, stunned the crowd at the NHRA Nationals in September with a 6.07 ET.

Ruth had his eyes on a 5-second pass as he entered the final round against Gary Beck, a gentleman whose license to drive a Fueler was only three weeks old. Ruth came out on the wrong side of a staging duel with Beck. Ruth built up too much heat in his Keith Black Hemi and hazed the tires when the light finally turned green. Beck took the win with a 6.11 ET, and Ruth missed his opportunity to run the first 5-second ET.

Don Prudhomme's Kent Fuller-built Yellow Feather *weighed less than 1,300 pounds. It was innovative, but national event wins proved to be elusive. Prudhomme raced the car into 1973 before he abandoned Top Fuel to concentrate on Funny Car. (Photo Courtesy Michael Pottie)*

Jerry Ruth's 6.0 ETs were made with a Keith Black Hemi and Lenco transmission in a Don Long chassis. Ruth hoped to be the first to break into the 5s, but he missed his opportunity. (Photo Courtesy Rich Carlson/ Grant Bittner)

Clayton Harris, driving Jack McKay's New Dimension *(a mobile home company) Fueler, was the top qualifier at Indy with a 6.13 ET. The Division 2 champion repeated the 6.13 ET here, at Ontario Motor Speedway in California, before he fell in the second round. The chassis was by Bill Stebbins. Note the two-stage rear wing. This car was plumbed for nitrous use. (Photo Courtesy Michael Pottie)*

Cragar 5-Second Club

Cragar (the manufacturer of blower manifolds, blower drives, headers, and S/S and Super Trick wheels) watched the chase to the 5s with a keen eye. It created the 5-Second Club and awarded the first 16 drivers who broke the barrier with a tailored leather jacket, an emblem of the club, and a portrait of the driver. An additional portrait was placed in the halls at Cragar's headquarters.

The first member of the club was "TV" Tommy Ivo. Ivo used a 473-ci Keith Black Hemi to run a 5.97 ET on October 22, 1972, at Pennsylvania's Keystone Raceway. Although Ivo's feat received little fanfare, he had the combination to get it done. In June, at the IHRA Longhorn Nationals, he set the class record with a 6.25 ET and won the event by defeating Carl Olson in the final. At Keystone, a sticky track and cool air worked in unison with Ivo's combination of a 225-inch Gilmore chassis, a well-tuned Hemi engine, and a Lenco 2-speed transmission.

During the 1972 season, Tommy Ivo concentrated most of his efforts on match racing. His stroked Keith Black Hemi carried parts by Cragar, Jahns, and Isky, and it was topped with a Larry Bower blower. (Photo Courtesy Grant Bittner)

Mike Snively, shown here at Ontario Motor Speedway, was the first racer with an ET in the 5s. Snively grew up racing some of the finest West Coast Fuel cars, so it wasn't a surprise to many when he broke the 5-second barrier. (Photo Courtesy Michael Pottie)

The One-Tire Idea

In the early 1970s, the AHRA's George Eisenhart proposed a one-tire rule to help curb the cost of drag racing. Eisenhart applied the same logic to the round tracks that he managed in Ohio, and it worked. Not only did it cut the costs but it also helped to level the playing field between the professionals and the amateurs.

Eisenhart's proposal had categories limited to a specific tire size and brand of tire that could be used. Eisenhart took his idea to AHRA President Jim Tice, who suggested scheduling a meeting with the NHRA's Wally Parks and the IHRA's Jim Carrier. Tice felt that if Eisenhart could get everyone to agree, they'd do it.

"We had the meeting, and they all listened intently," Eisenhart said. "Then, Wally Parks spoke up. He said, 'George, I have no doubt in my mind what you're saying is correct, and it will work. But, if you remember a number of years ago, I banned nitro from drag racing, and the guy sitting next to you shoved it right up my a––. I'll never go out on a limb again.'"

That brought an abrupt end to the proposed one-tire idea.

Four weeks later at the Supernationals, Dan Borre coated the Ontario track with the VHT traction compound, and the first NHRA 5-second run was realized. Mike Snively, in "Diamond" Jim Annin's Fueler, ran a 5.97 ET in a semifinal loss to Vic Brown, who ran a 6.03 ET in the *Creitz and Dill* car. In the final, Don Moody improved upon Snively's mark with a 5.91 ET and defeated a red-lighting Brown.

The use of the traction compound allowed for tighter clutches and contributed to less breakage and quicker times. Reportedly, neither Snively or Moody ran a full load of nitro on their 5-second runs. For the first time at a national event, the complete Top Fuel field was comprised of rear-engine cars. Half of those were said to run Donovan's aluminum Hemis.

First and Lasts at the Finals

At the NHRA World Finals in Amarillo, Texas, Jim Walther became the first to win the world championship in a rear-engine car and the last to do so with an early cast-iron block. He'd been running 6.40 ETs all weekend in his Connie Swingle–chassis car, but he ran a 7.23 ET in the final when his car broke.

"I left on my opponent Clayton Harris, and somewhere out there, he broke the rear end," Walther said. "I did not know that, and I was about 800 feet out when I

Ohio's Jim Walther spent his money wisely on a Woody Gilmore chassis, Hanna body, and an early 392 engine that was prepped by Ed Pink. (Photo Courtesy Grant Bittner)

broke the input shaft and blew the clutch, taking out the left rear tire. I coasted through the lights ahead of him."

Outside of the help of two or three hands, Walther did it all himself. He built his own engines and counted on parts from Ed Pink, among others, to get the job done. He prepped his own blocks, counting on the early Hemi because it was more in line with his budget and he felt that they were stronger. A 3/8-inch stroker crank gave his Hemi 437 ci.

The Vega body was a hit with the Funny Car racers. "Lil' John" Lombardo partnered with driver Steve Plueger to campaign this Donovan-powered beauty. Plueger and Richard Conklin formed the successful S&R Race Cars company that built numerous Funny Car chassis through the years. (Photo Courtesy J. R. Bloom)

Funny Car

With all of the Funny Cars weighing a minimum of 1,800 pounds, any advantage that one car had over another boiled down to driver skill, the correct parts

Canadian Terry Capp's Wheeler Dealer *Fueler made good while looking good. Seen here at Mission Raceway, the wheel pants added style. Note the upright wing, as everyone had their own ideas regarding what worked. (Photo Courtesy Rich Carlson/Grant Bittner Collection)*

Chris "the Greek" Karamesines tried the wedge design but quickly abandoned it when no positive results were seen. The Lester Guillory skin hid an early 392 engine and a Don Garlits chassis. (Photo Courtesy James Handy)

Chasing an Aerodynamic Advantage

Front-wheel fairings, or "wheel pants" first appeared in 1972, and they were created in an attempt to improve aerodynamics.

Although it's doubtful that wheel pants contributed to how well a Fueler cut through the air, they carried a significant cool factor. However, a few accidents were blamed on the pants because some figured that when crosswinds hit while the car was at its top speed, the pants acted as a rudder and steered the car off course. The NHRA agreed with that sentiment and banned the pants in 1977.

Another attempt to improve aerodynamics during this period involved enclosing the rear section of the Fueler into a wedge-shaped shell. The wedge enclosed the engine and slicks and removed the need for a towering wing, as the wedge created its own downforce. Several racers tried the design but quickly abandoned it because it did not have the desired effect and did nothing more than add undesired weight. It ended up in drag racing's dustbin of failed ideas.

Kenney "the Action Man" Goodell was a successful Oregon-based racer. His **Wynn's Stormer** *was as tough as it was good looking. The car earned wins at the Manufacturers Meet at Orange County International Raceway (OCIR) and Seattle's Northwest National Open. Kenney briefly fielded a matching Top Fuel wedge car. (Photo Courtesy Rich Carlson/Grant Bittner Collection)*

Mart Higginbotham and car owner Mike Burkhart joined forces in 1969 to field their first Funny Car. In 1972, Higginbotham defeated Tom McEwen with the Drag-On Vega to win the AHRA Gateway Nationals.

combination, the ability to fine-tune the combination, and money. As with the Top Fuelers, the majority of leading Funny Cars were running aftermarket aluminum Hemis by 1972. Nitro loads hovered around 90 percent, and blowers were usually 35- to 40-percent overdriven. The drivetrain combinations varied. Some used direct drive, but most used the 2-speed Lenco (more often than not with a reverser) that transmitted the power to the third member, which was usually a bulletproof 9-inch Ford rear end.

Whipple and McCulloch

In the case of Art Whipple and Ed McCulloch, their *Revellution* Dodge made use of a Bernie Wadekamper–tuned 473-ci Keith Black Hemi to dominate the NHRA season. Where their drivetrain combination varied from most was their use of a Halibrand quick-change rear end. The pair debuted the Revell-sponsored Demon at the NHRA Winternationals, and McCulloch won the class by defeating Dale Pulde in Mickey Thompson's Hemi-powered Pinto.

For McCulloch, the Winternationals wasn't without incident. According to eyewitness photojournalist Steve Reyes, McCulloch got into trouble when he went to the starting line to check the track conditions. A security guard came over and said that he couldn't be out there. McCulloch ignored him, and the guard became angry and began shouting at McCulloch. McCulloch tried to explain who he was and why he was there. By that point, two more security guards showed up to help remove him. A brawl ensued, and McCulloch punched out two of the three guards. It took six guards to subdue him before he was hauled off to jail. The next morning, he was back at the track with a group of police officers watching his every move.

Whipple and McCulloch split after the Winternationals win, but that failed to slow McCulloch, as he went on to earn wins at the Gatornationals, Bakersfield, and the Springnationals. In addition, he repeated his 1971 win at Indy. Due to the unorthodox way that the NHRA crowned its world champions at the time, a driver had to earn enough points through the season to make the top five in their respected division to earn an invite to the World Finals. Once there, a competitor had to battle through a 32-car field. The last man standing was crowned the world champion. Although McCulloch dominated Funny Car action throughout the season, at the World Finals, he fell in the semifinals and watched as Larry Fullerton won the title.

Ed McCulloch's 118-inch-wheelbase Demon hides a Woody Gilmore (Race Car Engineering) chassis. A Crower fuel pump fed a 90-plus-percent load of nitro to the Donovan blower that ran 30-percent overdrive. McCulloch enjoyed Revell sponsorship through 1977. (Photo Courtesy Rich Carlson/Grant Bittner)

The 1972 NHRA World Champion team of Kevin Doheny and Larry Fullerton used a 488-ci Ed Pink Hemi and a Lenco 2-speed transmission to realize 6.40 ETs. The 116-inch-wheelbase chassis was built by John Buttera. (Photo Courtesy Ed Aigner)

Dunn and Reath

Influenced by the success of the rear-engine dragster, a few Funny Car teams gave it a try, including the team of Jim Dunn and Joe Reath. Their mid-engine Plymouth 'Cuda was bestowed with the Best Engineered Car award at the 1972 NHRA Winternationals. It became the first and only rear-engine Funny Car to win a national event when Dunn took honors at the season-ending Supernationals.

The 'Cuda featured a Woody Gilmore Race Car Engineering 125-inch wheelbase chassis and a Don Kirby body that tilted skyward at either end. The early Hemi, which was built by Reath Automotive, was increased to 425-ci and ran power directly to a Halibrand quick-change rear end, which usually housed a 4.52 gearset.

In the Funny Car Final at the Supernationals, Dunn defeated a red-lighting Pat Foster, who was driving Barry Setzer's Vega. Foster, with Larry Wagner wrenching on the Ed Pink Hemi, previously laid down the low ET for the Funny Cars with an astounding 6.29.

Although Dunn had success with the 'Cuda, he retired the car in 1973 after running a best ET of 6.44. Hoping for greater success, he and Reath debuted a conventional front-engine Plymouth Satellite in 1974.

Fireman Jim Dunn earned a win at the 1972 Supernationals. The Barracuda featured a 125-inch Woody Gilmore chassis. (Photo Courtesy Michael Pottie)

Jim Dunn made the Funny Car's rear engine work. The body tilted at each end, but it was sometimes just easier to remove the body for maintenance. (Photo Courtesy Michael Pottie)

Jim Dunn toyed with the idea of running Top Fuel by placing this slippery Doug Kruse body over his Funny Car chassis. The best showing for the Top Fueler was a third-round finish at the 1973 PDA Meet at Orange County International Raceway. Its best ETs were in the 6.40s. (Photo Courtesy Steve Reyes)

Bruce Walker drove the Barry Setzer *Pro Stock Camaro. Booth-Arons Racing Enterprises took over building the big-block engine from Ed Pink. The Camaro's best showing was a semifinal finish at an IHRA race in Charlotte, North Carolina. (Photo Courtesy Michael Pottie)*

Kelly Brown drove the Barry Setzer *Vega during its debut at the 1971 NHRA Springnationals. Pat Foster would be handling the butterfly steering wheel by the end of the season. (Photo Courtesy J. R. Bloom)*

Barry Setzer

In 1971, North Carolina textile manufacturer Barry Setzer took his interest in drag racing to an entirely new level. That year, he debuted a Bruce Walker–driven Pro Stock Camaro. Later in the season, he debuted a Kelly Brown–driven Vega Funny Car.

With the rules of Pro Stock quickly evolving, the Camaro proved to be unremarkable. In 1973, a promising John Buttera–built, Frank Schmidt (Traco)–powered 331-ci Vega was introduced. Buttera's chassis work was outstanding and considered to be second to none, and it showed in the Vega. The car won the Best Engineered Car award at the NHRA Winternationals. This was partially because Buttera had the foresight to fabricate the car with the ability to strip the body of its panels in a heartbeat, which provided easy access for maintenance.

The future is now, or so Buttera thought. The exercise in forward thinking went nowhere. Pat Foster drove the Can-Am-influenced dragster a few times before they gave up on it. The car has since been restored. (Photo Courtesy Steve Reyes)

At the Vega Funny Car's debut during the 1971 Springnationals, Brown earned a runner-up finish to Don Schumacher and his 'Cuda. The Vega featured the standard Funny Car fare of the day. Innovations included extra driver protection, which was incorporated by fabricating a Top Fuel–style roll cage. Filling the Buttera-formed rails was an Ed Pink 473-ci Hemi, which was backed by a 2-speed Lenco that transferred power to a solid-mounted Halibrand quick-change rear end.

Pat Foster took over driving the Vega by the end of 1971, and the results through 1972 included wins at the Orange County International Raceway (OCIR) Manufacturers Meet and at the IHRA Pro-Am in Rockingham, North Carolina. Similar results occurred in 1973, with wins in Florida at the IHRA Winter Nationals and NHRA Gatornationals, where Foster set the class record with a 6.36 ET.

Looking to the future, Setzer took on the space-inspired Buttera, Louie Techenoff, and Nye Frank–built monocoque, Can-Am-influenced dragster. From its one-piece body, chassis configuration, wedge shape, narrow track, wings, and wheel fairings, the car was like no other. The 185-inch-wheelbase car featured a stroked Ed Pink Hemi.

How did it go? Well, reports are that Pat Foster made just one pass in the dragster that had it lifting the wheels. When it touched down, it damaged the tub. Repairs were made, but the car saw little track time afterward. The futuristic car was sold to parts unknown, but it reappeared years later and has since been restored. Setzer pulled out of drag racing in 1975, which ended his short-but-sweet involvement in the sport.

The Wonder Wagon

One of the sport's first major non-automotive sponsors was Wonder Bread. According to information compiled by Phil Burgess at NHRA.com, veteran California Fuel Altered racer Glenn Way set his sights on building a new Altered. However, with Funny Cars exploding in popularity, he had a change of heart. Way's friend, Bob Kachler of Racing Graphics, came up with the idea of using a Vega panel body. He was also the one who sold the idea to Wonder Bread. It was then up to Way to come up with a car.

Hot rodder extraordinaire Don Rackemann was

Kelly Brown pilots the Wonder Wagon at the 1972 Supernationals, where the car made its debut. Brown's 6.70 ET failed to advance. Poor handling characteristics of the 125-inch-wheelbase car limited its success. (Photo Courtesy Michael Pottie)

Work is well underway on the first Wonder Vega at John Buttera's shop. Unfortunately, the Vega's panel skin did not lend itself to being a Funny Car. (Photo Courtesy Steve Reyes)

The roof spoiler and rear window vents were added by Buttera in hopes to improve the panel's poor handling. They failed to make the desired difference, as did canards that were later installed. (Photo Courtesy Michael Pottie)

Don Schumacher was not the first to have a multi-car team, but his string of 'Cudas was one of the most successful. In August 1972, Bobby Rowe took over driving this car. (Photo Courtesy Michael Pottie)

With the Vega panel being a flop, Don Schumacher reverted to his proven Barracuda shell. He drove the car to wins at the NHRA Summernationals and Grandnationals. (Photo Courtesy Grant Bittner)

brought in to lend a hand with the ill-fated project. With hindsight being 20-20, it's easy to look back with today's knowledge and ask, "What were they thinking?" The Vega panel was not a good idea. Aerodynamically, it was about as streamlined as a brick. It would fly all right—but not in the manner in which they hoped.

Don purchased the ex–Stan Shiroma *Midnight Skulker* Barracuda Funny Car to use the chassis under the first of two Vega panels to be built. Don Kirby put the first car together, and John Buttera built the second. Kelly Brown was brought in to run one Vega and Way ran the other.

The fans loved the unique bodystyle, and a few loaves of bread were sold most likely. However, even with the best of parts and Ed Pink power, the panels couldn't overcome their poor handling characteristics. Their record was nothing to write home about, and at the end of the season, Way's deal with Wonder Bread ended. Don Schumacher picked it up for the 1973 season.

Pro Stock

By the end of 1971, Pro Stock had become a bore to many fans who were tired of watching the factory-backed Mopars do most of the winning. Advancements in the category were subtle over the first two seasons and were not enough to break Chrysler's stranglehold, as it won 12 of 15 NHRA national events during the period. If the category was going to survive, something had to change, and those changes came in 1972.

New Weight Breaks

In the fall of 1971, Bill "Grumpy" Jenkins sold NHRA Executive Director Jack Hart on the idea of allowing small-block subcompact cars to compete in Pro Stock. Jenkins did some testing with small-block Chevys in his *Grumpy's Toy V* 1969 Camaro and figured that if he could get the weight breaks he desired, a small-block Vega could end Chrysler's dominance.

Jenkins sold the idea to Hart from a marketing perspective. The buying public was purchasing small cars, and by racing the same, the crowds would pour into the stands. Hart agreed, and the new rules and weight breaks that were written by Jenkins were implemented for the 1972 season. Sensing that their domination of Pro Stock

Chassis builder Ron Butler was responsible for some of the finest scientifically developed Pro Stock cars that were built during the early 1970s. Bob Lambeck's perfect launch proves this. Lambeck's greatest success occurred at AHRA events. (Photo Courtesy J. R. Bloom)

Who would have thought that a high-revving, 331-ci Vega could squash the Hemis. Jenkins's small-block made 540 hp with the help of a 0.558-lift Sig Erson cam, modified Holley 660 carburetors, and a modified Edelbrock intake. (Photo Courtesy Michael Pottie)

Just like Top Fuel, Pro Stock was in a year of transition in 1972. As the sun set on Mopar's domination, Don Grotheer was one who provided hope. During the 1972 season, he had two NHRA semifinal finishes and an AHRA win. (Photo Courtesy Michael Pottie)

was coming to an end, Chrysler representatives protested the new rules—but to no avail.

Jenkins's weight breaks were as follows: Wedge-engine cars carried 6.75 pounds per cubic inch, inclined-valve engines carried 7.0 pounds per cubic inch, and all others (specifically single-overhead-cam Fords and Chrysler's Hemi) were required to carry 7.25 pounds per cubic inch.

"Maybe the Chrysler people had upset Jack Hart or something; I don't know," Jenkins said. "But, he didn't flinch when I presented the weight breaks to him."

Jenkins and his crew spent approximately 1,700 hours building his controversial Vega before the Winternationals.

Pro Stock rules required the driver to be protected from all angles, and reinforced step frames were permitted. As the Vega was of unibody design, Jenkins had S-W Race Cars weld up a step frame/roll cage. Contrary to popular belief, Jenkins's Vega was not a full tube-chassis car. The rocker panels on the stock Vega were key supports (frame rails, if you will), and Jenkins designed the 360-degree roll cage to tie into the inner rocker panels and rear step frame. Outside of the Pinto rack-and-pinion steering and Lamb components, the chassis (as required by NHRA rules) was all OEM forward of the firewall.

Ushering in the age of linked rear suspensions, Jenkins built the Vega with an adjustable 4-link. Shortly after the Winternationals, he updated the car with a 3-link. This was similar in design to the 1958–1964 Chevrolet rear suspension that incorporated a floating A-frame, tying the rear to the 4130 tubing. The rear-end housing was an acid-dipped and drilled Dana 60 with 5.57 gears.

To the surprise of many, the Vega passed the Winternationals tech inspection. The only issue was that the headers of the 331-ci engine that exited out of the lower fender took away from the stock appearance. Jenkins made a quick trip to Hooker Headers in Orange, California, where a new set of in-chassis headers were fabricated.

At the NHRA Summernationals, Jenkins continued to steamroll Chrysler's Hemi cars by defeating Dick Landy's Challenger with a 9.48 ET at 144.23 mph. Later in the year, Jenkins used a 354-ci engine to record a best ET of 9.19 while losing a West Coast match race to Butch "the California Flash" Leal. (Photo Courtesy Brian Beattie)

Jenkins managed to overcome suspension issues with the 4-link and battled his way through a field of Mopars to meet the Hemi 'Cuda of Don Grotheer in the final. Jenkins left the line first and never looked back. Shifting through the gears at 8,200 rpm, the Vega, which was dubbed *Grumpy's Toy IX,* downed the 'Cuda with a 9.68 ET at 140.18 mph to a losing 9.82 at 141.95. Jenkins's interpretation of the rules made every pre-1972 Pro Stocker obsolete, as well as any new car that wasn't a subcompact.

Jenkins single-handedly breathed new life into Pro Stock and went on to win 6 of the 7 NHRA national events that he entered in 1972. He lost at the Gatornationals on a red-light and watched from the sidelines as Don Carlton won the event in the *Mopar Missile.*

Jenkins won the World Finals by defeating Ken Dondero, who was driving "Dyno" Don's Pinto, to earn his first world championship. Overnight Pro Stock chassis building became big business. SRD Race Cars, Wolverine, and Don Hardy were a few companies that made Pro Stock chassis to feed the boom.

Ford's Better Idea

Unlike Chrysler, which did not have a subcompact or small-block program to take on the Vegas, Ford had the Pinto and the 351 Cleveland to play with. Don Nicholson debuted his Cleveland Pinto at the Gatornationals and then finished the season by winning the AHRA Pro Stock World Championship.

The Cleveland mill quickly proved to be superior to the small-block Chevy. By design, the engine featured heads that resembled the big-block Chevy, with canted valves measuring 2.19 inches on the intake and 1.71 inches on the exhaust. The best that could be done with the small-block Chevy was 2.05 inches on the intake valves. The downside of the Cleveland was the exhaust ports that featured a dogleg bend that hampered flow. Racers eliminated the problem by cutting out a portion of the exhaust side of the head and installing a drilled plate that raised the ports and eliminated the dogleg to provide a clean exit for the spent gasses. By trial and error, builders found additional horsepower and torque gains by reshaping the ports and experimenting with their size.

The season-ending Supernationals used the new 1973 weight breaks. Bob Glidden, running Gapp and Roush's old Pinto, provided a glimpse of things to come when it took a holeshot by Bill Jenkins with a 9.38 ET to defeat Glidden's 9.37 ET in the final round. Regarding Glidden, Jenkins crewman Ed Quay looked to the future and said, "He's going to be trouble."

The Pro Stock Pinto of "Dyno" Don led the Ford contingency in 1972. The mighty Cleveland engine was only beginning to show its capabilities. (Photo Courtesy Michael Pottie)

Exhaust-port plates that removed the power-robbing dogleg of the Cleveland head made a huge performance difference. This plate is bolted to one of Bob Glidden's heads.

Booth Drives for AMC

American Motors Corporation (AMC), which was generally more concerned with the human race than drag racing, changed its tune in 1969, when it contracted Hurst to build 52 drag race–only Super Stock AMXs. The company turned its attention to Pro Stock in 1971.

In October 1971, Bob Swaim was coaxed from Ford by AMC to lead the company's racing activities. His first task was to hire a proven winner for the Pro Stock program. Swaim set his sights on "Dyno" Don Nicholson, and the pair negotiated a deal. Swaim figured that the deal was done, but Nicholson had a last-minute change of heart. He couldn't bring himself to disappoint his Ford-Mercury fans.

At the recommendation of Dick Maskin, who was a Michigan-based Modified Production racer, Swaim spoke to Wally Booth. Booth liked the idea of racing on someone else's dime and saw potential in the AMC engine. A contract was signed late in 1971. At the 1972 Winternationals, Booth was in a Gremlin. It surprised many to learn that having no other option or car, he ran a 304-ci Gremlin in Stock Eliminator.

Dick Maskin and Rich La Mont joined Booth under the AMC umbrella. Swaim stated that La Mont "was a political move," as he was

AMC signed Chevy racer Wally Booth to lead its Pro Stock program. Booth's compact Gremlin was a sign of better things to come. The car's best ETs were in the 9.50s.

The powertrain of Booth's Gremlin consisted of a 340-ci engine, a BorgWarner T-10 transmission, and a Dana rear end. A 10-point cage provided plenty of protection.

The WIBG Buckley Broadcasting Gremlin of Rich LaMont was built by Holman-Moody with a Traco-built 366-ci engine. (Photo Courtesy Michael Pottie)

connected through Roger Penske. Penske had been under contract with AMC since 1970. In 1972, he campaigned a Matador in NASCAR for the manufacturer.

The three Pro Stock teams had a good starting point, as the NHRA's weight breaks favored Wedge-powered compacts. The AMC engine was designed with the ideal large-bore, short-stroke combination. It was only a matter of time before AMC became a genuine Pro Stock threat.

Rebellion Results in Payout Increase

The NHRA faced a rebellion of sorts in 1972, when Don Garlits presented the PRA National Challenge on Labor Day weekend. It was the same weekend that the NHRA hosted the Indy Nationals, which was the biggest race of the season.

"Show me the money" was what the professional racers (led by Garlits) told NHRA President Wally Parks in 1972.

"In 1971, with the Vietnam war raging, the United States motorsports community came together in a show of support for the troops during a United Service Organizations (USO) tour at the request of Admiral Emmet H. Tidd," drag racing historian Bret Kepner said. "The team featured the best of the best in all forms of racing and included the likes of Richard Petty, A. J. Foyt, Mario Andretti, and drag racing's Don Garlits."

Evidently, individuals in the group began to talk about earnings. When payouts were mentioned, Garlits discovered just how far behind the professional drag racers were. He felt that the payouts needed to be increased immensely for the sport to gain respectability.

Shortly after Gartlits's discussion with the other racers, he created the Professional Racers Association, which included several pro-class racers. The National Challenge race came to fruition after Garlits had an argument with NHRA President Wally Parks about the measly $3,000 that Steve Carbone received for winning the Nationals in 1971. Garlits told Parks that he felt the payout should

In 1972, Doug Walton, Wes Cerney, and Don Moody teamed up to present this Don Long car. The wheelbase measured 224 inches and was propelled by a Keith Black Hemi. Moody's National Challenge win was preceded by a win at the NHRA Summernationals. The best ET was 6.02. (Photo Courtesy Michael Pottie)

Butch Leal's Ron Butler-built Duster was a terror. Joe Allread assembled the Hemi that propelled the car to a class win here at the AHRA Winter Nationals. Class-legal ETs in the 9.40 range were realized by the close of the season. (Photo Courtesy J. R. Bloom)

have been closer to $25,000. Parks laughed at Garlits and told him that it would be years before the NHRA paid that kind of money.

So, Garlits told Parks that he could put together a race that paid $25,000 to the professionals. Parks told him that it couldn't be done, so the challenge was issued. Garlits reached out to AHRA President Jim Tice, who gave Garlits the Tulsa track to use and helped secure the $150,000 for payouts.

Garlits's National Challenge had three professional categories: Top Fuel, Funny Car, and Pro Stock. With a payout of $25,000 plus contingencies going to each category winner, the race had no problem presenting three fields of 32 cars. There were no Sportsman categories that ran over the weekend. Instead, they ran the preceding Tuesday through Thursday.

The PRA, which was renamed the Professional Racers Organization after 1972, carried onward with Garlits at the helm through 1974, after which he was no longer involved. Big winners at the 1972 Challenge were Don Moody in Top Fuel and Tom McEwen in Funny Car. In Pro Stock, the winner was Bill Jenkins, who also took class honors in 1973 and 1974. Was the National Challenge a money maker? It's not likely that it made money, but it made the point that it aimed to make. As a result, NHRA payouts increased, and it helped the sport of drag racing advance.

Indy

With the majority of the key players at Tulsa, everyone had a chance to win at Indy. Gary Beck, the transplanted American who ran out of Edmonton, Canada, won Top Fuel by defeating Jerry Ruth. Proving that it was no fluke, Beck repeated the win in 1973.

In Funny Car, Ed McCulloch defeated Canadian Gordie Bonin. Bonin enjoyed his first year as a professional in the *Pacemaker* Vega and only saw his light burn brighter. He earned the nickname "240 Gordie" while driving his 1977 Bubble Up–sponsored Trans Am, due to the ease in which he broke the top speed (MPH) barrier. In 1979, he earned his only win at Indy by defeating Kosty Ivanof.

In Pro Stock, fans were privileged to see the NHRA's first all-Chevy final. Ray Allen in his SRD Race Cars–built Vega defeated Bill Blanding's Fred Forkner–built Vega that was driven by Rich Miracki. Interestingly, if you excluded Bill Jenkins's many wins with his three Vegas, Allen's Vega was the only other Vega to win an NHRA national event.

Relatively unknown racer Gary Beck came to Indy in 1972, won class, and took home nearly $20,000. (Photo Mike Lacelle)

In 1972, Ray Allen drove the 331-ci** Truppi-Kling **Vega to a Pro Stock win at Indy. For all of the screaming about Vegas dominating Pro Stock, outside of Grumpy Jenkins's numerous wins, this was the only other Vega to win an NHRA national event. (Photo Courtesy Michael Pottie)

The Last Drag Race

The Los Angeles Harbor Commission, which owned the land where the famed Lions Drag Strip was located, announced on September 23, 1972, that it would cancel the track's lease on December 31 of that year. It was the inevitable end of an era, as from its earliest days, noise complaints were an issue. Long before 1972, housing began to creep up on the property. Weekly, the Harbor Commission dealt the complaints. During the last few months of the track's existence, racing was relegated to bracket events.

Lions Drag Strip, also referred to as "the Beach" or "Wilmington," opened its gates in October 1955 with an overflow crowd of 10,000, and it closed them in 1972 in similar fashion. Track Manager Steve Evans planned the final farewell for Saturday, December 2, 1972. Evans made radio advertisements that invited fans to come to Lions Drag Strip to get a piece of history, and they did.

The last drag race was more of an event than a race. With the gates locked due to a maximum-capacity crowd, eager fans who drove for miles weren't going to be denied entry. Barriers were no deterrent for the unexpected thousands.

Spectators who anticipated the first 5-second Top Fuel pass were disappointed and had to settle for Don Moody's 6.02 ET. Carl Olson in the Kuhl-Olson *Da Fast Guys* car defeated Jeb Allen with a 6.20 ET in Top Fuel. In Funny Car, Tom McEwen beat his Hot Wheels partner, Don Prudhomme, in his unpainted 'Cuda with a 6.39 ET. In Pro Stock, "Red Light Bandit" Bill Bagshaw defeated the Dodge Demon of Larry Breaux.

Mike Kuhl and Carl Olson, otherwise known as "Da Fast Guys," hold the record for the fastest trip down Lions Drag Strip, running a 6.02 on closing night. (Photo Courtesy Lou Hart)

"Red Light Bandit" Bill Bagshaw took Pro Stock honors at the Last Drag Race with his Ron Butler-built, Joe Allread-powered Dodge Challenger. (Photo Courtesy Lou Hart)

Steve and Rhonda Woods were dominant in BB/GS with their 331-ci Hemi-powered Prefect. *Steve won Comp Eliminator at the 1972 NHRA Winternationals (and repeated in 1973) and defeated the A/FC car of Jeg Coughlin with a 9.38 ET. (Photo Courtesy Rich Carlson/ Grant Bittner Collection).*

The Tentmaker *was driven by Omer Carrothers Jr. of Joplin, Missouri. Carrothers enjoyed a few rounds at the Last Drag Race in his Woody Gilmore-chassis Mustang. (Photo Courtesy Lou Hart)*

When it was all said and done, spectators took Steve Evans's advertisement literally and helped themselves to any piece of history they could get their hands on, including parts of the track's surface.

Comp Eliminator

In 1972, AA/Gas Dragsters, the Top Gas refugees, found a new home in the Comp category. Joining them were the B/Fuel Dragsters, Wedge-engine C/Dragsters, and BB/Funny Cars. They all battled existing classes that included the old Supercharged Gassers.

"Ohio" George Montgomery threw a little spice into AA/GS back in 1970, when he added a pair of Switzer turbochargers to his Boss 429 Mustang. Al Lidert did the same in 1972 and added twin turbos to his AA/D car, the *Golden Gator*. In 1972, Paul Pittman added a pair of Garrett Industries turbos to his *Sassy Gremlin* and had success in the BB/GS category. However, each racer felt the wrath of the NHRA, which showed little interest or understanding of the turbocharger at this point in history.

"Ohio" George Montgomery

When it came to adding the turbos, Montgomery wasn't alone in his effort, as he received back-door assistance from Ford Indy expert Danny Jones. The pair relied heavily upon the manufacturer's defunct Indy program for turbo parts and technology. In June 1972, George set the AA/GS top speed record in at 166.75 mph. Screams from the competition had the NHRA create a separate class for Montgomery: AA/GS-Turbo. The NHRA set a minimum for AA/GS at 163.63 mph. Montgomery's time followed him to AA/GS-T. In a previous interview, Montgomery stated it took a couple years to work out the bugs, but once the car was sorted, it cranked out 8.40 ETs at 175 mph.

The shell of George Montgomery's Mr. Gasket-sponsored Gasser was all fiberglass and was formed using a preproduction 1969 Mustang. In 1977, the year that the Mustang was retired, it won the Division 2 points championship. (Photo Courtesy Bob Martin)

With the support of Ford Engineer Danny Jones, "Ohio" George dipped into the manufacturer's Indy parts bin and came up with twin Schwitzer turbos. The unique setup had each turbo feeding two cylinders on opposing sides of the engine. Bendix delivered the fuel, and Mallory set the spark. The compression was about 7.0:1. (Photo Courtesy Michael Pottie)

As turbo technology was lagging at the time, the trick was to kill some of the top-end power to compensate for the lag. Each turbo on Montgomery's Boss produced more than 30 pounds of boost and beat everyone. Due to the Mustang's killer midrange and top end, he drove around cars that were quicker off the line.

Winning the Gatornationals in 1973 and 1974 didn't make the NHRA happy.

"[The NHRA] didn't understand turbos and were afraid of them," Montgomery said. "In not so many words, they let me know that the car was no longer welcome."

Montgomery parked the Mustang and went to a BB/FC Mustang. A turbocharged Pinto was his final car before he retired.

Golden Gator

In the AA/D category, Al Lidert found himself in a similar boat, as Montgomery, Lidert, and partner Chase Knight were doing their part to advance the sport by campaigning the blown and twin-turbocharged, 464-ci Hemi-powered *Golden Gator*. As with Montgomery's ride, Lidert's dragster produced 30 pounds of boost

Before turbocharging his Hemi Gremlin and being designated as a BB/GS-Turbo car, Paul Pittman ran Hilborn injection. Turbocharged best times were reported to be in the 8.80s. M&S Welding prepped the chassis. (Photo Courtesy Rich Carlson/Grant Bittner)

Tuning these twin turbochargers and GMC blower was difficult before the age of computers. Managing the turbo boost, fuel delivery, and blower drive speed was a chore. (Photo Courtesy Robbie Robertson)

from each turbo. Knight stated that with an entirely mechanical fuel-injection system, the most difficult part was managing the fuel curve.

The car was campaigned into the 1980s, when it ran a copious amount of alcohol through the Hilborn injectors. A win at the 1973 Gatornationals was the highlight of the *Golden Gator's* run.

Convention Wins Out

In the end, convention won out. Bob Durban won in the Jegs-sponsored A/FC 'Cuda at the Gatornationals, Jim Oddy's AA/GS Opel won the US Nationals, and Colorado's Wayne McMurtry's Donovan-powered Gas Dragster won the world championship. Each win came with a more conventional blown Hemi.

Modified Eliminator

In 1972, the Modified category saw an influx in participation, as Stock had a mass exodus with its new Pure Stock format. With the variety of classes and cars and the caliber of talent found in Modified, it's difficult to pick out any single competitor who stood ahead of the pack. Joe Williamson and his Ford 6-cylinder-powered Altered and Bob Riffle in his Modified Production, Rod Shop–sponsored Dodge were multiple national event winners. However, no one shined like Paul Blevins and his D/Gas Corvette.

Scotto & Blevins

On any given weekend, at any given Division 1 meet, if the team of Joe Scotto and Paul Blevins showed up, the

In 1972, Wayne "Mr. Bud" McMurtry was the Comp World Champion, and he had had a magnificent career. For a few years, he enjoyed the sponsorship of Budweiser. Off the track, he became NHRA's facilities manager and was responsible for bringing new tracks into the NHRA fold. (Photo Courtesy John Pattison)

Throughout Bob Riffle's career, he campaigned winners in Street, Modified, Comp, and Pro Stock. In 1972, he had a great season with his Modified Production Dodge, as his de-stroked Hemi produced 9.80 ETs, countless class wins, and national event wins at the NHRA Summernationals and Grandnationals. (Photo Courtesy Todd Wingerter)

The Nomad of Scotto & Blevins was a consistent AHRA, NHRA, and UDRA winner. A BorgWarner 2.54-first-gear transmission was backed by an unbreakable 1957 Oldsmobile rear that housed Summers axles and anywhere from 5.12 to 6.17 gears. (Photo Courtesy Carl Rubrecht)

chances of anyone else going home with the gold were greatly diminished. The pair's effort during the season was rewarded with the division championship and the Modified world title.

In 1968, Scotto and Blevins came together to campaign a G/MP 1955 Chevy Nomad. Immediately, the wagon paid dividends by winning meets and setting records through 1972. The wagon was powered by a punched-out 283 engine that could rev to 10,000 rpm and usually left the line at 9,000 rpm. Backing the 283 was a slick-shifted, 2.54 first-gear BorgWarner transmission and an Oldsmobile rear housing gearing anywhere from 5.12 to 6.17.

According to Scotto, the team was hounded by sponsors that wanted their name on the car and by Chrysler, which wanted them on its team.

"[The sponsors] led to plenty of free parts and directly to us building the world championship–winning [1965] Corvette," he said.

The pair was inspired to build the Corvette by Division 2's Bob Callaham, who was the first to see any real success in the Modified category, with the second-generation Corvette.

These Corvettes, with their short 98-inch wheelbases, superior aerodynamics, and a favorable weight bias of 52/48 (front to back), compared to a first-generation Camaro's 56/44, were ideal candidates for the category. The Corvettes grew in popularity as the decade progressed and had success in the Modified Production, Altered, and Gas classes.

The *Scotto & Blevins* Corvette ran a stock-bore 327 as

Former Junior Stock racer Bill Izykowski was hired to drive the Scotto & Blevins Corvette that earned a runner-up finish at the 1971 World Finals. In 1972, Blevins won the title while driving the car. (Photo Courtesy Bob Boudreau)

well as the 287 out of the Nomad on occasion. Completing the driveline was a 30-pound flywheel, a 2.64 first-gear BorgWarner transmission, and a Dana 60 rear end. Blevins followed Callaham's lead when it came to the rear suspension and installed a 4-link.

"Callaham was the man when it came to 4-links, and he had a lot of input on this one," said Bill Izykowski, who drove for the team.

Scotto & Blevins sold both the Nomad and Corvette at the end of the 1972 season to finance Blevins's move into Pro Stock. Blevins's first Pro Stocker was an SRD-built Vega that was powered by the Corvette's 327. Scotto retired at the end of 1972.

Bugging Out

The Volkswagen Beetle, the underpowered people's car from Germany, was the scourge of the Modified category in the early 1970s. As often happened, the West Coast paved the path, and leading the charge was the *Inch Pincher* of Darrell Vittone and Dean Lowry's *Deano's dynoSoar*.

Jim Colson took over driving the* Inch Pincher Too *when EMPI was sold to Filter Dynamics in 1972. The body features a chop of nearly 4 inches. A 4.44 ring and pinion helped produce wheels-up launches. (Photo Courtesy Steve Reyes)

EMPI

Engineered Motor Products Inc. (EMPI), owned by Joe Vittone (Darrell Vittone's father), can be credited for breathing life into the flat-four-powered Bug, as the company offered performance parts for the car in the late 1950s. One of Joe's first hires was Dean Lowry. Lowry's key responsibility was to design and develop the parts that EMPI sold. His hands were all over EMPI's first drag-racing effort, which was the *Inch Pincher* VW. The I/Gas Bug ran a 2,000-cc (122-ci) engine that was capable of ETs between 12.13 and 12.19 by the end of the decade.

Dean Lowry's purple* dynoSoar *was an H/G record holder and was capable of mid-11-second ETs. The Volkswagen won the Best Engineered Car award at the 1970 NHRA Springnationals. (Photo Courtesy Steve Reyes)

Lowry parted ways with EMPI in October 1968 to start his own company, which was called Deano Dyno-Soars. Darrell did a great job of filling Lowry's shoes and continued to develop new EMPI products. In early 1970, his skills showed when he debuted the *Inch Pincher Too* and proceeded to set his own I/G record at 12.12.

Joe sold EMPI to Filter Dynamics in the spring of 1971, and the *Inch Pincher Too* was part of the deal. Darrel drove the Bug through the early part of 1972, before Jim and Rick Carlson took over driving and maintaining the car. Darrell parted ways with Filter Dynamics not long after to set up his own business, called the Race Shop.

With Lowry long gone and Darrell exiting the scene, the Filter Dynamics–owned EMPI was a shadow of its former self. Filter Dynamics looked to maximize returns and seemed to be content selling popular bolt-ons and chrome parts. By 1974, EMPI closed.

Lightning Bug

In 1972, Lowry moved away from campaigning his Bug because it did his business no good to compete against his customers on the track. Lowry's employees, Paul and Mark Schley, took his place in the record books with their own Volkswagen. In October 1972, their *Lightning Bug 2* became the first H/G Volkswagen to crack the 10s when Paul ran a 10.97 ET, and he backed it up with a 10.94 ET at Fremont.

With its 2,180-cc engine, the Bug fit the H/G category's 8-pound weight break perfectly at 1,065 pounds.

Don Kirby laid the paint on the Schley's Bug back in 1970, and Nat Quick did the lettering. The body panels were hand-laid fiberglass, while the sunroof and windows were Lexan. The front wheels weighed a mere 3 pounds each while the rear rim and tire combination weighed 9 pounds each. (Photo Courtesy of Schley Brothers)

The little 2,180-cc pancake-4 engine was built by the Schleys, and it made nearly 250 hp. (Photo Courtesy of Schley Brothers)

As with its fellow Volkswagen competitors, weight was reduced in the usual manner. This junkyard Bug was stripped and dipped in a backyard vat of acid. Outside of the center tunnel, the floor pan was cut out to make room for aluminum flooring. Steel body panels were replaced with fiberglass parts, and the heavy side and rear glass were swapped for Plexiglas.

The frame head joined the pan on the cutting-room floor, which gave way to a fabricated tube axle. Designed by the brothers, the axle was attached to the main unibody with two 10-inch-long modified torsion springs. Paul recalled that after all the front-end modifications were complete, the suspension weighed a mere 28 pounds. They had removed 130 pounds.

Unlike a typical cast V-8 or 6-cylinder engine, the VW block is comprised of two halves that are bolted together. The Schley's engine case was extensively modified, welded, and a homemade cradle was fabricated to hold it all together. It was something that anyone running a modified Bug wouldn't or couldn't do without. The brothers added more support to the block around the flywheel, where there was a tendency to crack.

Extensive modifications were made to the oiling system that directed oil to the bottom of the piston. It squeezed out 15.1 compression, and a lot of heat was generated. The heads were ported, and the exhaust-valve guides were moved so that larger valves could be fitted. The intake valves measured 48 mm, while the exhaust valves measured 42 mm. To help reach maximum RPM quicker, the pushrods were drilled. The Weber carburetors that were used began at 48 mms but were opened up to 51 mm. Lighting the fire was a Joe Hunt magneto. All told, the engine produced 250 to 260 hp and was shifted at 8,000 rpm.

Completing the *Lightning Bug*'s driveline was a Porsche 741 box, which, unlike the Volkswagen box, had individual gearsets that allowed the Schleys to mix and match to suit conditions. The flywheel weighed 7 pounds. M&H slicks provided the traction, while the rims were welded two-piece, spun aluminum and were made by the brothers. The Schleys felt that they had reached the limit with the *Lightning Bug* and still wanted to go faster, so they sold the car in January 1973 and built the first Volkswagen-powered, 9-second dragster.

The Ned Bug

In addition to the successful Volkswagens on the West Coast, there were also successful Volkswagens on the East Coast. Bill Mitchell and his Motion Performance–sponsored *Thunder Bug* out of New York won several races and was a record holder with an 11.09 ET. The *Ned Bug* of John "Skip" Hamm and Dennis Grove from Hanover, Pennsylvania, can take credit for earning the Beetle its first national event category win. Grove grabbed Modified honors at the 1972 NHRA Gatornationals by defeating the B/Gas Maverick of Eddie Schartman.

As with the Schley *Lightning Bug*, the *Ned Bug* ran in the H/G class with a 2180-cc engine. Modifications included EMPI-prepped, dual-port heads; an Engle cam and valve gear; and Weber 48 IDA carbs. Power was transmitted through a 1964 Porsche transaxle. The *Ned Bug* left the line at 5,500 rpm and was shifted by Hamm at 8,000 rpm. Recognized as the *Inch Pincher*'s eastern counterpart (check out the matching paint), the Bug was capable of low-11-second ETs.

John Hamm and Denny Grove said that the West Coast's Dean Lowry, the Schley brothers, and Darrell Vittone were some of their influences. Grove's Gatornationals win came with an 11.14 ET. (Photo Courtesy Michael Pottie)

Super Stock

What a difference a year makes. To make room for last year's Stockers, the NHRA dropped its 1963-or-later requirement for Super Stock and opened the category to any year. To handle the onslaught, the NHRA increased the number of classes in the category from 16 to 40. While the post-1963 models handled the upper and middle classes, the new lower classes became home to the pre-1963 Stock models.

The new, more-liberal rules of Super Stock could have played havoc on the early, weaker driveline components if not for the aftermarket developing stronger, more-durable parts. Duane Brock and Larry Nelson incorporated these parts, and their '55 Chevy won the Summernationals and was runner-up to Dave Boertman at the World Finals. Nelson drove the SS/T, 265-ci-powered sedan to a record 13.20 ET with no issues.

Oregon's Mark Coletti had a 383 engine in his 1971 SS/JA Riddler *'Cuda, which was capable of 11.60 ETs. In 1972, well-established Coletti Racing Enterprises, which was led by Joe Coletti, had four Mopars under its banner. (Photo Courtesy Bob Martin)*

During a two-week period in the summer of 1972, Larry Nelson won more than $8,500 with this old Chevy. Two of those wins came against future Pro Stock standout Bob Glidden. Time marched on, and fewer of these old Tri-Five Chevys saw the winner's circle. (Photo Courtesy Bob Martin)

Dave Boertman's best year was 1972. He dominated the IHRA with his 273-ci Dodge Dart and won the NHRA World Championship with his Charger. (Photo Courtesy Todd Wingerter)

There's no denying that 1972 was Boertman's best year of his career. Along with the NHRA Championship, he owned the IHRA's Junior Stock category as well. He drove his 273-ci-powered 1967 Dodge Dart to victory at four of the sanctioning body's five national events, and he was runner-up at the fifth.

Stock

With the NHRA's Stock category running to Pure Stock rules and a limit of no cars older than 10 years, the field was open to Detroit's latest offerings. Pure Stock opened the door to a slew of new young guns to guarantee the sport a bright future.

Initially, the new format was unable to coax enough contestants to present a full field at most events. To alleviate the problem, the NHRA increased purses and began to relax the category rules as early as 1973.

Dave Benisek and his 1972 Stage 1 Buick Skylark won the C/SA class at the 1972 season-opening Winternationals as well as the season championship. Benisek did a fine job of interpreting the rules, and his blueprinted 455-ci Buick ran steady 13.50 ETs at more than 101 mph. There were rumors that Buick lent some backdoor support.

In 1972, Dave Benisek and his C/SA 1972 Stage I Buick dominated the new Pure Stock category. He started the year well by winning here at the Winternationals.

CHAPTER THREE

1973:

CRUNCH TIME

Bill "Grumpy" Jenkins, the 1972 NHRA Pro Stock World Champion, found things to be significantly more difficult in 1973. Jenkins's Vega received a new coat of paint to start the 1973 season. The car only lasted a few months before it was destroyed in a match race. (Photo Courtesy Bob Snyder)

With a gas shortage due to the Middle East oil embargo, the price for a barrel of crude oil quadrupled from $3 to $12. A portion of that increase was passed on to American consumers, who saw pump prices jump nearly 50 percent. For the Fuel racers, a barrel of nitromethane now cost $300, which lasted about 20 runs.

The result of this was that many low-budget Fuel teams disappeared, the dedicated Sportsman racers stayed close to home, and fans prioritized their spending. In spite of the hit, drag racing carried onward and continued to produce highlight-reel material.

Top Fuel

Although many racers took their engine building in-house, others, including Keith Black, Ed Pink, and Sid Waterman, made a killing by serving the Fuel ranks. Those with deep pockets or a generous sponsor could source a complete car that was ready to race from a number of builders, but it would cost about $25,000 (not including the necessary spare parts). A spare motor, tow rig, fuel, etc., previously cost about $25,000 but now approached $100,000. Top Fuel was not for the faint of heart.

Someone Has to Win

There were eight NHRA national events in 1973, including the Supernationals, and the only repeat winner was Garlits, who took honors at the Winternationals and year-end Supernationals. It was a great year for Garlits, who also won his third of four AHRA world titles in a row. The 1973 title would be the toughest of them all.

John Wiebe, the 1970 AHRA Top Fuel Champ, probably would have won the title in 1973 if it wasn't for his horrific crash with Jeb Allen at the National Challenge

Fuel racer "Slam'n" Sam Miller's 1973 experiment in streamlining didn't work as well as he expected. S-W Welding fabricated the chassis to Miller's design. (Photo Courtesy Bob Martin)

A year that saw so much promise for John Wiebe ended at the National Challenge. Prior to his wreck, he won the NHRA Springnationals and a pair of AHRA-series events. (Photo Courtesy Rich Carlson/Grant Bittner Collection)

in August. Injuries from the crash sidelined Wiebe for the season and seemingly ended any hope of winning his second world title.

However, AHRA rules stated that the earned points stayed with the car and not the driver, whereas NHRA points stayed with the driver. In an unheard-of move, the team of Warren, Coburn, & Miller stepped up to keep Wiebe's hopes alive. The team dressed its car in Wiebe likeness (name and all) and carried on for their friend. They won the Grand-Am race at OCIR and put Wiebe 450 points ahead of Garlits.

Garlits appeared at the race with his short-wheelbase (180 inches) *Swamp Rat 17* and his inventive-but-disappointing full-bodied *Wynn's Liner*. He bowed in the first round, and the *Wynn's Liner*, driven by Butch Maas, failed to qualify.

According to *Car Craft* magazine coverage, "Garlits was irate at the sudden development, and ignoring the fact that the precedent for transfer of points due to driver injury had been set in his own case back in 1970, [he] began to attack the AHRA through the news media.

"To soothe Garlits's feathers, a plan was announced whereby double points would be awarded in Top Fuel at the World Finals in Fremont. When it was realized that Warren/Wiebe would still win the title if Warren made it as far as the semifinal round, Garlits was suddenly awarded 200 points for the OCIR race."

In succession, the* Swamp Rat 19 *followed the* Wynns-Liner*, and the experimental, short-wheelbase* Swamp Rat 17*. The new car had a 240-inch wheelbase, and its Milodon Hemi was backed by a B&J 2-speed transmission. (Photo Courtesy Rich Carlson/Grant Bittner Collection)

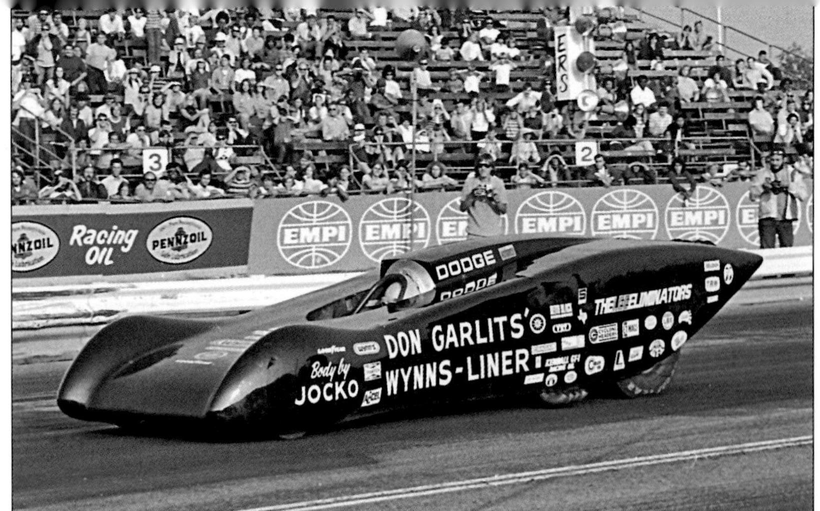

The Garlits* Wynns-Liner *featured a body by Robert "Jocko" Johnson. The streamliner handled poorly, as the rear had a tendency to lift at speeds of greater than 180 mph. The experiment was shelved in short order. (Photo Courtesy Steve Reyes)

The story went on to state that the points were awarded to Garlits because the streamliner qualified, which contradicted the race results. I doubt that anyone was happy with the result.

Garlits narrowly won the 1973 Top Fuel Championship by defeating Warren in the rain-delayed final at Fremont. Both had been running the fairly new Milodon aluminum block, but Warren fried his in the semifinal and had to switch to his iron-block backup motor.

Garlits's Milodon engine used a Keith Black stroker crank and measured 485 ci. Garlits's engine used less nitro, less overdrive, less spark lead, and more compression to record 5.70 ETs. In the final round, Garlits recorded a 5.95 ET at 234.98 mph to Warren's 6.35 at 213.76.

In the Rod Dunne and Jerry Johanssen Chevy Fueler, Larry Dixon became the seventh member of Cragar's Five-Second Club. Real Don Steele, the car's sponsor, was a popular West Coast disc jockey during the 1960s and 1970s. (Photo Courtesy Michael Pottie)

Don't Count Out the Chevys

In November 1973, Larry Dixon became the seventh member of the Cragar Five-Second Club by recording a 5.94 ET while qualifying at the Supernationals. What made Dixon's feat so unique was that he accomplished it using a big-block Chevy.

The Chevy wasn't dead yet in the Fuel ranks by a long shot. Jim Bucher and his aluminum 470-ci Chevy ran a 6.07 ET at the Gatornationals and then qualified number one at Indy with a 6.07 ET. Many predicted that Bucher would be the first driver in the 5s, and he might have been if it wasn't for some bad luck.

Nick Arias kept Chevy's hopes alive in the Fuel ranks by introducing aluminum Hemi heads for the Chevy engine in 1973.

Muldowney Earns Unlimited Fuel License

Shirley Muldowney became the first woman in drag racing to earn an Unlimited Fuel driver's license. In 1973, she received her license over the Easter weekend at Dragway Park in Cayuga, Ontario, Canada.

Muldowney made use of Bobby "Poncho" Rendon's *Frito Bandito* Top Fuel car and recorded a 6.60 ET at 221 mph on her licensing run. Present to witness the accomplishment were Muldowney's then-partner Connie Kalitta and fellow racers Tommy Ivo and Don Garlits.

Breaking drag racing's glass ceiling, Shirley Muldowney became the first woman to receive her Fuel license. A summer of match racing followed. (Photo Courtesy Rob Potter)

Funny Car

The AA Funny Car category enjoyed immense popularity through the 1970s. The cars were loud and had character. In addition, with names such as "Jungle" Jim, the *Chi-Town Hustler*, and the *Blue Max*, they were easily identifiable, even if they looked a little less like production models. The added bonus was that their speeds approached those of Top Fuel cars.

Jeg's High Performance was founded in 1960 by Jeg Coughlin Sr. Today, it is one of the leaders in mail-order parts. In 1973, Jeg's sponsored several drag cars, including this AA/FC, which is being driven by Dale Emery. The Camaro appeared in 1972 and is said to be the first with wheel bumps for front tire clearance. (Photo Courtesy Bob Martin)

Thompson's Grand Am

With yesterday's Funny Cars regulated to gas and injected circuit racing and the growing bracket-racing scene, the popular body choices in the AA class

One of the most unique Funny Cars of the period was Mickey Thompson's Grand Am. Here, Butch Maas boils the hides at the 1973 AHRA Winter Nationals. (Photo Courtesy J. R. Bloom)

for 1973 were the Chevy Vega and Ford Mustang. However, Mickey Thompson was different. He debuted a Pontiac Grand Am at the end of 1972 with Butch Maas at the wheel. Fans either loved or hated the car, but there was no denying that it stood out and received attention.

The Grand Am went up in flames at the Gatornationals, leaving Maas with bad burns and destroying the Ron Pellegrini body. The car was rebuilt and Dale Pulde took over driving. By Thompson's own admission, the car was too heavy. Even running a 540-ci engine, the Buttera-chassis car failed to meet expectations. It won one national event when Pulde defeated Art Ward at the AHRA Spring Nationals. The Grand Am was finally retired in 1976.

Schumacher's Trio of Cars

Helping to move the sport forward in 1973 was the predominant Funny Car team assembled by Don Schumacher. By the end of the 1972 season, Don had three 'Cuda Funny Cars in his stable. He drove one himself, and the others were driven by Raymond Beadle and Bobby Rowe, who later gave up the seat to Ron O'Donnell. The team made national events with all three sanctioning bodies and won a dozen events over the span of the 1972 and 1973 seasons, which culminated in Schumacher winning the 1973 AHRA Funny Car World Championship.

After Schumacher took over the Wonder Bread sponsorship in the spring of 1973, he made one attempt at running the ill-handling Vega panel before he switched back to his old 'Cuda shell.

"The car flew backward at half-track," Crewman Tim Grose recalled. "Minutes later, I jumped in the truck and trailer and drove to the shop in Park Ridge [New Jersey], slid the 'Cuda body into the trailer, and returned to

Raymond Beadle began the 1973 season behind the wheel of Don Schumacher's red Barracuda. Ed Pink supplied the power for Schumacher's cars. (Photo Courtesy J. R. Bloom)

finish our match race obligation with "Broadway" Bob Metzler."

Schumacher repainted all of his 'Cudas in the Wonder Bread polka-dot paint.

Schumacher's Aero Wonder

In August, Schumacher debuted his latest creation, the Wonder Bread–sponsored Vega coupe, at the PRO National Challenge. Although it lacked any wind-tunnel testing, Buttera and company relied upon common sense and judgement to come up with a pretty slick piece. Schumacher's Vega sat approximately 3 inches lower in the front and 5 inches lower in the rear when compared to the Vegas that he competed against. The low silhouette forced a 3-degree recline in the driver's position, which lowered the roll cage 9 inches. A Lexan window positioned in the roof helped Schumacher see the tree.

Don Schumacher's Vega coupe was groundbreaking. It was significantly different from the Funny Cars that preceded it. Of course, that doesn't mean it all worked as planned. (Photo Courtesy Bob Martin)

To cut down on drag, the Vega grille was open, and air passed through a louvered hood. Lexan side glass was installed, and the rear glass area was louvered to provide a way for trapped air to escape. Wheel discs were added, but when Butch Leal tried them on his Pro Stock Duster the previous year, they were soundly rejected by the NHRA in the name of safety. The NHRA surmised that the wheel discs would become dangerous projectiles if they came loose.

Don Prudhomme won his first NHRA Funny Car national event at Indy in 1973, becoming the first person in the sanctioning body's history to win a national event in Top Fuel and Funny Car. Prudhomme (and Tom McEwen) agreed to a sponsorship with Care Free chewing gum in 1973.

At the National Challenge, Schumacher qualified the Vega in the seventh position with a 6.596 ET. In an odd chain of events, Schumacher found himself in the final round against Prudhomme's 'Cuda after previous-round-winner Jim Nicoll's Vega broke while heating the tires. So, Schumacher, the previous round low ET loser, was alive again due to the break rule. Without taking the time to properly heat the slicks, Schumacher handed Prudhomme an easy win. At the NHRA Nationals (now referred to as the US Nationals by the NHRA), the Vega was given the Best Engineered Car honors.

As with Thompson's Grand Am, the Vega failed to meet expectations. However, you have to applaud Schumacher for the effort. He and Buttera looked outside the proverbial box in an attempt to advance the Funny Car category. Schumacher felt that time in a wind tunnel and a lighter body would have made a

difference. The car was nearly 400 pounds on the heavy side.

"The principles were phenomenal, but it was really my fault for asking for a stiff car," Schumacher said during an interview with the NHRA's Phil Burgess. "I had Buttera build the car with a stiff chassis because for all of the [match-race] dates I used to run, I got tired of rolling the car out of the trailer and finding something broken. We didn't know how critical it was to have a flexible car. It just didn't react well."

Schumacher's drag racing efforts were supported by Schumacher Electric as well as a list of sponsors.

In 1973, Don Schumacher calculated that he spent $287,000 of his own money. That's equivalent to $2,071,438 today. Continental Baking, the maker of Wonder Bread, pulled its sponsorship at the end of 1973.

The *Green Elephant*

In early 1973, Jim Green purchased Joe Pisano's Don Long-built Vega, painted it green, and labelled it as the *Green Elephant*. Dispelling the belief that green race cars were bad luck, Frank Hall drove the *Elephant* to the Division 6 Funny Car title in 1973 and won the world championship.

With the ever-capable Jerry Verhuel pulling wrenches, the team took the world title by defeating Bobby Rowe. Rowe began the season driving for Schumacher and closed it driving the *Mr. Ed* Plymouth Satellite of Ed Willis. At the World Finals, Rowe qualified number one with a 6.54 ET. Close behind him in the number-two spot was Hall with a 6.67. In the final, Rowe took both ends of the class record with a 6.38 ET at 228 mph (altitude corrected to a 6.28 ET at 232 mph), but Hall's slight holeshot won the race with a 6.39 ET at 224 mph.

Jim Green's Green Elephant Vega featured a Don Long chassis and a 484-ci Hemi with approximately 1,800 hp. Jerry Verheul and Mark Dentler maintained the car. Power passed through a Lenco transmission to a Ford rear end. (Photo Courtesy Rich Carlson/Grant Bittner Collection)

In 1973, West Seneca, New York-based Glenn Lazzar made the move from Gas to BB/FC and debuted his S&W Race Cars Funny Farmer *Pinto. (Photo Courtesy Michael Pottie)*

Concerned about the rising cost of drag racing, Schumacher walked away from the sport after 1975 and focused his attention on family and the family business. He returned in 1998, with coaxing from his son, to build one of drag racing's great enterprises.

Pro Stock

After Jenkins had the run of Pro Stock in 1972, the NHRA ensured that things were different in 1973. It hoped that an adjustment in weight breaks would balance the field. The new breaks saw "true wedge" (inclined-valve) engines running at 6.50 pounds per cubic inch and Hemi and SOHC engines at 7.00 pounds per cubic inch.

As was habit, the NHRA revisited the rules after the Gatornationals. At the time, the minimum weight for Pro Stocks with a wheelbase over 100 inches dropped from 2,400 to 2,300 pounds. Speeds now approached 150 mph, at which point a parachute was required and aerodynamics played a greater role. Dry-sump oiling systems allowed for a lower silhouette. In addition, tucked bumpers and fenders, drooping front clips, and the removal of drip rails all contributed to a clean path through the air, greater stability at speed, and quicker times.

The Pro Stock Lenco

In 1973, The Lenco planetary transmission became standard fare in Pro Stock after Leonard Abbott added another case to his 2-speed Fuel car unit to give it four forward gears. Some called the transmission the great equalizer because it took a racer's ability to be a good shifter out of the equation. With the introduction of the Lenco transmission, Ronnie Sox, who was considered by most to be the best 4-speed man in drag racing, had to find other ways to get an advantage.

The three levers of the Lenco transmission meant serious business. The transmission was a game changer and helped to put the "Pro" into Pro Stock.

Melvin Yow is credited with using the first Pro Stock Lenco after he tried it out in the spring of 1972. By the Winternationals in 1973, the transmission proved to be the next thing. (Photo Courtesy Bob Martin)

In a Pro Stock car, the Lenco carries three shift levers (one for each case). From first gear, each following gear is engaged by pulling down on one of three levers. Just like the Fuelers, the shift levers move the clutch pack together to engage the gear in each housing. The transmission cost about $2,500 and eliminated the chance of missed shifts, allowed for tighter engine tolerances, and, like the Fuelers, was said to reduce ETs by 2/10 of a second. There's no denying that the transmission contributed to the growing expense of building a competitive Pro Stock vehicle and the demise of the low-on-bucks racer.

Year of the Pinto

The new NHRA weight breaks worked out well for the Ford racers who figured out what made the canted-valve Cleveland run and survive. Head plates cured the

The Gary Dyer-driven Mr. Norm's Mini Charger *Colt featured a Romeo Palamides chassis. ETs in the 8.70s at 155 mph were produced. (Photo Courtesy Bob Martin)*

Terry Hedrick competes in the short-lived Colt that he campaigned with Red Sullivan. A crash ended the life of this Logghe-chassis car, which was the last car that Hedrick campaigned. (Photo Courtesy Bob Martin)

Mini Missile

The Hemi Colt was a monster! In 1973, Hemi-powered Colts began to appear on the scene, but, according to the NHRA rule book, they were not eligible to compete in Pro Stock unless the engine measured 366 ci or less (as manufactured). This meant that no de-stroked Hemi engines were accepted. If the Colts were to compete in NHRA Pro Stock, it had to be with an LA-series engine. For owners who chose the Hemi route and wanted to compete in Pro Stock, there was always the more-accommodating AHRA, IHRA, or UDRA.

In 1972, Logghe Chassis was contracted by Chrysler to prepare five de-stroked Hemi Colts. Chrysler hoped to convince the NHRA to legalize them for use in Pro Stock. Chrysler turned to Dan Knapp in 1973 to build five new cars. The advantage of the new Colts was that they weighed less than the Logghe cars. Knapp and his shop, Chassis Dynamics, got as far as building three complete cars before Chrysler pulled the contract. Those three cars were the Ted Spehar and Don Carlton Hemi-powered *Mini Missile*, a 340-powered car for the Rod Shop, and a small-block car for the team of Joe DeSantis and Francis Crider. One car not finished was to go to Butch Leal, and the final car, which was to go to Dick Landy, never made it off the drawing board.

breathing issues, and a reconfigured oiling system kept the thirsty bottom end alive.

"Dyno" Don Nicholson set the tone by winning both the AHRA and NHRA winter meets and set the class record at both with a 9.27 ET and a 9.01. Nicholson was on fire! He followed his Pomona win by driving down to Florida to win the Gatornationals.

The team of Wayne Gapp and Jack Roush competed in their Wolverine-chassis Pinto. The pair joined Pro Stock in 1970 and campaigned two different Boss 429–powered Mavericks before they saw the light. They won the 1973 NHRA World Championship by defeating Bill Jenkins at the World Finals with a 9.17 ET at 149 mph to Jenkins's 9.35 at 145.86.

The World Finals ran by the new 1974 rules and weight breaks, which

Bob Glidden went to Pro Stock racing full time beginning with the 1973 season. He had previously focused on Stock and Super Stock cars. Glidden provided a taste of things to come when it took a holeshot by Bill "Grumpy" Jenkins to defeat him at the 1972 Supernationals. (Photo Courtesy Bob Martin)

The Mopar Missile team innovations included magnesium and titanium parts that reduced the Duster's weight to the bare minimum. Prior to the season-ending Supernationals, Chrysler once again walked away from NHRA Pro Stock. (Photo Courtesy Bob Martin)

Mopar Missile Madness

Through the mid-1970s, the Motown Missile/Mopar Missile team was a step ahead of most. This made sense because the team consisted of several factory employees who were on a mission to put Chrysler at the forefront of Pro Stock. The 1973 *Mopar Missile* Duster was the pinnacle of its investment, as it pulled back its involvement in 1974.

As early as 1972, the *Missile* crew was one of the first teams to use computers to gather real-time track data. By 1973, it was able to measure wheel slippage, wheel speed, suspension travel, fuel pressure, oil pressure, and engine speed. Author Geoff Stunkard takes a fascinating look at the *Motown Missile* and *Mopar Missile* in his book, *Chrysler's Motown Missile: Mopar's Secret Engineering Program at the Dawn of Pro Stock*, which was written for CarTech.

Wayne Gapp and Jack Roush's first Cleveland effort resulted in a 1973 NHRA World Championship and a 1974 IHRA title. The team's reputation resulted in Gapp and Roush building winning powerplants for numerous customers. (Photo Courtesy Bob Martin)

In June 1973, "Dyno" Don Nicholson's Pinto became the first Pro Stocker to record an 8-second ET when he completed a run in 8.98 seconds in Connecticut. The same year, the Pinto held the NHRA ET record for six months with a 9.01. Although it was considered to be illegal, on rare occasions, Nicholson mixed his fuel with one part aviation gas to four parts Sunoco 260. He mentioned this to his friend Butch Leal while waiting in the staging lanes at the Gatornationals. Leal's response was, "Is that it? I run 50-50." (Photo Courtesy Bob Martin)

Colorado-based Irv Beringhaus was the 1973 Division 5 Champion with his Kent Fuller, Dick Landy-built Duster. The Dick Landy Industries 396-ci Hemi produced 9.30 ETs. (Photo Courtesy John Eichinger)

had the Hemi cars running at 7 pounds per cubic inch, small-block-powered big cars at 6.45 pounds per cubic inch, and Vegas and Pintos at 6.65 pounds per cubic inch. At Chrysler's request, all the factory-backed cars (outside of the West Coast–based Butch Leal and Dick Landy) sat out the World Finals. Leal was tossed at tech inspection due to his Duster's staggered wheelbase, and Landy couldn't get dialed in. The only Mopar racers to make the show were Larry Huff and Reid Whisnant, and they failed to make an impact.

Those Are the Breaks

With no subcompact or LA-series engine (small-block) program to speak of, Chrysler and its racers had little choice than to rely on its compact Dusters and Darts to keep it in contention. The top echelon found that running de-stroked Hemis in the 366- to 396-ci range was the best option. The smaller Hemis allowed them to run at a reduced weight, and when compared to a larger-inch Hemi, the horsepower drop in the useable range was insignificant. Using the new Harry Weslake–designed aluminum D-5 Hemi cylinder heads (with their smaller, round ports and raised exhaust) in conjunction with a new-profile camshaft from Crane provided the best results.

Although the Mopar contingency wasn't happy with the 7-pounds-per-cubic-inch break, nothing in the foreseeable future was going to change—not after Don Carlton ran a 9.22 ET in his *Mopar Missile* Duster at the NHRA Winternationals,

In 1973, Butch Leal wowed spectators with his 396-ci, Ron Butler-built Duster. Features included a narrowed front clip and magnesium and titanium parts. (Photo Courtesy Bob Martin)

In late 1973, Herb McCandless hitched a ride with Rufus "Brooklyn Heavy" Lee, driving this Dart Sport. With an aluminum Milodon 7-liter engine under the scooped hood, Herb recorded a jaw-dropping 8.51 ET during a match race session at Atco Dragway. It's a shame that aftermarket blocks were not Pro Stock legal. (Photo Courtesy Gary L. Anderson)

Although "Grumpy" Jenkins's Vega may have received all the ink, several Vegas competed in Pro Stock during 1973. Jeg Coughlin campaigned this 327-equipped subcompact that ran 9.40 ETs. (Photo Courtesy Bob Martin)

where he was runner-up to Nicholson. In addition, at the AHRA winter meet, Ronnie Sox, in the *Sox & Martin* Duster, qualified number one with a 9.17 ET and carried the AHRA's required 6.85 pounds per cubic inch.

Carlton wowed them at IHRA's Rockingham in April when he recorded an 8.98 ET with his de-stroked Hemi. He won the NHRA Springnationals and defeated Butch Leal, who gave Chrysler its only other win of the NHRA season by defeating Bob Glidden at the Grandnationals. Leal, in his Ron Butler–built Duster, had a phenomenal season going. He won a few AHRA series events, was runner-up at numerous events, and won the Popular Hot Rodding meet.

Outside of NHRA competition, it was a great year for Chrysler. Don Carlton went to all eight IHRA national event final rounds and won five of them. "Dandy" Dick Landy, in the beautifully constructed Ron Butler Dart Sport, captured the AHRA world title.

Comp Eliminator

The Comp category provided a good mix of old and new, and 1973 was more of the same. New Jersey's Pete Shadinger, who seemingly had been around forever, competed in the category as early as 1965. He drove his straight-8 Buick-powered D/Dragster to honors at the NHRA Summernationals.

Glenn Lazzar was the Division 3 points champion with his Chevy-powered, BB/FC *Funny Farmer* Pinto. The West Seneca, New York, farmer is well remembered for his fine line of Gor-Den Automotive–sponsored rides. When the season drew to a close, the world champion honors went to

The AHRA mimicked the NHRA when it came to Comp Eliminator and had two Supercharged Gas classes. Don Toia's Hemi-powered Maverick was tough on the competition. (Photo Courtesy J. R. Bloom)

category standout Paul Smith. Smith and his A/FD defeated Roy Rasetter's A/Altered in the final round at Amarillo.

Modified Eliminator

The NHRA added two Modified Compact classes to Modified Eliminator in 1973, which increased the total number of classes in the category to 26. The sanctioning body found it necessary to clarify what transmissions could and couldn't be used in Modified after Francis Crider took category honors at the Gatornationals with a Lenco 4-speed.

In 1972, Carroll Caudle parked his potent Modified Production '55 Chevy and debuted this Vega, which had been his wife's daily driver. Don Hardy back-halved the car, and Caudle built engines of 331 ci and 287 ci to run B/MP, C/MP, and E/Gas. Division 4 wins and class records followed. (Photo Courtesy John Eichinger)

Crider's Critter

Crider's A/SR, often referred to as a Pro Stock in a Ford Model T roadster skin, dropped more than a few jaws when it debuted early in 1973. Crider reset the class record of 9.37

Francis Crider's Street Roadster *featured a Hemi that put the wheelie bars to work. The tall front tires aided roll-out. In 1974, Crider's partner Joe DeSantis drove the car. (Photo Courtesy Bob Martin)*

with a 9.08 ET and won Modified at the Gatornationals. Powering the Roadster was a twin-plug Hemi, the aforementioned Lenco 4-speed, and a narrowed Dana rear end mounted in a Ron Fournier chassis.

The NHRA banned the Lenco from the Modified category immediately after the Gatornationals. The new rules stated, "Aftermarket transmissions accepted as long as a clutch is necessary to shift all of the gears in a conventional stick-shift manner."

Although the rule change slowed Crider, he marched on and reinstated the class record with a 9.27 ET in May. Crider went on to win class at the Summernationals with a 9.39 ET, and he won class at Indy with a 9.37 ET to defeat Jerry Hays.

Modified Compact

The new A/MC and B/MC classes were for 4-cylinder-equipped cars with a maximum displacement of 151.5 ci. The caliber of cars varied from Pete Brock's Winternationals B/MC-winning Datsun 510 to Chris Lawrence and Jeff Leininger's World Finals–winning Volkswagen fastback.

Lawrence and Leininger, proprietors of Chris and Jeff's Bug Shop in Houston, Texas, won class at Indy before the World Finals at Amarillo. At the World Finals, Leininger took the wheel of the B/MC fastback and defeated John Preston's M/Gas Karmann Ghia. Interestingly enough, Lawrence is credited with the win and should have been driving, as he was the one who earned the points to qualify for the race. Apparently, the two felt that Leininger was the better driver, and no one was the wiser.

The Bug Shop team of Chris Lawrence and Jeff Leininger brought Volkswagen its one and only World Championship. While Beetles were a common sight on the track, the fastback versions were not. (Photo Courtesy Steve Reyes)

Carroll Fink debuted his SS/EA Hemi 'Cuda in 1971 and campaigned it into the 1976 season. The Chrysler-supported car set out to crush the Ray Allen-driven Truppi-Kling *Chevelle. With a Ron Mancini Hemi in place of the original 340 engine, it did just that. (Photo Courtesy Michael Pottie)*

Chrysler Executive John Tedder, a drag racer at heart, earned the nickname "Mr. MoTech" due to his success in recruiting for MoTech Automotive Educational Center in Livonia, Michigan. Tedder was a Division 3 champion and earned multiple class wins. (Photo Courtesy Bob Martin)

Super Stock

Looking back on Super Stock in the 1970s, one can see how each of Detroit's Big Three manufacturers had cut out its niche. Chevy, with its multitude of small-block combinations, dominated the mid and lower classes, the Cobra Jet Mustangs retained a solid grip on classes F through H, and classes A through D were considered Hemi territory.

Unlike General Motors and Ford, which decreased their support of racers at the beginning of the decade, Chrysler remained deeply involved. It retained its grip on Super Stock and tossed cars and parts to the likes of Judy Lilly, Ron Mancini, Carroll Fink, and Steve Bagwell. Each of them found their way into the winner's circle during 1973.

Bagwell-Earwood

In Steve Bagwell's SS/EA Hemi 'Cuda convertible, Terry Earwood won what is and always has been considered to be the most prestigious race of the season: the US Nationals. Terry's final-round victim was the SS/HA Camaro of Bill Felker.

To begin the 1973 season, Earwood drove the same convertible for the Bowers brothers. At Earwood's suggestion, Bagwell bought the 'Cuda from the brothers. Bagwell added fancy paint that, according to Earwood, cost $5,500, which was the same amount that he paid for the car. Bagwell's home improvement store allowed him to spend and fulfill his dream of being out there and racing with the professionals.

Bagwell stated that outside of the old "Dyno" Don Comet wagon that he match raced through the

Driving for Steve Bagwell, Terry Earwood was nearly unbeatable. Few moments were prouder than his Indy win in 1973. Check out the Cragar spun aluminum wheels. It seems that everyone had a set by the mid-1970s. (Photo Courtesy Terry Earwood)

The 1973 NHRA World Championship car of Bill Hanes is seen here in 1974 winning the Popular Hot Rodding meet in Martin, Michigan. The Impala and its 350-ci engine produced 12.30 ETs. (Photo Courtesy Bruce Nelson)

mid-1960s, the 'Cuda convertible was the most successful, money-making car that he campaigned.

"We campaigned the car as a '71, even though it was a '70," Bagwell said. "The car was a record holder at 11 seconds flat in 1973."

Things only got better in 1974.

Chevy Comes Through

Bill Hanes, a long-time Michigan racer who was a part of the famed Chevair racing team in the early 1960s, won class at the Winternationals and Indy in 1964 with his 327-equipped 1962 Bel Air. In 1973, Hanes, with his wife, Irene, by his side, campaigned an SS/PA 1969 Impala. Hanes earned the season's world championship when he defeated Ron Peters's SS/B 1965 Plymouth in the category final.

Hanes ran the Impala with the ever-popular 255-hp-rated, 350-ci engine that produced mid-12 ETs through 1974 before he swapped the Impala body for a lighter Biscayne body. The combination moved the Chevy into the SS/LA class. Eventually, the Biscayne was turned into a Pro Gas car that ran a 454-ci small-block.

The AHRA did things a little differently than the NHRA. Allen Patterson won the Super Stock Championship with his Braswell 2-barrel-equipped Camaro. ETs in the 11.50s were common. (Photo Courtesy Allen Patterson)

Stock

The NHRA ran Stock at just three national events in 1973, plus the World Finals, which was won by Jerry McClanahan in his 1966 Chevy wagon. Rules remained nearly unchanged to start the year, which meant that headers and reground camshafts were not allowed. However, offset cam keys were now allowed. The biggest increase in power came from blueprinting an engine. Superseded carburetors were now allowed, but throttle bore and venturi had to match the original part. There were numerous carburetor gurus in business who knew how to draw some extra power out of a stock part.

Street tires were the only type of tires available to start the season, and those tires had to fit the stock wheel

The *Hard Times* Firebird

In 1968, Truman Fields bought this Ram Air I Firebird brand new. As a result of his success, he raced for Pontiac in 1972. (Photo Courtesy Bill Truby)

wells. Classes that ran to P/S in 1972 now ran through Y/S, with all classes running at half-pound increments. The new Pure Stock format slowly gained competitors.

Truman Fields won the Labor Day weekend Indy Nationals with his *Hard Times,* Ram Air I 1968 Firebird. The Firebird, which was sold to Mike McKinney in 1976, would rack up 10 straight NHRA Indy class wins between 1970 and 1979. Powering the Firebird was a Ram Air I 400-ci engine that was rated at 340 hp from the factory.

Days of Future Past

The *Battery Box* electric vehicle (EV) dragster of Roger Hedlund was ahead of its time. The short-wheelbase dragster clocked low-13-second ETs and is believed to be the first EV to break the 100-mph barrier. A GE 9-inch DC-series motor with 12-volt Diehard batteries that produced 192 volts provided the power, which was transferred to the rear wheels via a chain.

An unusual car out of the Sacramento, California, area was the Battery Box *of Roger Hedlund. This electric vehicle was ahead of its time. (Photo Courtesy Roger Rodgers)*

CHAPTER FOUR

1974: GETTING TO THE POINT

Hot Rod magazine featured a series of articles that focused on the build of C. J. Baker's 1969 Chevelle. Baker campaigned the car with great success in multiple 2-barrel and 4-barrel classes. (Photo Courtesy Rich Carlson/Grant Bittner)

Between 1965 (the year of NHRA's inaugural World Finals) and 1973, each category of World Champion was determined by who won the World Finals. Making it to the World Finals was a chore because it required an invite, and only the top five point-getters from the seven divisions were invited.

In 1974, the NHRA implemented a season-long points system for the professional categories to determine the world champions. It was similar to the Grand-American series that the AHRA introduced in 1970. With the NHRA, points were earned at regional meets and national events. The Sportsman categories retained the old format, where the World Finals determined the season champion. In 1981, all categories went to the season points–chase format.

Top Fuel

New NHRA rules that affected mainly the Top Fuel racers stated that only water could be used for burnouts, which ended the spectator-loving fire burnouts.

Another safety-minded rule change stated that all new Top Fuel and Funny Cars had to carry a full-floating rear-end assembly. The floaters all but eliminated stray busted axles and errant wheels bouncing down the track or into spectators. With a floater, the wheels are bolted to a hub, which is independent of the axle. If an axle snapped, the wheel remained with the car.

Another new safety rule that was required in all blown and Fuel classes stated that valve-cover vent tubes had to expel into a catch container. This benefited drivers

Gary Beck and Ray Peets scored a major sponsor deal when they landed Canadian cigarette brand Macdonald. By 1974, it was becoming more difficult to survive in the pro ranks without sponsorship dollars. (Photo Courtesy Mike Dimery)

who still sat behind the engine.

Another issue discussed by the rule makers was the ongoing rising costs of drag racing, specifically in the Fuel classes. In November 1974, the NHRA met with several racers to discuss banning nitromethane as a way of lowering costs. Although the NHRA had a strong case, the majority of Fuel racers balked at the idea, and it was quickly dropped.

Beck and Peets Top the Heap

Gary Beck was the first world champion under the new points-chase system. Crew Chief Ronnie Capps helped Beck earn the title. Capps spent the previous year wrenching for Jerry Ruth and was instrumental in Ruth earning the Top Fuel championship in 1973. Ironically, Ruth and Capps defeated Beck in the Top Fuel final that year to win the world title.

Ray Peets was the majority owner of the Beck-driven Woody Gilmore car. Nestled between the frame rails was a Keith Black Hemi and Lenco transmission. Beck said that a good ring seal, Peets cylinder head prep, and the crew at Reliable Engines in Edmonton, Alberta, Canada, kept him in front of the

Gary Beck, a native of Seattle, Washington, married a Canadian woman from Edmonton, Alberta. This contributed to many believing that Beck was Canadian. On both sides of the border, he was a winner. (Photo Courtesy Rich Carlson/ Grant Bittner Collection)

Journeyman Dave Settles drove the Keith Black-powered Top Fuel car for Paul Candies and Leonard Hughes in 1974. He won the Gatornationals and was the runner-up at three more national events. (Photo Courtesy Mike Lacelle)

pack. By Beck's own estimates, the horsepower rating approached 2,500 at this point.

As it was nearly impossible to race on your own dime, Peets searched for a major sponsorship and found one in Macdonald, a Canadian tobacco company. The Macdonald Export "A" cigarette sponsorship began in 1974 and carried through 1975. A deal was in the works with the company for the 1976 season but fell through due to increasing pressure from the Canadian government regarding tobacco advertisements. Peets quickly agreed to a deal with Thrush Performance Products, which is a Rexdale, Ontario, Canada–based aftermarket manufacturer that also provided the NHRA with its track dryers.

Dave Settles, driving for the team of Candies & Hughes (Paul Candies and Leonard Hughes), made a great showing by finishing second in the points standings. As with the Peets and Beck Fueler, the *Candies & Hughes* car featured a Woody Gilmore chassis and a Keith Black aluminum Hemi that was stamped on the block with serial number 002. At the World Finals in October, Settles faced Beck in the semifinals. In a run that both competitors would love to do over, Settles pulled a red-light, and Beck crossed the centerline. In doing so, Beck disqualified himself, and Settles was reinstated. Garlits took care of Settles in the final.

John Rodeck proved that his aluminum Chevy block could survive the world of Top Fuel. Here, his short-wheelbase car attempts to qualify at the World Finals, but the attempt fell short. (Photo Courtesy Robert Runne/Stephen Justice)

The Rodeck Rat

John Rodeck introduced his aluminum Chevy Fuel motor and gave hope to the Chevy faithful. In 1974, he briefly ran the engine in this short-wheelbase Top Fuel car. The car lasted about a half-dozen runs before Rodeck crashed it. He headed back to the shop and emerged later with a conventional long-wheelbase car.

After Herm Petersen recovered from a horrific crash at Orange County International Raceway in 1973, he returned to action in 1974 with partner Sam Fritz in this Can-Am-inspired Top Fueler. Under the blue anodized skin was a Woody Gilmore chassis. Petersen said that the car handled well, but the Donovan Hemi couldn't overcome the added 200 pounds of body weight. A best ET of 6.24 was realized before the car was retired at the end of the season. (Photo Courtesy Rich Carlson/Grant Bittner Collection)

Don Prudhomme's Army sponsorship ran from 1974 through 1980. Here, he is back in his old 'Cuda after the winter meets. (Photo Courtesy Rich Carlson/Grant Bittner Collection)

Funny Car

Slight NHRA rule revisions allowed Funny Cars to shrink from a minimum of 65 inches in width to 62 inches. Top chops remained 2 inches, and due to the low ground clearance of some cars that tripped the lights early, ground clearance at the front spoiler was set at a minimum of 3 inches.

Chain Lightning

The 1974 NHRA World Finals was one to remember. In the Funny Car final round, Dave Condit, in the Plueger and Gyger Donovan-powered Mustang, defeated Dale Pulde, who raced Mickey Thompson's Grand Am that turned a slower 6.19 ET to a 6.17 ET. However, the real story of the event was Shirl Greer's return after a blower explosion that happened during qualifying, sending him to hospital and nearly destroying the body of his Mustang.

Greer was having a great year. He won rounds and earned a category win at the Grandnationals in Canada, defeating the Chevy Vega of Kosty Ivanof. Heading into the World Finals, Greer trailed Paul Smith in the standings by 174 points. Greer received a huge break when Smith failed to qualify. Hot on Greer's heels was Prudhomme, who also had a shot at the title. Greer needed more than a little luck to pull off a championship win.

Any hopes that Greer had looked to be snuffed out during qualifying, when a massive top-end fire sent him to the hospital with second-degree burns to his arms, hands, and face. The Mustang barely survived, due to extensive fire damage to the back half of the car. Laid up in the hospital, word reached Greer that he still had a chance at the title if he could get out of bed and if the Mustang could be pieced back together.

In a show of camaraderie that had engulfed the sport from the beginning, dozens of people worked to piece the Mustang back together in anticipation of Greer's return. The rear body was rebuilt using sheet aluminum, a boatload of rivets, and yards of racer's tape. Against his doctor's wishes, Greer signed himself out of the hospital the next day and intended to climb back into the Mustang, and he did just that. Greer donned a pair of gloves provided by Prudhomme, took his one shot at qualifying, and made it. He was up 270 points on Prudhomme.

In the first round of eliminations, Greer defeated Leroy Chadderton in the *Chadderton & Okazaki* Vega. This gave him the points needed to clinch the title, as Prudhomme lost in the second round to Dale Pulde. It's interesting to note that Greer was the last one to win a Funny Car championship without the support of a major sponsor. Times were changing.

On Shirl Greer's way to capturing the NHRA Championship, he won just one national event in 1974. Here, driving* Chain Lightning*, he failed to qualify at Indy. (Photo Courtesy Ed Aigner)

More Lil' John's

In early 1974, two more of Lil' John Buttera's lowrider Funny Cars appeared: Larry Huff's Richard Tharp-driven *Soapy Sales* Dart and Don Prudhomme's Army-sponsored Vega. Prudhomme was never comfortable in the car, and he ran it at the AHRA and NHRA winter meets before hopping back into his proven Barracuda. With the new (old) ride, Prudhomme won the US Nationals and the AHRA Funny Car Championship.

Larry Huff was one of the first racers to campaign cars in all three Pro categories. Dave Uyehara drove the Soapy Sales Dart through 1974. The low-slung Funny Car's chassis was built by John Buttera. (Photo Courtesy Michael Pottie)

The John Buttera-built Vega wasn't a comfortable fit for Prudhomme. Tom Hoover purchased the Vega and had success running it as* Showtime*. (Photo Courtesy Grant Bittner)

No one expected Shirl Greer to return from this qualifying fire. It took many hands to rebuild the car and a signed release to get Greer out of the hospital. (Photo Courtesy Howard Koby/Lou Hart Collection)

Surviving another fire while qualifying, Shirl Greer defeated Leroy Chadderton in the first round. Greer secured the win when Don Prudhomme lost in the second round. (Photo Courtesy Michael Pottie)

Chi-Town Hustler *Success*

The Chi-Town Hustler crew, who made half-track burnouts a common occurrence in Funny Car to the delight of drag racing fans everywhere, deserves a mention for its trackside accomplishments.

Amidst its robust match-race schedule, the Chi-Town crew, consisting of Austin Coil, John Farkonas, and driver Ron Colson, won enough IHRA national events to win the season's Funny Car Championship. The unique fuel-delivery system developed by Farkonas and Coil helped make the team a consistent winner.

By 1974, most racers ran 16 nozzles: 8 to the hat and 8 to the ports. The Chi-Town Hustler crew developed a 24-nozzle fuel-delivery system that worked in conjunction with the Enderle lid atop a Gary Dyer blower. The 8

By 1974, Ron Colson was driving the famed Chi-Town Hustler. *Romeo Palamides built the 119-inch chassis. Austin Coil and Tim Wilson built the stroked Hemi. The Charger looks good on polished Super Trick wheels. (Photo Courtesy Michael Pottie)*

additional nozzles fed the ports, which were controlled by a two-stage valve that opened at 80 psi. The additional nozzles helped increase low-end and midrange power without affecting the top end. The results were 6.30 ETs with less breakage.

Jake Johnston worked in conjunction with Cragar Industries and experimented with pressurized air induction in 1974. Cragar's setup did away with the huffer altogether and pumped a mixture of pressurized air and alcohol into the engine. It went nowhere. (Photo Courtesy Rich Carlson/Grant Bittner Collection)

64 Funny Cars

How popular were Funny Cars during the 1970s? Well, during the early part of the decade, the Northwest was known for its wet weather, lush forests, and the abundance of bumper stickers that read, "The Last Person Leaving Seattle, Turn Off the Lights."

However, the tide began to turn when promoter Bill Doner rolled in from Southern California to take over Kent Pacific Raceway. Doner renamed the track the Seattle International Raceway and introduced the Northwest region to 64 Funny Cars, the fox hunt, and a party atmosphere. Doner created what is known as the West Coast Swing by booking high-profile drag racers into tracks up and down the West Coast.

Under the circumstances, lining up 64 Funny Cars, 32 nitro cars, and 32 alcohol burners was a fairly easy endeavor for Doner. The 1974 event drew more than 25,000 fans, which was an unheard-of number for a one-day drag-racing event. The show with 64 Funny Cars ran into the 1980s before it petered out due to the costs and a lack of touring cars.

Pro Stock

Revised rules allowed the use of full-tube chassis, which raised the ire of those who felt that the Pro Stock category was heading the same way as Funny Car. The

"Dyno" Don Nicholson's new-for-1974 Mustang II made a good showing during its debut at the NHRA Gatornationals but fell to class-winner Wally Booth. By 1974, most Pro Stock cars were constructed using body panels (as opposed to manufactured body shells). Nicholson held the IHRA record for a period of time in 1974 with an 8.845 ET at 151 mph. (Photo Courtesy Michael Pottie)

The "64 Funny Cars" events that Bill Doner promoted in the Northwest were more than just a race–they had a party atmosphere. (Photo Courtesy Rich Carlson/ Grant Bittner Collection)

new rule was a bonus for chassis manufacturers, which found themselves with an instant backlog.

The NHRA weight breaks were changing again, and Ford's Cleveland was the winner. The breaks, which were split over and under a 105-inch wheelbase, made for some odd combinations.

Something Different

Don Nicholson cashed in his two Pintos after the Winternationals in favor of the new Mustang II. Although the new Mustangs looked significantly better than the Pinto, they were no better aerodynamically. Then, to take advantage of the over/under wheelbase weight breaks, cars with a wheelbase less than 105 inches had to carry 6.85 pounds per cubic inch. Cars with a wheelbase of more than 105 inches only had to carry 6.45 pounds per cubic inch. Nicholson had Don Hardy build him a 1970 Mustang.

Others who built long-wheelbase cars included Harvey Cohen, who campaigned a Don Hardy 1970 Mustang with driver John Healey, and Gapp and Roush, who chose a slightly different route by having Don Hardy build them a four-door Maverick.

Gapp and Roush chose the Maverick, as opposed to a Mustang, as the team felt that the smaller, narrower car had a distinct advantage at speed, as it would push less air. With Wayne Gapp at the helm of the car, the team backed up its 1973 NHRA world title by winning the IHRA Championship in 1974.

"Dyno" Don Nicholson campaigned the longer-wheelbase 1970 Mustang to take advantage of the NHRA weight breaks. His Mustang II saw action in AHRA and IHRA competition. The first pass in the Mustang netted a 9.07 ET. (Photo Courtesy Bob Boudreau)

In 1974, you would be hard-pressed to find a quicker ride in Pro Stock than the Juana Taxi of Gapp and Roush. A 366-ci Cleveland that was nestled in a Don Hardy chassis propelled the Maverick to 8.80 ETs. (Photo Courtesy Michael Pottie)

Glidden's Finest Hour (The First One)

Drag racing's "Mad Dog" Bob Glidden debuted his own 1970 Mustang in 1975. Glidden won the 1974 NHRA Championship and closed the season in his year-old Pinto. It was an amazing come-from-behind win for Glidden, as up until the final month of the season, he wasn't even in contention. After his win at the US Nationals, Glidden's 5,689 total points lagged behind Gapp's 6,272 and Wally Booth's 6,019.

By the time of the final points meet at Beech Bend, Glidden moved into contention when he won the meet and set both ends of the record with an 8.83 ET at 154.90 mph. Heading to the World Finals, the points now stood as follows: Booth 7,277; Gapp 7,230; and Glidden 6,947. To win the championship, Glidden had to outlast Booth and Gapp and set at least one end of the class record.

Glidden made up the points quickly. He set the ET record and qualified with an 8.81 ET. "Dyno" Don Nicholson took care of one of Glidden's problems by eliminating Booth in the second round. Glidden had to take care of Gapp in the final round. Glidden had the momentum and wouldn't be denied. In the final,

Bob Glidden was a man on a mission. Few racers were as dedicated as Glidden or had a comparable work ethic, and it paid off for him. (Photo Courtesy Bob Martin)

Bill "Grumpy" Jenkins's completed Vega raised the bar regarding how future Pro Stocks should be built. The Vega posted mid-8-second ETs before it was retired in 1975. (Photo Courtesy Bill Truby)

Glidden took the win with an oh-so-close 8.89 ET to Gapp's 8.91 ET.

Jenkins's Most Innovative Toy

With Chrysler boycotting Pro Stock, the season battles raged between the Chevys (Jenkins), AMCs, and Fords. Jenkins and his aging Vega *Toy X* won the season-opening NHRA Winternationals by defeating the Pinto of Gapp and Roush. Then, Jenkins won the Summernationals with a new Vega, (*Grumpy's Toy XI*). Jenkins down played the significance of the new car, but the Vega was by far the most innovative Pro Stocker to date. The car incorporated an SRD tube chassis, McPherson strut suspension, rack and pinion steering, and a dry-sump oiling system. All were significant innovations and remained Pro Stock staples for decades to come.

Booth Captures the Gators

Wally Booth brought American Motors Corporation (AMC) its first national event victory when he won the Gatornationals in March. Booth found new power for his 362-ci Hornet by bolting on a set of Bob Schaeffer cylinder heads. The combination saw Booth win all five Division 3 points meets. At the Gatornationals, Booth defeated the Mustang II of Jack Roush with an 8.97 ET. The team of Gapp and Roush had two cars in the program to contend with. Wayne Gapp drove the team's 1973 world championship–winning Pinto.

SRD built some of the decade's finest Pro Stock cars. The nearly complete skeleton of* Grumpy's Toy XI *is seen here perched on the chassis jig. The total weight of the completed chassis was a shade over 100 pounds. Note the high strut mounting that changed on later cars and allowed for an even lower profile.

By 1974, AMC was a genuine Pro Stock threat. Here, at the NHRA Winternationals, Wally qualified with a 9.03 ET, and Dave Kanners qualified with a 9.10 ET. Both racers fell victim to Bob Glidden (Kanners in the first round and Booth in the second round). (Photo Courtesy Rich Carlson/Grant Bittner Collection)

Pro Comp Eliminator

Pro Comp was a new heads-up NHRA category that was created in 1974 by dividing Comp Eliminator. According to the NHRA, the category bridge the gap between the Pros and the Sportsman. The category went through its initial growing pains as new combinations were sorted.

The category consisted of six classes: A/FD, B/FD, AA/D, BB/FC, A/FC, and AA/Altered. The propellent that was allowed varied among the classes, and the rules stated that Fuel was optional in A/FD, B/FD, and A/FC. In AA/D, it was pump gas only, and for the remainder two classes (BB/FC and AA/A), it was alcohol.

The Pro Comp category was trialed at the 1973 Supernationals, where Don Enriquez (in Gene Adams's A/FD) defeated Ken Veney's injected nitro-burning Vega in the final round. The category's official introduction came at the 1974 Winternationals. The AHRA introduced its own Pro Comp category the same season, while the IHRA waited until 1976 to join the party. As with most situations, the best rise to the top. Initially, the proven

Brad Anderson began his career in the Stock category before he moved into Comp and then Pro Comp in 1974. His candy-red cars were always tough competition. Anderson formed Brad Anderson Enterprises (BAE) in the 1980s, which continues to do business to the present day and manufactures aluminum Hemis and related parts. (Photo Courtesy Rich Carlson/Grant Bittner Collection)

In the first year of Pro Comp, the Mack and Dorr AA/D dragster was one of the best. It was powered by a Milodon Hemi. Dave Mack raced the dragster at AHRA and NHRA events and took honors in May at the AHRA Grand-American race at Dragway 42. (Photo Courtesy Michael Pottie)

dragster combinations of Adams and Enriquez as well as Al Weiss and Jimmy Scott led the charge. However, once the racers in Funny Car sorted their new blown alcohol combinations, the names Dale Armstrong, Veney, and Brad Anderson became familiar.

AA/Dale

Dale Armstrong, nicknamed "AA/Dale," arrived from Canada in the mid-1960s and established a strong reputation around Southern California tracks by driving an early blown Chevy II. Due to his success in Pro Comp, he is recognized as the category's winningest driver, and his list of wins is long. Between 1974 and 1980, the year he moved to Top Fuel, Armstrong won an NHRA world title in 1975, an AHRA world title in 1974, and two IHRA world titles. He won a dozen NHRA Pro Comp national events, a dozen IHRA events, and at least five AHRA series events.

Dale Armstrong teamed with Ken Veney in 1974. Here, at the Winternationals, Armstrong qualified number two with a 7.09 ET. Then, he ran the quickest time ever for an unblown Fuel car (a 6.89 ET at 196.50 mph), defeating Veney's Vega in the final round.

In a competitionplus.com interview, Armstrong said that the first Pro Comp car he drove was Veney's injected nitro dragster. Then, Armstrong drove a Pro Comp Funny Car for car owner and tuner Jim Foust. Foust's *Alcoholic* Plymouth Satellite was powered by a blown 505-ci Donovan that was backed by a 3-speed transmission. When fluctuating weight breaks made the car uncompetitive, Armstrong switched to a dragster.

Ken Veney

Ken Veney may be Pro Comp's most recognized name. Throughout his career, he won 13 national events (9 in Pro Comp alone). His best year was in 1976, when

Ken Veney began the 1974 season by winning the AHRA Winter Nationals. In the final round, he faced and defeated Dave Mack in the Mack and Dorr AA/D with a 6.99 ET. (Photo Courtesy Michael Pottie)

Dale Armstrong was the 1974 AHRA Pro Comp World Champion. The Plymouth's Donovan Hemi produced more than 1,600 hp and 1,200 ft-lbs of torque at 7,000 rpm. This was good for 6.50 ETs. (Photo Courtesy Michael Pottie)

he won four national events. With payouts falling far short of the investment, Veney barely broke even. He walked away from the sport at the end of the season and sold everything to Frank Hawley.

Veney took up truck driving, bought himself a Kenworth, and hauled steel. When he was stuck in an early February blizzard on the Ohio Turnpike while the racers were enjoying the warm temperatures of Southern California at the Winternationals, he realized that quitting drag racing wasn't such a good idea.

Ken Veney and Kenny Cox were responsible for designing and welding the chassis and forming the fiberglass body of Veney's Challenger. The Keith Black Hemi with 11.1 compression was backed by a Lenco 3-speed. (Photo Courtesy Hilak Bros. Photography)

He returned to the sport in mid-1977 and raced AA/DA in the former Speelman and Cottrell (John Speelman and Len Cottrell) *Chicken Chokers*. It was Veney's first ride in a dragster. On his third outing with the blown Cleveland-powered car, he won the NHRA Summernationals, defeating Scott Weney with a 6.76 ET at 201 mph.

The AA/DA venture was brief, and Veney returned to BB/Funny Car in 1978 with a Dodge Challenger. The Keith Black Hemi was a study in Veney's handiwork and featured a modified 8-71 blower. It was lengthened so that it was closer in size to a 12 or 14-71. The blower sat on a fabricated intake, featured a fabricated injector, and rode in a Veney-designed chassis. Topping it off was a fiberglass shell that Veney made himself using a rental car. He debuted the Challenger in fine fashion at the Sportsnationals and won the event.

In 1978, Veney created the first set of aftermarket billet aluminum Hemi cylinder heads. Using Chrysler blueprints and an old Bridgeport mill, he created seven sets of heads. Veney bolted a pair onto his Challenger and promptly went out and set both ends of the BB/FC record with a 6.55 ET at 214.28 mph. In no time, he had Fuel guys, such as Kenny Bernstein and Darrell Gwynn, knocking on his door.

Veney took a hiatus at the end of the 1979 season and returned the following summer with a Hemi-powered alcohol dragster. He hadn't lost a step and won the 1980 NHRA Pro Comp Championship.

The NHRA dissolved Pro Comp in 1981 and split the classes (as the AHRA had done in 1977 and the IHRA had done in 1980). Veney moved on and campaigned alcohol and fuel Funny Cars through 1985. In September 1988, he reappeared as the crew chief of Darrell Gwynn's Top Fuel effort. Veney's debut at the Keystone Nationals helped Gwynn win class.

Comp Eliminator

With the addition of Pro Comp and a shuffling of classes, the NHRA added two Econorail classes to Comp Eliminator in 1974. Econorail was created to give a home to those who wanted to run a budget dragster. The rules were clear and stated that no Hemi engines or blowers were allowed and a single 4-barrel carburetor was required. The class was popular and took know-how and innovative thinking to build a competitive car. By the end of the decade, the category consisted of four classes. Surprisingly, the rules changed little over this period.

The world champion was David Majors, whose E/A defeated Ray Cunningham's D/A 1967 Camaro in the finals. Majors's Music City Rod Shop–sponsored 1923 Ford Model T was powered by a Ford 6-cylinder engine that featured a fancy fabricated Cleveland cylinder head.

The Jesel and Clark Camaro, built by SRD Race Cars, appeared more like a Pro Stocker than the Altered that it was. Wayne Jesel pulled the levers on the Lenco, and the transmission was later swapped for a Doug Nash 4+1. Danny Jesel built the 302-ci engine that ran a record 9.87 ET at 137.33 mph. (Photo Courtesy Michael Pottie)

David Majors was the 1974 Comp World Champion. His Music City Rod Shop-sponsored 1923 Ford Model T was powered by a hybrid 310-ci Ford 6-cylinder engine. The car regularly ran ETs in the 9.60s at 145 mph. (Photo Courtesy Michael Pottie)

Modified Eliminator

The new year featured a shake-up in Modified, as the four Altered classes (B through E) joined AA/Altered in Comp Eliminator. They were replaced by four new Gas classes (K/Gas through N/Gas). These new classes were reserved for flatheads, inline sixes, opposed sixes, and straight eights. The 6-cylinder-powered cars with fabricated heads down in the lower Gas classed (excluding N) were forced to carry an additional 1/2 pound per cubic inch by the NHRA.

Can't Lose for Winning

Perennial Division 3 winners Bob Seibert and John Bugenski didn't need a fabricated cylinder head on their inline six N/G Vega to win a pair of national events in 1974. The Vega was powered by an inline GMC 302 that was bored 0.125 inch and de-stroked, using a 248 crank. The final displacement was 306 ci. Famed C. J. Batten was called on to rework the factory cylinder head that helped produce mid-11-second ETs. Seibert said that Batten wanted to take things a little further, so Batten took two cylinder heads and cut one low through the ports and one high through the ports. Then, he welded them back together to create a high-port head.

Bill Mitchell's Thunder Bug *featured a 2,180-cc engine, Porsche box, and 4-link suspension. In similar fashion to Funny Cars, the front clip tilted forward, as did the main shell. The* Thunder Bug *weighed 950 pounds and produced 10.60 ETs. (Photo Courtesy Michael Pottie)*

Between the years 1972 and 1975, Bob Seibert and John Bugenski dominated their class with a GMC Jimmy 6-cylinder-powered Vega. They earned eliminator wins at the Gatornationals and Summernationals in 1974. Their best ET was 11.47. (Photo Courtesy Bob Boudreau)

It would have been great—had the class rules allowed for it. Seibert and Bugenski had no desire to go that route and preferred their current winning combination. Weber carburetors on a fabricated intake completed the induction system. A Nash 5-speed transmission and an early Oldsmobile rear end with 5:38 gears completed the package.

The combination worked well for the guys, and they won their division title twice between 1972 and 1975. In addition, during that period, class wins came at the Gatornationals (twice), Springnationals (four times), Sportsnationals (twice), Summernationals (three times), and US Nationals (three times).

More Revisions but Little Change

Additional rule revisions resulted in the end of crossbred cars in Modified Production. For example, if you wanted to run a Chevy engine in your Ford vehicle and still wanted to run Modified Eliminator, you had to do it in the Gas class. It seemed that no matter what the category or combination was, the Chevys kept winning in 1974. On the national-event level, Chevy's yearlong dominance was broken only by Joe DeSantis, whose *DeSantis-Crider* Hemi-powered A/SR defeated the Corvette of Jerry Ault at the Springnationals.

Lee Shepherd scored his first national event victory at the NHRA Winternationals behind the wheel of the F/Gas, Chevy-powered Maverick of Reher and Morrison. He defeated the A/MP Hemi Dart of Jim Marshall in the final round. Shephard debuted the team's E/MP Corvette at the following Gatornationals.

David Reher and Buddy Morrison took possession of the Ray Martin and Hokie Holcomb 1967 Corvette in early 1974. They campaigned it through 1975 (painted black and then painted white) before they sold it to Tony Christian. Christian went on a tear with the car and won the 1976 Sportsnationals, Summernationals, and Grandnationals. (Photo Courtesy Todd Wingerter)

The Sportsnationals

The 1974 season featured the addition of the Sportsman-only NHRA Sportsnationals. Hosted in Bowling Green, Kentucky, the inaugural race saw Paul Mecure in the Mecure-Keener *Check Mate* Camaro win the Modified category by defeating the A/MP Barracuda of Ken Montgomery in the final. Mike Keener referred to the mid-1970s as magical. Their Camaro was considered to be nothing short of revolutionary, and some labeled it as an all-steel Pro Stock.

The Check Mate *Camaro is remembered as one of Modified's finest-constructed cars. In 1974, ETs in the 9.90s were common.*

Powered by a 331-ci engine and backed by a Chrysler 4-speed transmission, the Camaro used a 4-link rear suspension that was marked as illegal by the NHRA immediately after the Sportsnationals. The sticking point was that the 4-link was located outside of the frame rails. The Camaro ran as an E/Gasser through the remainder of the season, at which point, Mike Fons, who built the suspension, replaced the 4-link with a ladder-bar setup.

And Your Champion Is...

The World Finals moved from Amarillo, Texas, to Ontario Motor Speedway, where it ran concurrently with the Supernationals, which was previously a Pro-only show. Larry "Doc" Dixon used various-inch small-blocks in his 1969 Camaro and became the world champion in 1974. At the World Finals, Dixon defeated Gene Dunlap's C/Gas Dodge in the category final.

Larry "Doc" Dixon debuted his 1969 Camaro in the 1973 season and focused on running AHRA and IHRA races. Turning his attention to the NHRA in 1974, Dixon won the Grandnationals and World Finals. (Photo Courtesy Bill Truby)

Super Stock

Rule revisions in Super Stock allowed engine builders to bore the cylinders 0.065 over (an increase from the previous limit of 0.030 over). This was initially a problem for those running Cobra Jet–powered or Cleveland-powered Fords, due to the thin cylinder wall castings. It was recommended by seasoned builders that the cylinders not be bored more than 0.020 to 0.030 over. If the cylinders were bored more than that, distortion, poor seal, and cracked cylinders were the result. To get around the issue, several racers cut out the thin cylinders and installed thick sleeved barrels.

Other rule changes now allowed the use of any transmission—as long it was built by the same manufacturer and carried the same number of forward gears. In addition, racers could now swap out the rear end for a stronger unit, although no truck axles were allowed. Another new and welcome rule stated that unibody cars could tie their front and rear subframes together.

On the 1320

Chrysler's boycott of Pro Stock saw it move its contracted drivers into Super Stock. The most successful of the bunch was the A-990 SS/B 1965 Plymouth that was campaigned by Butch Leal. Dubbed the "Most Feared Car in Super Stock" by *Super Stock & Drag Illustrated* magazine, the factory lightweight posted a 9.80 ET to break the 10.40 ET record on its second pass. The ability to run that far under the previous record equated to many

The Nitro 9 Mustang of Brandon and Turnage was the car to beat in 1974 and 1975. The Mustang had a Cobra Jet engine, Toploader transmission, full-floating 4-link, and 9-inch rear end, which propelled the Mustang to ETs of 10.60. (Photo Courtesy Bob Martin)

Direct Connection

Manufacturers came alive with one-off parts. More accurately, they continued with one-off parts for select racers. Chrysler's Rapid Transit and clinic program faded in 1972 but bounced back in 1974 with the introduction of its Direct Connection parts and technical support program.

The premise of the Direct Connection program was to let racers build a combination based on Chrysler's testing and research. The program had one goal in mind: to put Chrysler in the winner's circle in drag racing, oval-track racing, and road racing.

Chrysler made it easy to go racing with its Direct Connection special parts program. From advice to parts to complete cars, Direct Connection had the Mopar racer covered.

class wins. Leal won class with the car at all of the national events that he entered.

Leal built a new Duster for 1975 and sold the 1965 Plymouth to Steve Bagwell. Steve converted the car to an automatic and ran it through the 1979 season. He initially shared driving duties with Terry Earwood before Terry retired after the 1977 season.

Butch Leal's 434-ci, single 4-barrel Hemi was responsible for the wheels-up starts. The 4-link-equipped Ron Butler car recorded a jaw-dropping 9.80 ET on its second pass. (Photo Courtesy Bob Martin)

Through the 1970s, several remarkable Mopars ran under the Steve Bagwell name. Barnett Automotive built Bagwell's Hemis and prepped the chassis. Bagwell's Hemi Barracuda hid 300 pounds of lead weight in the gas tank.

Bobby Warren: S/S Champ

The world title went to Bobby Warren of Clinton, North Carolina. His attention to detail and interpretation of the rules made him a dominant Division 2 racer. Warren, who had been tearing up tracks since the 1950s, won his first world title in 1970, when he drove a 350-ci-powered Nova Stocker before stepping up to Super Stock in 1972.

Bobby Warren's Camaro waits to compete at the Sportsnationals. Warren eventually won Super Stock by defeating Terry Earwood in the final. A World Finals win earned Warren his second of three World Championships. He also won in 1970 and 1978. (Photo Courtesy Michael Cochran)

Stock

New rules for 1974 included the welcome return of exhaust headers to increase horsepower. It was still a trick to get the power to the ground, as racers were limited to running street tires. It helped that street/strip tire advancements were being made.

Station wagons and four-door cars, with their favorable weight bias, seemed to gain popularity. No wagons were as predominant as the mid-1960s Chevys (Chevy IIs, Chevelles, and full-size Chevys). These cars had a lock on the lower classes, due to the number of available combinations. To prove this point, you only need to look to the Division 6 and 7 racers, including Jerry McClanahan, Cal Method, Tom Taylor, Bruce McNicol, Les Young, and Larry Peterson.

Jerry McClanahan

McClanahan ran his 1966 Chevy wagon in numerous variations and repeated his 1973 World Championship in 1974 and 1978. McClanahan used the 283 in 2-barrel

Oregon's Larry Peterson was one of the West Coast racers that set and reset the R/SA class record. Times in the mid-15s were common for the 283-equipped wagon. (Photo Courtesy Rich Carlson/Grant Bittner Collection)

Jerry McClanahan was the world champion again. Here, at Fremont, McClanahan takes a handicap start against the Cobra Jet Mustang of Jeff Powers in R/SA. (Photo Courtesy Dave Kommel)

(195 hp) and 4-barrel (220 hp) configurations. His available combinations increased to as many as a dozen, as he also ran the wagon at different times as an Impala, Bel Air, and Biscayne by simply changing the trim. It was a six-passenger wagon by design, and by adding the optional third seat, he could run yet more classes.

There was nothing overly unique about McClanahan's wagon because strict rules hampered modifications. With headers now welcome in Stock, he used up to five different sets of various length and diameter. This went along with the approximately 20 different Quadrajet carburetors. Behind the 283 engine was a 2-speed Powerglide transmission from a 6-cylinder car, as they were built with a lower first gear.

Cal Method

Cal Method ran the gamut of full-size Chevys and won more than his share with multiple combinations. In 1972, Method won his first Division 6 crown with a 1966 Impala. The Impala began Method's journey of using full-size Chevys to earn class wins and set records into the 1980s.

"Back when they gave you points for the record, I would switch combinations," said Method, who had been an experienced Stock class racer since the early 1960s. "When one record got a little too difficult, I'd switch to another combination."

Method's potent little 283s wreaked havoc on the chassis of the big wagons. He recalled replacing frames because the cross-member to which the rear upper control arms bolted would break. He discovered that the solution was to add 12x12-inch triangular gussets on all four corners of the cross member.

Washington's Cal Method made running a Stocker into a science. He won in everything, from a '57 Chevy wagon in the 1960s to a Nova that is still campaigned today. (Photo Courtesy Rich Carlson/Grant Bittner Collection)

CHAPTER FIVE

1975:

ON PAR

Rick Barratt's Cleveland-powered Pinto was a consistent class winner. In 1975, he defeated the Street Roadster of Neil Mahr in Modified at Indy with a 9.28 ET. Note the "Machine Work By Bob Glidden" on the front fender. (Photo Courtesy Bob Martin)

In 1975, the NHRA introduced its new index numbers system, which was a dramatic change. The new Par system was a method of handicapping various classes of cars based on their calculated performance potential (as opposed to using handicaps with changing class records). The new system affected the cars of the Comp, Modified, Super Stock, and Stock categories.

NHRA National Tech Director Jim Dale said, "The indexes were determined by a computer system that took into account not only the scientific data on a car/engine combination but also the accurate performances at points meets across the country of cars in the various classes. With the new system, there will be no breakouts, as in the present system. With no breakouts and without a national record to protect, there should be no reason for on-the-brakes racing because the quicker cars will not be, in effect, penalized."

To reflect their handicaps against each other in this no-breakout system, the eliminator's fastest class, such as A/Dragster in Comp, had an index of 0.00, B/Dragster's index was 0.25, etc. The system was adjusted for 1976, and the calculated index number was replaced with an actual ET.

In 1975, Winston signed on to be the series sponsor for the NHRA. The partnership lasted 26 years and helped to advance the sport immensely. Thanks to Winston, payouts saw a major boost as well.

Year-end champions Don Garlits and Don Prudhomme each received a $20,000 bonus, while Pro Stock champion Bob Glidden received $12,000. The first race under the Winston Series title was the Springnationals at Ohio. Pro winners were Marvin Graham, Don Prudhomme, and Bill Jenkins. The NHRA held 8 national events in 1975, 8 regional meets, and 35 divisional races.

Winston signed on as a major sponsor of the NHRA in 1975. The cigarette manufacturer's financial support took drag racing to a new level. The relationship ran through 2001.

Top Fuel

The rules remained unchanged from 1974, so as far as the racers were concerned, no news was good news. All of the action took place on the track, and all eyes were on Garlits. He was at his peak and on a mission to show that he could still get it done. Garlits did so by becoming the first to win championships with two sanctioning bodies (the NHRA and IHRA) in the same season.

Garlits Shocks the Troops

Looking back on Top Fuel in 1975, no story came close to topping the phenomenal 5.63 ET that Garlits ran at the Supernationals. His feat came after a season-long, see-saw battle for the championship that took place between himself and Gary Beck, the 1974 world champion. It took until the Supernationals to determine the 1975 world champion.

Beck's season did not get off to the start that he envisioned. At the AHRA Winter Nationals, he fell in the semifinal round. Then, at the NHRA Winternationals, he bowed out in the second round. Garlits set some lofty goals for himself at the beginning of the season and stated that he wanted both the NHRA and IHRA world titles and to break the 250-mph barrier. He opened the season by winning the NHRA Winternationals with his *Swamp Rat 21*.

Beck was runner-up at the Summernationals and Grandnationals (to Garlits), and he won the inaugural Fallnationals. Beck had a verbal agreement with IHRA President Larry Carrier that he would run four of the sanctioning bodies national events, one being the Bristol race in September. Midway through the season, the NHRA added the Fallnationals in Seattle, which was scheduled to take place the same weekend as Bristol. To pursue the NHRA title and race in front of his hometown fans, Beck swung a deal with Carrier, where the two agreed that Beck could pass on Bristol and race at Amarillo in June.

After Amarillo, where he was runner-up to Garlits, Beck's four-race agreement with Carrier was done. Garlits hit the roof. He had it out with Carrier and said that he (Carrier) and Beck had agreed that Beck would run

Shirley Muldowney made her first final-round appearance at the NHRA Springnationals. She qualified ninth in the 16-car field with a 6.14 ET. In a final-round loss to Marvin Graham, Muldowney's chute failed, and she went off the end of the track. (Photo Courtesy Rob Potter).

Garlits began the season in Swamp Rat 21*, which was a car that didn't fit him well because it was initially built for Funny Car pilot "Jungle" Jim Liberman. Garlits debuted* Swamp Rat 22 *after the Gatornationals. He opened the World Finals by tying his top speed record of 249.30 mph. Not happy with Gary Beck at several races during the season, Garlits offered a $1,000 bounty to anyone who eliminated Beck. (Photo Courtesy Dan Williams)*

It was a battle to the finish with a reported $37,000 in prize money up for grabs. Gary Beck stated that he grossed $135,000 in 1975. After paying his expenses, he was left with $20,000. (Photo Courtesy Mike Dimery)

Bristol, not Amarillo. Remember, Garlits, and Beck were both after the NHRA title. It was in Garlits's best interest if Beck didn't (or couldn't) run in Seattle. Beck refused to run Bristol, as he and Carrier had a verbal agreement. Carrier, under pressure, sued Beck in federal court to prevent him from competing in the Seattle race.

Beck went to Seattle, where, upon his arrival, he was served with an injunction that stated he could not compete in the race. Well, he not only competed but he also qualified number one with a 5.92 ET. Then, he beat Marvin Graham in the final. The win gave Beck a 148-point lead over Garlits with just the Supernationals remaining. Beck was charged with contempt of court and fined $1,000 for ignoring the injunction. It took a few years, but the whole matter was eventually dropped.

At the World Finals in Ontario, Garlits continued to protest. He felt that the points Beck earned at Seattle should be erased since Beck was ordered by court to not compete in the race. Garlits filed suit against the NHRA and Beck. The court, nor the NHRA, saw things as Garlits did, and the suit was quickly dismissed. Do you think that Garlits was a little hot under the collar? Imagine how he felt when Beck qualified number one with a 5.69 ET and backed it up with a 5.74 ET to break Garlits's existing 5.78 ET record. Beck credited his improved performance to the new TRW slugs that he ran, which were lighter and stronger. He said that it was the first time he ran ETs in the 5.60s.

Garlits was a man on a mission. He had a few tricks up his sleeve, including a new set of high-compression pistons and a trick new camshaft. Garlits meant business. He qualified right on Beck's heels with a 5.71 ET at 249.30 mph. When qualifying ended on Saturday, Garlits had laid down a

At Ontario Motor Speedway, fans anticipated a final-round showdown between Gary Beck and Don Garlits. (Photo Courtesy Rich Carlson/Grant Bittner)

After defeating Herm Petersen here at the World Finals, Don Garlits did not compete in any of the NHRA's events in 1976. He sat out in protest of weak purses and a dissatisfaction with its points program. (Photo Courtesy Dave Kommel)

Contrary to what some may believe, Top Fuel racers were making money, as is evident by Chris "the Greek" Karamesines's gold-plated Fueler. Karamesines had a reported $250,000 into this car. (Photo Courtesy John Eichinger)

blistering 5.63 ET. His 250.63 mph top speed on the run was a new record and good for a few hundred points.

In discussing the run in his 1976 autobiography, Garlits said, "The air was right, the wind was right, the car was right, the engine was super strong, [and] everything was nice. It was the perfect time. I let it warm up real well and built some heat [into the engine]. I let the clutch out on that baby, and it carried the wheels out there 400 feet and just pulled like a ripper. I shifted it, the front end came up again, and I knew I was on my way. I went through the traps, and by the time I got lifted, I was 150 feet through the traps. I knew I must have some kind of record because it seemed like the fastest ride I'd ever taken."

Heading into Sunday's eliminations, Garlits was a mere 97 points behind Beck. Both men easily won their opening round. In round two, Beck dropped James Warren with a 5.74 ET before Garlits defeated Dale Funk with a 5.65 ET at 249.30 mph to back up his previous 5.63 ET for a new class record. This robbed Beck of his record points. At this stage, Garlits had the lead in the points standings: 9,293 to 8,990. For Beck to win the championship, he had to reset the record, hope that Garlits would fall in the semifinals, or defeat him in the final and win the meet. It was not to be.

In the semifinals, Garlits unleashed a fine 5.67 ET at 249.30 mph to eliminate Marvin Graham and gain a berth in the final round. The pressure was on Beck, who faced Herm Petersen. Off the line, Beck shook the tires but kept on it. Fate reared its ugly head when Beck tossed a blower belt at mid-track. Petersen sailed onward for the win and deprived the crowd of a much anticipated Garlits-versus-Beck showdown. In the final, Garlits easily defeated Petersen with a 5.74 ET.

It was Garlits's finest hour. He accomplished everything that he set out to do at the beginning of the season. He won his first (of three) NHRA world championships as well as the IHRA championship (the first of three in a row), and he was the first to break the 250-mph barrier. What's truly amazing is the fact Garlits's record ET of 5.63 stood until March 1981, when Jeb Allen lowered it at the Gatornationals with a 5.62 run.

Funny Car

Don Prudhomme had an amazing season—especially considering the competition of Tom "the Mongoose" McEwen, Tom Prock, Gordie Bonin, and Raymond Beadle (among others). Don "the Snake" Prudhomme was coming off an AHRA world championship and won his first of four consecutive NHRA titles in 1975.

One of the last chassis that Woody Gilmore built was under the Phil Castronovo Custom Bodies Enterprises Dart. Driver Tom Prock closed the NHRA season as the runner-up at three national events. (Photo Courtesy Michael Pottie)

Shirl Greer carried the number 1 on a new Mustang II in 1975. Un-Chained Lightning *featured a Jaime Sarte chassis and a 484-ci Keith Black Hemi. Greer began the year by winning the AHRA Winter Nationals. However, he wasn't able to replicate his success at the IHRA Summer Nationals. (Photo Courtesy Dan Williams)*

The Snake

Don Prudhomme and his chief wrench, Bob Brandt, made it all look easy. They began the season by defeating Mike Miller in the *Green Elephant* Vega at the NHRA Winternationals and finished with a win at the Supernationals by defeating the Denny Savage–driven *Chi-Town Hustler*. In between were another four national event victories. The win at the Supernationals was overshadowed by Prudhomme's qualifying top speed of 241.53 mph (a Funny Car's first 240-mph run) and his third-round 5.98 ET (a Funny Car's first 5-second pass). Just as in 1955, when scientists theorized that the quickest a man could travel the distance of a quarter mile before passing out was 167 mph, some felt that aerodynamics prevented a full-bodied car from

Prudhomme lost only two NHRA national events in 1975, which earned him the first of four consecutive world championships. The secret was in the setup of his clutch and the fuel delivery. Of course, great driving and a top wrench helped. (Photo Courtesy J. R. Bloom)

Jim Liberman, who had competed in drag racing since the early 1960s, won his first NHRA national event at the Summernationals in 1975. NHRA rules that year dictated that Funny Cars had to weigh a minimum of 1,950 pounds, which was increased from 1,800 pounds in 1974. The weight remained at 1,950 pounds through the remainder of the decade. (Photo Courtesy Michael Pottie)

In 1975, you were traveling in style if you had a setup like this. The trailer appears to be a Don May unit, and the tow rig was a Chevy dually that was most likely powered by a 454-ci engine. By 1980, semitrailer rigs became more common. (Photo Courtesy Rich Carlson/Grant Bittner Collection)

covering the quarter-mile in less than 6 seconds and in excess of 240 mph.

In speaking with Prudhomme about this period, he credited his success to the fuel system that he and Brandt had developed as well as clutch management. Prudhomme said that they did a lot of match racing during this period, which allowed them to refine and perfect the fuel delivery. Consistency came by using the best of parts, including a John Buttera and Pat Foster chassis, and a 480-ci Keith Black Hemi that was backed by a 3-disk Crower clutch and 2-speed transmission.

At the Supernationals, eliminations proved to be little more than a cake walk for Prudhomme. His final-round opponent, Denny Savage, shut off early, and Prudhomme took the win with a 6.15 ET at 240.64 mph.

Pro Stock

NHRA Pro Stock now featured 16 different weight breaks, and Ford's Cleveland, its SOHC 427, and Chrysler's Hemi carried the most weight. The class minimum weights, which now included the driver, were set at 2,250 pounds for small-block-powered cars and 2,450 for big-block-powered cars. Rules allowed for 100 pounds of ballast.

Glidden Pours It On

Bob Glidden ran four different cars through the 1975 season while trying to find his way. That included a 1970 Mustang that he drove to wins at both the AHRA and NHRA Winternationals, a pair of Mustang IIs, and his aging Pinto.

Scott Shafiroff parked his Pro Stock Vega in favor of this Cleveland-powered Mustang II. His 8.80 ETs won him the IHRA Spring Nationals at Bristol. (Photo Courtesy Michael Pottie)

In a 1975 *National Dragster* interview, Glidden stated that because he raced two cars simultaneously (a Don Ness Mustang II for IHRA races and the 1970 Mustang in NHRA competition), his engine program suffered a series of failures. Glidden blamed this on the toll that it took to run two cars. This setback caused Gapp and Roush to briefly take the lead in the NHRA points standings. Gapp had a great season and closed it out with three national event victories and three runner-up finishes.

Glidden got back on track by restructuring his operation. He sold both Mustangs and borrowed his old Pinto

The NHRA added 0.35 pound per cubic inch to the long-wheelbase Cleveland Fords in mid-1975, which killed the advantage that racers, such as Bob Glidden and the team of Gapp and Roush, enjoyed while running the long-wheelbase cars. (Photo Courtesy Michael Pottie)

Of the eight NHRA national events in 1975, Bob Glidden won four of them. He used a variety of cars to do so. Here, at the IHRA Summer Nationals, Glidden and his Don Ness Mustang II are guided from the water box by Etta Glidden. (Photo Courtesy Dan Williams)

Herb McCandless drove this Don Hardy-built Mustang II before owner Lou Oleynik sold it to Bob Glidden in the spring of 1975. Glidden ran the car for four races in 1975. (Photo Courtesy Rob Potter)

from Brandon and Turnage in time for the Fallnationals. There, he faced a world-traveling-weary Wayne Gapp in the finals. After Gapp won the US Nationals, he hauled his Maverick to Brazil for a match race. The all-expenses-paid trip was covered by Ford Motor Company, whose best-selling model in Brazil was the Maverick. A win at the Fallnationals would have sealed the season championship for Gapp & Roush.

Just like 1974, it wasn't meant to be. In the too-close-to-call final round, Glidden eked out the win with an 8.84 ET at 155.44 mph to Gapp's 8.85 at 153.06.

Head Games

When rules regarding cylinder heads state that anything goes, expect the extreme. Chrysler introduced its twin plugs per cylinder D-series head in 1970, Ford introduced raised port plates

Little changed for the team of Gapp & Roush in 1975. It earned three national event wins and three runner-up finishes. The team of Gapp & Roush was Glidden's toughest competition. (Photo Courtesy Bob Boudreau)

Looking to squeeze as much air and fuel into his Chevys, Bill "Grumpy" Jenkins experimented heavily with port shape and size. The small-block Chevy was hampered by the small chambers that limited the intake size to 2.05 inches.

Wally Booth went to extremes and sliced his cylinder heads lengthwise to raise the ports. This worked wonders, and Booth nearly won the NHRA title. (Photo Courtesy Arvid Svendsen)

Looking at the exhaust face of Wally Booth's modified heads, one gets the feel as to how much the ports were raised. (Photo Courtesy Arvid Svendsen)

Paul Blevins got a lot of miles out of his Vega. He debuted it in 1973 and campaigned it through 1975. Blevins found life in Pro Stock more difficult than in the Modified ranks. A new NHRA rule for 1975 required hood scoops to be attached to the hood. (Photo Courtesy Bob Boudreau)

in 1972, and Chevy had Bill "Grumpy" Jenkins help develop the turbo head and the famed Bow Tie head. Jenkins said that he had "gone up to Saginaw and took a bunch of 292 water jacket bores and filed away where we didn't want the water to be, and this allowed for additional room to port." The new heads appeared in 1976.

AMC (specifically the team of Maskin and Kanners and the team of Booth and Arons) were up to tricks of their own during the 1974–1975 season. Maskin took a similar route to Ford and sawed into a set of AMC NASCAR cylinder heads. Maskin cut into the intake side and back to the spring seats to install a formed aluminum plate that raised the ports. Offset rocker shafts and a matching tunnel-ram manifold were created.

Wally Booth raised the ports of his heads by taking four heads and cutting them in half. Two halves of the heads were cut 1/2 inch above the head centerline, and two were cut 1/2 inch below the centerline. Halves were swapped and furnace brazed back together. Booth used the heads to run an 8.75 ET at Indy in 1975. The results were better than expected, but word from the NHRA was that no welded heads would be accepted in 1976.

World Finals Showdown

The old adage that history repeats itself was proven once again in 1975 (just like in 1974), as Bob Glidden and Wayne Gapp battled for the championship. Heading into the finals, Gapp held a slight lead over Glidden. In the first round, it looked like Gapp and Roush had secured the championship when Glidden red-lighted against

When it came to Pro Stock Chevys in the 1970s, Bill "Grumpy" Jenkins was the leader. He debuted his Grumpy's Toy XII *Monza in August at the Popular Hot Rodding meet. Those headlight covers were not allowed by the NHRA.*

Paul Blevins. However, after the run, Blevins was disqualified because his Vega was underweight. This meant that Glidden was back in the hunt for the title.

In the second round, Glidden advanced with a fine 8.67 ET against Lee Hunter. Gapp faced opponent Stacy Shields and his Gapp and Roush–powered Mustang II. In an upset, Gapp had the lead before tossing a few rods, allowing Shields to take the win.

In the semis, Glidden ran an 8.78 ET and defeated a red-lighted Shields to clinch the championship. In the somewhat anticlimactic final, Glidden faced low-qualifier (8.79) Bill Jenkins. It was a great Chevy-versus-Ford race, and Glidden won with an 8.851 ET at 154.63 mph to Jenkins's 8.853 at 153.84.

Pro Comp

NHRA rule revisions saw turbocharged classes added to the Pro Comp category: AA/DA(T), BB/FC(T), and AA/A(T). In an attempt to level the playing field, the turbocharged cars were required to carry an additional 0.60 pounds per cubic inch.

What can one say about Pro Comp in 1975? Ken Veney's and Dale Armstrong's NHRA domination continued. Weight breaks were tinkered with, but when it came to winners and losers, little changed. Armstrong and his Donovan-powered *Alcoholic* Plymouth Satellite won the world championship, running a 6.60 ET in the final round at Ontario to defeat Veney, whose Vega ran a red-light 6.78 ET. In AHRA competition, the Pro Comp world title went to Wayne Stoeckel and his AA/DA.

At the NHRA Grandnationals in B/FD, Ken Cook (in the Cook and Thorn car) dropped a few jaws when his injected, small-block Chevy–powered car ran a 6.92 ET to become the first car in the B category to run an ET in the 6s. For comparison, the ET was quicker than Dale Armstrong's A/FD class record of 6.99.

Comp Eliminator

As with Pro Comp, and to the pleasure of those campaigning cars in BB/A and BB/GS, the NHRA created separate classes for the turbocharged cars: BB/A(T) and BB/G(T). The weight per cubic inch remained the same for

"Wild" Wilfred Boutilier was one of the first Pro Comp racers to break into the 6s in 1974. Always a tough competitor, he won the NHRA Fallnationals in 1975. (Photo Courtesy Michael Pottie)

Joe Williamson dominated in his E/A car. The Division 3 racer won the 1975 Gatornationals. Throughout his career, he won seven NHRA national events. Later in his life, Williamson raced stock cars. (Photo Courtesy Bob Martin)

each (5 pounds for the BB/Altereds and 7 pounds for BB/Gas). The Econorails grew in popularity as the low-buck category added a third class, C/ED, for 4-cylinder and rotary engines.

Richie Rosen

Louisiana's Richie Rosen, a two-time Division 4 champion, won the world championship with his California Concepts front-engine rail by defeating the rear-engine car of Jeff McCoy, which was driven by Mark Prudhomme (Don "the Snake" Prudhomme's cousin), in the all A/ED final. Seeing that no Hemis were allowed in the class, the big-block Chevy was the only way to go, and both cars made use of one. Rosen took it to Prudhomme's cousin with an 8.18 ET.

Modified Eliminator

The big change in NHRA Modified Eliminator for the 1975 season was a rule that allowed aftermarket clutch-operated transmissions to be used in the Modified Production category. It was a welcome rule change for

Richie Rosen and George Bazile proved the value of a 10-year-old Automotive Specialties chassis when they used one to win the world championship. A bored and stroked 447-ci Chevy powered the car to low-8-second ETs. A Holley dominator on an Edelbrock dual-plane intake and Airflow Research-prepped heads were used on top of the mill. A Turbo 400 transmission and Chrysler 4.10 rear end rounded out the package. (Photo Courtesy Dave Kommel)

Dick St. Peter built engines down to 277 ci to race in various Modified Production classes with his Nova. This car had a Doug Nash 5-speed transmission and a 6.50-geared Ford 9-inch rear end. St. Peter later installed an underdriven transmission in the Nova. (Photo Courtesy Rich Carlson/Grant Bittner Collection)

many, as the combination of a large amount of power and the shock of high-RPM launches spelled doom for OEM transmissions.

Although various transmission choices were available, the Doug Nash 5-speed was favored. First introduced in 1972, the Nash was far superior to the factory hardware that was offered by Chevy, Ford, or Chrysler. Besides its unmatched strength and reliability, the Nash offered a 3.76 first-gear ratio. It was perfect for launching those small-inch cars in a hurry.

Although Modified Eliminator (Modified Production, more specifically) was moving further away from the grassroots that it once represented, it gained in popularity as the decade progressed.

Sizing Up

Bruce Sizemore, in his I/G Pinto, won the 1975 Modified World Championship. Lee Shepherd in the Reher-Morrison 1967 Corvette was his final-round victim. This was the final Modified race for the RMS team, as it jumped into Pro Stock in 1976.

Bruce Sizemore's Pinto was an I/Gas and J/Gas record holder. His I/Gas record (a 9.79 ET at 136.98 mph) was set in 1976 and stood through 1978. The Pinto held the J/Gas record with a 10.11 ET at 133.13 mph, which Sizemore set in September 1977. (Photo Courtesy Bill Truby)

Bruce Sizemore's Pinto was powered by a 306-ci 6-cylinder engine that featured a modified Cleveland head and three Weber carburetors. The combination was good for about 500 hp and capable of 9,000 rpm. (Photo Courtesy Dan Williams)

The Sizemore Pinto was built around a Don Hardy Pro Stock chassis and recorded a best ET of 9.70 due to the 306-ci, 6-cylinder engine that carried a C. J. Batten–hybrid Cleveland head and Hilborn injection of Sizemore's own design. Power was transmitted through a Doug Nash transmission that carried a 3.05 first gear. The 5.14-equipped 9-inch Ford rear end was supported by a ladder-bar suspension.

Welcome Super Modified

Concerned with the growing expense of drag racing, *Car Craft* magazine staffers John Dianna and Rick Voegelin created the Super Modified Eliminator category. The concept was to field a poor man's Pro Stock, which was a class with minimal and cost-conscious rules. The pair presented the idea to the NHRA, which accepted the format with only minor tweaking.

A/Super Modified rules dictated that cars had to be 1967 or newer. A weight break of 9.00 pounds per cubic inch was assigned to the class, and the minimum weight was 2,850 pounds. Saddled by a maximum carburetor size of 750 cfm, most of the competitive cars ran well below the allowed 366 ci.

To help keep the cost down, a rule stated that only production-line cylinder heads could be used. Although, the ports could be matched to a 1/2-inch depth, and the chambers could be modified. All other internal engine modifications were accepted.

An OEM transmission case had to be used, but any gear was allowed. Harnessing the power was left to a pair of slicks that measured no more than 10.5 inches wide and 30 inches tall.

Super Stock

The Super Stock category made progress of its own with rules that allowed aftermarket transmissions (4-speed only). In addition, the rear frame rails could be moved inboard for tire clearance, and rear ends could be narrowed.

Oddly, rules now stated cars could be lightened to the class minimum. Racers no longer had to find a car that best suited class or fell closest to the break. To be clear, the NHRA stated that no weight reduction of body parts was allowed. It seems to be that the NHRA caught on to rule interpretations and how the envelope was being stretched. The NHRA had to make clear that the "lightening" that was being performed needed to be obvious.

In the year where Gary Herman and his Hemi Dart put the SS/A class record into the 9s, it was tough to

The Super Modified category debuted at the 1975 Winter Nationals. Norm Mayersohn, driving Rick Voegelin's 1967 Camaro with a 316-ci engine and Muncie 4-speed transmission won class and continued to do so at the next four Winternationals. (Photo Courtesy Dave Kommel)

Carl "Captain Cobra Jet" Holbrook ran this SS/GA Mustang convertible in 1975. The Instant Action Mustang was a class winner and record holder with an 11.07 ET. (Photo Courtesy Bob Martin)

Carl Holbrook worked with Edelbrock to create an intake manifold. However, Holley released an intake for the same application before Holbrook worked the bugs out of his fabricated piece. (Photo Courtesy Bob Wytosky)

find any single car that grabbed the headlines. Check out the following cars.

Agaman's Missile

Bernie Agaman and partner Claude Urevig would tread where few men dared. Chrysler all but owned the top Super Stock classes—from SS/A through SS/EA. Agaman's low-compression, 454-ci 1971 Corvette fell squarely into SS/DA. He debuted the 425-hp Corvette at the 1974 Gatornationals, where he won class with a 10.58 ET but fell in the category final to Judy Lilly.

At this point in drag racing history, Corvettes weren't standouts due to their independent rear end and suspension. Agaman spent a good part of 1974 dealing with breakage issues that related to the rear suspension and housing. When building the car, Agaman went with a live Dana rear with the understanding that it was legal. However, that was not the case. The NHRA clarified the rule and stated that it would only accept the Dana center section. The Corvette independent suspension itself had to be retained.

With the help of SRD Race Cars, a bulletproof rear end and suspension were built for the Corvette during the winter of 1974–1975. To cure the Corvette's ills, SRD used a Dana 60 center section, fabricated trailing arms, and half shafts that carried Chevy C60 truck U-joints. The Dana center section had 5:13 gears.

Refactored to SS/CA in 1975, the Corvette dominated the class through the season and won the Summernationals, Grandnationals, and World Finals. At the World Finals, Agaman defeated the Hemi Barracuda of Paul Rossi with a 10.29 ET to earn the title. At Atco Dragway in September, Agaman reset his own class record with a 10.21 ET at 132.15 mph. The record stood until the NHRA erased it in April 1978.

Jack Mullins's Pontiac Wagon

Like Agaman, Jack Mullins was a graduate of the Stock category. Also like Agaman, Mullins campaigned an unusual Super Stocker—his in the form of an SS/U 1963 Pontiac station wagon. Jack's wagon took him to category wins at the Sportsnationals, Springnationals, US Nationals, and a runner-up finish at the Summernationals.

The wagon was powered by a 4-barrel-equipped, low-compression 389 engine that was backed by a BorgWarner transmission with a 2.96 Doug Nash first gear. Out back was a bulletproof Dana rear end that housed gears ranging from 5:13 to 5:88. A Cam Dynamics shaft that featured 0.700 lift rotated the valvetrain. A fabricated girdle kept the big-block Chevy rockers aligned and allowed Mullins to come off the starting line at 8,000 rpm. Mullins custom-made his own intake manifold by fusing two back halves of an Edelbrock Torker together with his own plenum. By design, the Torker was a compromised manifold designed by Edelbrock for both street and strip use. By welding the two back halves together, this eliminated the long, narrow front

Bernie Agaman took a bye for the class win here at Indy and let it all hang out with a 10.51 ET. Note the 1969 Corvette's domed hood on Bernie's 1971 model. This hood was never available on a 1971 Corvette. It seems insignificant, but the actual 1971 big-block hood is about 4 to 5 inches shorter. Later, the NHRA clarified the rules. (Photo Courtesy Bob Martin)

Business was booming at Jack's Garage thanks to Jack Mullins's Pontiac station wagon's success (12.60 ETs). To Mullins, class losses were foreign. (Photo Courtesy Dave Kommel)

runners. Topping the intake was the required factory aluminum 4-barrel (AFB) carburetor.

The NHRA couldn't leave well enough alone and refactored the wagon for 1976. A repeat win at the Sportsnationals and a few runner-up finishes for Mullins were the result. He made a move to Modified with an Opel Gasser that was powered by a Pontiac 4-cylinder. A fire sidelined his career until 1985.

Pooling Resources

Larry Tores and Gary Bosz found the right combination for SS/HA in their 327-ci, 275-hp (refactored to 285 hp) 1967 Chevy II. It's amazing what a low-on-bucks pair can accomplish when they pool their resources.

The pair built much of the car themselves in Tores's single-car garage. They took advantage of the rules and fitted the car with a full roll cage and a Ron Butler–designed 4-link rear suspension. Although they were battling the almighty dollar, Tores knew they had to do something a little more sophisticated, as unibody Chevy IIs flexed quite a bit and had to be fought to go down the track straight. Before the suspension was installed, Tores and Bosz went through the painstaking steps of moving the frame rails inboard 2¾ inches per side to make room for the 11.5-inch slicks that they planned to use. Tores fashioned drill bits to knock out the factory welds, and the pair went to work. They swapped out drills when they got too hot and carried onward.

The pair debuted the Chevy II at the 1975 NHRA Winternationals, where they ran an 11.30 ET to earn the class win over the 'Cuda of Ron Debler. Tores built the 327 engine, which was backed by a Marv Ripes Powerglide. The Powerglide initially ran the factory 1.82 low gear before they made a switch to 1.98. The change helped set the class record at Fremont in July, when the Chevy II recorded an 11.10 ET at 121.62 mph. By the end of the summer, Tores had the fastest and first SS/HA car in the 10s when he recorded a 10.94 ET at Sacramento.

At the end of the season, John Lingenfelter purchased the Chevy II and was to take possession at the 1976 Winternationals. In a storybook ending, Lingenfelter, in the *Graf Enterprise* SS/MA Corvette, met Tores in the Super Stock final. Tores took the win with a 10.83 ET and the $10,000 prize that came with it. After Tores treated

A Ron Butler-designed 4-link rear suspension helped the Larry Tores and Gary Bosz Chevy II hook and go. The 275-hp, 327-ci engine was backed by an A-1 Powerglide transmission and was capable of 10-second ETs. (Photo Courtesy Dave Kommel)

everyone to dinner, Lingenfelter paid the $10,000 purchase price for the car. Lingenfelter campaigned the Chevy II for a year and opened by winning IHRA's first ever Super Modified eliminator.

Ed Hamburger

In the Chrysler camp, few racers or builders made the impact that Ed Hamburger did during this period. Hamburger did a good job of covering the Chrysler camp with his string of 340- and 360-powered A-bodies—possibly to the chagrin of Chrysler and the racers who enjoyed factory support.

Hamburger became serious about drag racing in 1970. That year, he looked for a car that would make a significant impact and enable him to build a business. That car turned out to be a 340 Duster. Hamburger eventually built an aftermarket empire that began with his fabricated oil pans. By the mid-1970s, business was booming, and he was the go-to shop when it came to aftermarket goods for Chrysler's LA-series engine.

In total, Hamburger eventually had eight team cars under his umbrella. The blue and white Mopars had Stock, Super Stock, and Super Modified covered. Each car and its owners benefited from Hamburger building and preparing the cars and keeping them tuned at the track. He was definitely a busy man.

In 1975, Hamburger was supposed to receive a tricked-out, lightweight, 360-ci-powered Duster directly from Chrysler, but it ended up in the hands of Judy Lilly instead. Feeling shafted and looking for some retribution, Hamburger and his partner, Carlos Lawrence, purchased their own 360-ci Duster to battle head-to-head with Lilly in SS/LA. The move didn't sit well with the manufacturer.

This situation erupted approximately a month prior to the Sportsnationals. Hamburger prepared the

John Lingenfelter's low-compression, 350-powered 1973 Corvette was the SS/LA record holder with an 11.38 ET at 117.18 mph when this photo was taken at the 1976 Winternationals. Running in the SS/MA class here, it was Lingenfelter's last event in the Charles Graf Corvette. He purchased the Tores Chevy II (in the far lane) prior to the race. (Photo Courtesy Dave Kommel)

By 1975, the NHRA had increased the horsepower rating of Chrysler's 360 engine to 280 hp (the factory rating was 245 hp). However, that didn't slow down Ed Hamburger. Mid-11-second ETs came easily for him. (Photo Courtesy Rob Potter)

Tommy Auger, still racing Mopars, campaigned this Ed Hamburger-prepped 340 Duster in 1975. Capable of running 10-second ETs, the Duster was once billed as the world's quickest 340. (Photo Courtesy Rob Potter)

Judy Lilly had the most successful season of her career in 1975, as she won the Gatornationals and Fallnationals. She ran quick 11.60 ETs. (Photo Courtesy Bob Martin)

Duster in about three weeks, ran it at one division race, and won it. Lawrence hauled the Duster to Bowling Green for the Sportsnationals, where it failed tech inspection. Lawrence was told that the car had the wrong transmission in it. The Duster had a 727 transmission, which is what the 360-ci-equipped cars came with.

The problem was that Lilly had already passed tech inspection with a 904 transmission in her Duster. She had the paperwork from Chrysler to prove that it was the transmission that came with the car. It was common for the manufacturers to create bogus paperwork to show that such combinations were legitimate. The advantage of running the 904 over a 727 was that it robbed less horsepower and was good for at least a tenth of a second on the track.

Hamburger flew into Bowling Green and was not a happy camper. Upon arrival, at 1 a.m., he immediately headed to Tech Director Jim Dale's hotel suite. Hamburger woke Dale and explained that the 727 is the transmission that came in the car and said that he could prove it when they arrived at the track later that morning.

Once there, they crawled under a few cars in the parking lot. Hamburger was proven to have the correct transmission, and the Duster sailed through tech. In the class final, the two remaining combatants were Hamburger and Lilly. The Chrysler representatives in the stands had to watch Hamburger tree Lilly and beat her with a slower 11.69 ET at 114.79 to a quicker and faster 11.67 at 115.38.

Not making friends with Chrysler or Lilly, Hamburger checked out Lilly's Duster at the following Summernationals, where he discovered the too-light sheet metal. Hamburger doesn't like to lose and likes it even less to lose to a cheater, so he suggested to acting tech inspector Greg Xakellis that he may want to check her spare tire. It was discovered that the tire was hiding 150 pounds of lead.

Through his career, Hamburger competed using three different cars: a 1970 Duster, a 1971 Demon, and a 1975 Duster. During his heyday, it wasn't unusual to see multiple Hamburger cars in the winner's circle at any given meet. He retired in 1983 to focus on his business.

Stock

By the mid-1970s, things were looking up in the Stock category. Headers, reground camshafts, slicks that were 9 inches wide, and DOT–approved tires up to 12 inches wide were welcomed. No one car dominated the category, which saw a variety of national event winners. Tom Tereau won the Winternationals with his I/S 1969 Camaro, and Tim Ekstrand won the World Finals driving Bob Lambeck's 360-powered Duster. In between, Bob Shaw won the Sportsnationals. Shaw's Z/S 1967 Corvair stood out because of its uniqueness and the fact that it always seemed to win. He was regularly protested because of the Corvair's ability to outrun the competition with its ETs of 16 seconds flat.

Bob Shaw's 95-hp 1967 Corvair was such a terror in the Z/Stock class that the NHRA factored in his pancake six, adding another 5 hp. Shaw received so much flack that he was eventually bumped to W/Stock. Then, a rule was created that stated no 6-cylinder cars could compete in Y/Stock or Z/Stock. (Photo Courtesy Bill Truby)

Duster Do

In 1974, Chrysler introduced its 360-ci engine as a replacement for the 340. According to a *National Dragster* interview with Bob Lambeck, "Chrysler had just come out with its new, low-compression, 360-ci engine for 1974 and wanted to prove that it could be competitive."

As history shows, the engine in a Duster was a perfect fit in the SS/I and I/S classes.

With Chrysler supporting the cause, Lambeck and Tim Ekstrand set to work to prove the 360's worth. Lambeck began by boring the block 0.020 over. From there, he added a Crane legal "cheater" camshaft. Rules stated that replacement camshafts had to meet factory lift and duration specifications. Rules did allow for a greater ramp rate. Behind the 360 was a TorqueFlite with an 8-inch B&M converter. The 8.25 rear end with its 4.88 gears managed to survive the increase in power.

Ekstrand won the NHRA Fallnationals in 1975 by defeating the A/S Ford Fairlane of Jim Waldo in the final round. At the World Finals, Ekstrand qualified number one with a 12.72 ET. Then, he marched to the final, where he faced Waldo again. Ekstrand took the handicap start, never looked back, and took the win with a 12.67 ET. Lambeck and Ekstrand obviously liked the combination, as they were back in 1985 to win the world title in another 360-powered Duster.

Bob Lambeck turned his showroom-fresh Duster with a 360-ci engine into an immediate I/SA class threat. Tim Ekstrand drove the Duster to record-holding 12.50 ETs. (Photo Courtesy Dave Kommel)

CHAPTER SIX

1976: CELEBRATE GOOD TIMES

Don Coonce, driving the Albert Clark and Don Coonce G/Gas 1966 Corvette, survived a strong field of Modified cars to win at Indy in 1976. A 277-ci engine propelled the car to consistent 10.40 ETs. (Photo Courtesy Bob Martin)

The year 1976 was a year of celebration for America: 200 years of independence. Patriotism was alive and well, and from shore to shore and border to border, the nation showed its pride.

On the racetrack, there was a diverse list of winners. Women made greater inroads, as Shirley Muldowney and Charlene Wood won national events and joined previous female winners, including Shirley Shahan, Judi Boertman, Mary Ann Foss, and Judy Lilly.

Top Fuel

The push start, which was once an integral part of the Top Fuel show, was regulated to memory in 1976, as new rules mandated self-starters. The NHRA cited safety concerns for the new rule, but there was no denying that the use of starters sped up the program.

Remote starters that spun off the blower have been around since the latter part of the 1960s. Former Top Fuel driver Jim Davis is generally credited as the one who introduced the starter. Davis purchased surplus P-51 12-volt aircraft starter motors in bulk, made the necessary modifications to suit drag racing's needs, and resold them.

The cost to drag race continued to increase, especially in the pro categories. Those running on fuel saw a barrel of nitromethane climb to $425 (a $100 increase over the 1975 price). With the price for commercial customers sitting at a reported $180 per barrel, many asked questions. Veteran Funny Car racer Kenny Safford, driving Mr. Norm's Charger, talked of filing a class-action lawsuit against Commercial Solvents of Terre Haute, Indiana, which was the nation's sole producer of nitromethane at the time.

Track Action

Shirley Muldowney, Richard Tharp, and Frank Bradley each won their first Top Fuel national event in 1976.

Howard Haight surprised many behind the wheel of Jim Johnson's Chevy-powered Hemi Hunter. *The car featured many factory high-performance parts, including the block, which proved that they could survive the rigors of Top Fuel. (Photo Courtesy Michael Pottie)*

In 1976, Shirley Muldowney won the NHRA Springnationals, making her the first woman racing in the pro categories to win a national event. (Photo Courtesy Dave Kommel)

The always-potent team of Warren, Coburn, and Miller won the Gatornationals, which was the team's first national event victory since the 1968 Winternationals. At the Gatornationals, James Warren defeated Jim Bucher with a 6.24 ET to Bucher's 6.45 ET. (Photo Courtesy Michael Pottie)

Jeb Allen let the masses know that he was back and won the Fallnationals, which was his first victory since his fiery crash at Tulsa in 1973.

Muldowney

With Ronnie Capp and Connie Kalitta in her corner, Shirley Muldowney won her first national event: the NHRA Springnationals. Muldowney showed them all that she was ready for business when she qualified number one (another first for a woman) with a 6.03 ET.

Her march to the final was well earned, as she defeated Frank Holden and Paul Longenecker and then beat Ted Wolf (in the *Jade Grenade*) in the semifinals. Her final-round opponent, Maryland's Bob Edwards, was making only his third national event appearance. The odds were on Muldowney, and she didn't disappoint. She took the win from Edwards with a 5.96 ET at 243 mph.

Tharp

Richard Tharp was a man with an abundance of experience behind the wheel of Fuel cars that dated back to the mid-1960s. In 1975, he was hired by Candies and Hughes to replace Dave Settles in their Keith Black–powered Top Fuel car. Settles had been driving for Candies and Hughes since 1973, when they campaigned both a Top Fuel car and a Funny Car. He decided to go his own way and build a Top Fuel car of his own.

Tharp won his first Top Fuel national event in 1976 by defeating Pat Dakin at the IHRA Winter Nationals. On the NHRA trail, he earned his first national event win at Summernationals, where he defeated Jeb Allen in the Top Fuel final with a 5.99 ET to a 6.04 ET. Tharp followed with a win at the US Nationals and defeated John Wiebe.

In a hard-fought season battle, the always-entertaining (on and off the track) Tharp won the NHRA Top Fuel Championship, and Frank Bradley was the runner-up. Tharp proved to be no flash in the pan, as he won IHRA Top Fuel Championships in 1981 and 1983.

Richard Tharp, in the Paul Candies and Leonard Hughes Fueler, competes at Pomona. Woody Gilmore built the chassis of this one. By 1976, a Top Fuel car that was running well hit 60 mph in 1 second. (Photo Courtesy Michael Pottie)

After Jeb Allen's wreck in 1973, his return was highly anticipated. Allen was rewarded with wins at the NHRA Fallnationals (where he defeated Hank Johnson) and the AHRA Summer Nationals (where he defeated Flip Schofield). (Photo Courtesy Mike Dimery)

Bradley

Frank "the Beard" Bradley's season got off to a great start, as he won the AHRA and NHRA Winternationals. In AHRA competition, Bradley and John Wiebe were in full control and swapped wins all season. When all was said and done, Wiebe repeated his 1975 Top Fuel

Along with Frank Bradley's NHRA Winternationals victory (where he defeated James Warren), Bradley won three AHRA series events in 1976. Bradley was the last member of the Cragar Five-Second Club, after he ran a 5.96 ET in June 1974. (Photo Courtesy Rich Carlson/Grant Bittner Collection)

The versatile Paul Longenecker competed in numerous categories–from Super Stock to Pro Stock and finally Top Fuel. The Longenecker rail closed the 1976 season in the top 10 of the standings for all three sanctioning bodies. (Photo Courtesy Michael Pottie)

Championship. Through the 1970s, Frank saw his greatest success running AHRA events, and it's amazing that the Napa Valley, California, resident never won a world title.

Funny Car

Rule revisions for 1976 were minimal. The minimum weight of an NHRA Funny Car remained at 1,950 pounds, whereas the AHRA set its minimum at 1,700 pounds. The two sanctioning bodies varied in minimal wheelbase as well, with the NHRA set at 100 inches and the AHRA at 110 inches.

Snake Bites

Entering the season, Don Prudhomme hadn't lost a national event since Indy in 1975, when Raymond Beadle defeated him in the final. Prudhomme continued the streak and won the first five national events of the 1976 season before he lost, again at Indy, to Gary Burgin and his *Orange Baron* Mustang. Burgin recorded a 6.25 ET to the Prudhomme's tire-shaking 6.46 ET. It was Prudhomme's only loss of the season, as he went on to win the Fallnationals and World Finals. Burgin, who created the "Orange Baron" nickname while trying to land an orange-juice sponsorship (but never did), closed the season second in points behind Prudhomme.

Tom McEwen, coming off an AHRA Championship season, was hard-pressed to pick up a win in 1976. McEwen campaigned two Funny Cars between 1974 and 1976, with John Collins in the second car. (Photo Courtesy Rich Carlson/Grant Bittner Collection)

The "Orange Baron" Gary Burgin earned the biggest win of his career by defeating Don Prudhomme in the Funny Car final at Indy. (Photo Courtesy Rich Carlson/Grant Bittner Collection)

Blue Max

Raymond Beadle, owner and driver of *Blue Max* won three IHRA Funny Car championships: 1975, 1976, and 1981. These went hand in hand with the three consecutive NHRA Funny Car titles that he collected in 1979, 1980, and 1981.

The *Blue Max* story is difficult to follow. However, for a brief history, Harry Schmidt gave birth to the car and then the name in 1970. By 1973, he was burned out and decided to step aside and hand the reigns to his driver Richard Tharp. Shortly after, a fire burned the Buttera-chassis car to the ground. It was replaced with a short-lived Vega-bodied *Blue Max*.

In an NHRA.com interview with Phil Burgess, Richard Tharp stated that Schmidt was a very smart man who was ahead of his time. "He was the first one to put a quick-change (rear end) in a Funny Car and the first to run a big fuel pump and hang a lot of weight on the clutch."

Raymond Beadle won his second IHRA Funny Car World Championship in 1976. Beadle was also busy match racing (which was still a big deal in the 1970s) nearly every weekend. (Photo Courtesy Mike Dimery)

In 1974, Schmidt was coaxed out of retirement by Raymond Beadle, who convinced him to turn wrenches on the 'Cuda that Beadle ran under Don Schumacher's name. In 1975, the pair decided to revive the *Blue Max* name. That year, they earned their first national event victory by defeating Prudhomme at the US Nationals. The *Blue Max* was so popular with fans that by the end of the year, Schmidt and Beadle received requests to compete in match races and received $2,500 for those match-race bookings.

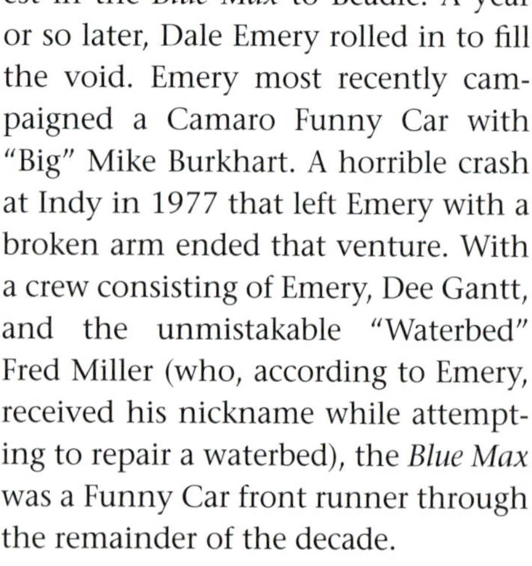

In 1976, Schmidt sold his interest in the *Blue Max* to Beadle. A year or so later, Dale Emery rolled in to fill the void. Emery most recently campaigned a Camaro Funny Car with "Big" Mike Burkhart. A horrible crash at Indy in 1977 that left Emery with a broken arm ended that venture. With a crew consisting of Emery, Dee Gantt, and the unmistakable "Waterbed" Fred Miller (who, according to Emery, received his nickname while attempting to repair a waterbed), the *Blue Max* was a Funny Car front runner through the remainder of the decade.

From Fuel Altereds and wheel-standers to Funny Cars, there was nothing that Dale Emery couldn't tune or drive. In 1977, he drove this Camaro for "Big" Mike Burkhart. The Roger Carrier body was destroyed in a spectacular crash at Indy. (Photo Courtesy Bob Snyder)

Pro Stock

Things were chaotic in Pro Stock, which seemed to be the norm. The causes were the shifting weight breaks and rules that prohibited certain cylinder head modifications. The new rules stated that heads could not be more than 0.250 inch above the stock height. This was in direct response to the modifications that were being performed by Wally Booth.

Southern California's Bob Anderson liked his Novas. In 1970, Bob campaigned them, all with big-block power, in Pro Stock. This 1974 model saw double duty and ran as a C/Gasser as well. (Photo Courtesy Bob Snyder)

Further rule revisions did away with the drooping front ends. Builders did what they could to cheat the wind, but the habit of dropping the leading edge of the front end was getting out of hand. The NHRA felt that it was time to curtail the practice and restore the stock lines. One can take a look at today's Pro Stock to see how far the category has deviated from stock through the years.

Wally Booth

Wally Booth borrowed Andy Mannarino's Vega to start the season. He figured that without his welded AMC heads, there was no way that his Hornet could be competitive. It turned out that only Booth's heads were affected by the rule, as nothing else changed. In April, the rule revisions allowed cylinder head height to be 0.250 above stock. Booth bypassed the Gatornationals in March but competed at the Springnationals in the Hornet with his welded heads.

Booth went on a tear and won the Springnationals, US Nationals, Fallnationals, and World Finals. He closed the season third in points behind World Champion Larry Lombardo and Warren Johnson. It's safe to say that losing out at the Winternationals and missing the Gatornationals likely cost Booth the championship.

Andy Mannarino lent Wally Booth his Wolverine Chassis-built Vega to run at the Winternationals. There, Booth fell in the first round to Bob Glidden.

Back in the Hornet, Wally Booth went on a tear and had the best year of his career. He won three NHRA national events and a few IHRA races. (Photo Courtesy Todd Wingerter)

Maskin-Kanners

Speaking of AMC, in a previous conversation with the author, Richard Maskin relayed how both he and Booth simultaneously worked on modified cylinder heads without either realizing it. Maskin, like Booth, raised the roof, enlarged the ports, and changed the angles.

"The first heads appeared in 1976 during test sessions at Irwindale prior to the Winternationals," Maskin said.

Maskin went to AMC with the modified heads, and the manufacturer gave him its full support and allowed modified tooling so that the heads could be cast. The cast heads appeared in 1977 and incorporated all of the changes that Maskin was unable to make with the welded heads.

Glidden in a Chevy

Two-time NHRA World Champion Bob Glidden, frustrated by seeing his Cleveland-powered Fords being hammered by the weight breaks, dropped the jaws of fans and fellow competitors when he debuted a Chevy Monza at Indy. The car was all about the weight breaks, as he ran the Monza at a lighter weight than his previous Pinto. Don Hardy built the chassis for the Monza, while Glidden built a de-stroked big-block. In a first for Glidden, he failed to qualify at Indy, as his 9.00 ET at 148 mph landed him as the first alternative. Undetected timing issues and leaking cylinders hampered his effort. Frustrated, he sold the Monza to Comp Eliminator racer John Lingenfelter shortly after Indy.

Dave Kanners wheeled the Maskin and Kanners Hornet X *into 1977. At the 1976 NHRA World Finals, the only all-AMC Pro Stock final ever at a national event, Kanners ran a quick 8.76 ET but fell to Booth's 8.78 ET. (Photo Courtesy Michael Pottie)*

Bob Glidden had only four runs on his Chevy Monza before selling his car. His best run was an unqualifying ET of 9 seconds flat at Indy. (Photo Courtesy Dan Williams)

The Reher and Morrison team's Monza was rebuilt after the Lee Shephard crash, and it showed up at the 1977 NHRA Winternationals with Richie Zul behind the wheel. Zul's existing Camaro Pro Stocker was sold to Dennis Ferrara. (Photo Courtesy Bob Snyder)

Although Glidden failed to capture the NHRA crown in 1976, he cleaned house in IHRA competition using his Cleveland-powered Pinto to win 9 of 10 national events. Nothing came easy for Glidden and his crew, which consisted of his wife, Etta; employee, Fred Flagle; and two growing sons. The Gliddens worked up to 16 hours a day, 7 days a week by Glidden's own admittance.

RMS Pro Stock Debut

Reher, Morrison, and Shepherd entered the world of Pro Stock in 1976 with a Chevy Monza. The first race for the car was the inaugural Cajun Nationals on April 23, and they couldn't have asked for a better debut.

Lee Shepherd, who gained a reputation as having one of the best reaction times in the sport, defeated Wally Booth in the class final. Shepherd beat Booth off the line and hung on with a 9.07 ET to Booth's 8.88 ET. Sadly, the Monza, which had so much potential, met its demise quickly. At the 1976 Summernationals, a Heim joint in the four-link broke and caused the Monza to crash.

Jenkins Double Whammy

After Bill "Grumpy" Jenkins's semifinal round loss at the NHRA Winternationals, the reins of his 331-ci Monza were turned over to Larry Lombardo. It was a smart move for the aging Jenkins, as Lombardo went on to win the world championship. The win went in hand with the 1975 and 1976 AHRA World Championships that Ken Dondero won while driving Jenkins's second car.

While Dondero's 1976 World Championship was a walk in the park

Bill Jenkins and his line of Grumpy's Toys never failed to draw a crowd. The 1976 season proved to be driver Larry Lombardo's finest. (Photo Courtesy Bill Truby)

The versatile Ken Dondero was left to his own devices and earned Bill Jenkins two AHRA World titles while driving Jenkins's second Monza.

With his 1974 Camaro and its 396-ci engine, Warren Johnson came close to earning the NHRA Pro Stock title. The 1976 Gatornationals saw the first all-Chevy NHRA Pro Stock final since 1972. There, Lombardo defeated Warren Johnson with an 8.71 ET to an 8.76 ET. Johnson's Camaro left the line at 10,000 rpm and was shifted at 6,500 rpm.

(winning 7 of 10 series events), Lombardo's title was tougher to collect. At the season-ending World Finals, Team Jenkins saw its opportunity for the world championship threatened by upstart Warren Johnson and his de-stroked 427-equipped Camaro. Johnson hadn't won a single national event during the eight-race season, but due to points gained during the year, he found himself in the enviable position of being a possible upset victor. If he could outlast Lombardo by three rounds, he would go home with the title.

Johnson, who held the number-2 qualifying position with an 8.82 ET, and Lombardo, who qualified the Monza in 10th position with an off-pace 8.93 ET, met in the first round of eliminations. A holeshot by Lombardo clipped Johnson's Camaro with a 9.00 ET to a losing 8.91 ET.

Pro Comp

Pro Comp enjoyed immense popularity. It was not an issue to run a 32-car field, and the spectators loved the close racing. Indy had its first all-6-second field, which saw Dave Settles defeat Dale Armstrong in the final to give A/FD only its third national event win in NHRA history.

Relatively unknown in the South, Brent Bramley raced out of Alberta, Canada, with his AA/DA to win the

By the mid-1970s, leasing the name of a known driver was common. Here, Indiana's Norm Day carries Don Garlits's name on his BB/FC car. Ken Cox built the chassis, and a Donovan Hemi provided the power. Carrying the Garlits name increased bookings for Day and put extra cash in his pockets as well as the pockets of Garlits. (Photo Courtesy Michael Pottie)

In 1976, Brent Bramley brought the Pro Comp World title home with him to Canada. He made his one national event win of the season count. The AA/DA car featured a big-block Chevy and a Mark Williams chassis. (Photo Courtesy Rich Carlson/Grant Bittner Collection)

Norwin Palmer turned more than a few heads with his Ford Cleveland-powered Corvette. Palmer was a serious threat in 1976 in D/Altered class. It makes the Datsun (Nissan)-powered D/ED entry that he drove later seem not so unusual. (Photo Courtesy Bill Truby)

World Finals. Brent pulled off the win by defeating a broken Doug Kerhulas in the final round. It was no easy task, as the Canadian first had to face and defeat last year's World Finals runner-up, Ken Veney. Although Bramley relied on a blown Chevy for a good part of the season, by the finals, he was using a Billy Williams–built Donovan Hemi to record 6.80 ETs.

Comp Eliminator

In the name of bringing balance to the category, more shuffling of classes and weight breaks occurred. Gas Dragster classes were reduced from four to three, and weight breaks were adjusted accordingly. Econorail went in the opposite direction, increasing from three classes to four.

The AA/GS class disappeared, and Econo Altered was added. The new category consisted of two classes for non-supercharged cars that ran a single engine on gas. A/EA ran at a 5-pounds-per-cubic-inch break with a maximum carburetor size of 850 cfm. B/EA ran at a 6.50-pounds-per-cubic-inch break that allowed a maximum carburetor size of 750 cfm. B called for Wedge-head engines only, so no Hemis were allowed.

Wayne Clapp: World Champion

Wayne Clapp, in his Gapp and Roush Cleveland-powered B/D, walked away with the 1976 World Championship.

Clapp became a full-time points chaser in 1975 and campaigned a Chevy-powered B/ED. He closed the season with a win at the Fallnationals.

"That win gave me enough confidence to tour with the car and race at national events back east," Clapp said during an interview. "I wanted to see how I'd do against the other top Comp racers in the country."

Wayne Clapp, seen here driving the Dean Thompson B/D at the 1977 Popular Hot Rodding meet, carries the number one in recognition of his 1976 Comp World Championship. Pro Stock's Gapp and Roush supplied the Cleveland engine. (Photo Courtesy Tom Kosiara)

Seeing that Comp payouts weren't going to pay the way, Clapp stayed with friends and hoped to win rounds so that he could replenish parts and eat.

Clapp teamed up with Dean Thompson in 1976, and the pair debuted its B/Dragster at the Summernationals. Clapp had a semifinal finish at Indy and a final-round loss at the Fallnationals before he defeated Wally Jacobsen's D/A Camaro with an 8.05 ET to win the World Finals.

This isn't the car that fans expected to see "Ohio" George Montgomery driving. The AA/MC turbo Pinto was capable of running 0.4 seconds under the class index. The "MXP" on the door stood for Malco Extraordinary Pinto. (Photo Courtesy Bob Martin)

Modified Eliminator

Little changed in Modified for 1976, as it still offered the same excitement. Weight was adjusted in all classes, and the cars of Gas, Street Roadster, and Modified Production all received an extra 0.5 pound per class. The Modified Compact classes were hit with 1.5 pounds.

Super Modified expanded to three classes in 1976. Weight breaks came in at 8.50 for A/SM, 9.50 for B, and 10.50 for C. A minimum weight of 3,350 pounds was set for A, and a minimum weight of 3,000 pounds was set for B and C. The A/SM allowed an unlimited engine size, while the maximum engine size for B and C was 366 ci.

Racers, being the fierce lot that they are, went to extraordinary lengths to gain a competitive edge. Super Modified seemed to lose its way and its affordability. Those with money turned to pro-built engines and cylinder heads. This may have been the beginning of the end of the category. At the very least, it pushed the guys with thin wallets out of competition.

Larry Kopp, World Champion

Journalist Rick Voegelin wrote a great piece on Larry Kopp, where he referred to Kopp as "the uncrowned king of NHRA Modified Eliminator," and that he was. Kopp was the most successful racer in the category's 12-year history (1970 to 1981). He won a total of nine national events, and the world championship in 1976.

Larry Kopp campaigned his 1964 Corvette in multiple classes–usually the 12.50-pounds-per-cubic-inch classes of H/Gas and D/MP. This put the engine of the world championship car down in the 280- to 290-ci area. Ignore the 1967 Corvette front clip. The fender vents were swapped for 1964 vents. (Photo Courtesy Michael Pottie)

Kopp won the Division 1 title in 1976 behind the wheel of his small-inch H/G 1964 Corvette. He picked a great time to win his first national event, when he defeated Tony Christian in the final round at the World Finals. Larry qualified fourth (0.05 under his class index), with Christian right behind him in the ex-Reher and Morrison G/Gas Corvette.

In the final round, Kopp recorded a 10.84 ET at 106 mph, while Christian ran a 10.64 ET but hit the brakes too soon and watched Kopp sneak past.

Chevrolet All the Way (Almost)

Chevy was dominant in the Modified category. Looking at the year-end class record holders for 1976, of the 60 records (ET and mph), Chevy held 39; Ford, 7; Volkswagen, 6; Dodge, 2; Mazda, 2; and 4 were open. The remaining two records (K/G and the A/SM top speed records) were open.

Outside of the first-generation Camaros that showed in most every category, the Corvette held favor in the majority of Gas and Altered classes. The slippery design and built-in engine setback made it a natural winner. Add a small-block engine that the aftermarket catered to, loved to rev, and could be bored and stroked or de-stroked to make it fit any class, and it's easy to see why the cars were so prevalent. Few Corvettes were as consistent at winning as the 1963 split-window that was campaigned by Dayton, Ohio's Jerry Ault.

The Frizzell brothers and their Camaros (they had two) were a Division 6 threat through the 1970s. The Quaker State-sponsored Camaros featured small-block engines that measured from 292 to 331 inches. Carl Fizzell has fond memories of coming off the line at 10,500 rpm and recording mid-10-second ETs. A Doug Nash 5-speed and Ford rear end completed the bulletproof drivetrain. (Photo Courtesy Derk Frizzell)

Ault and James

Ault built the Corvette in 1970 and raced it through 1978. Unlike the majority of his competitors who ran tunnel ram manifolds with twin Holley carburetors, Ault went with Crower injection from the beginning. His engines ranged from 277 to 292 ci. During the 1976 season, the driveline in the Corvette consisted of a 3.05-first-gear Doug Nash 5-speed transmission and a Dana 60 rear end that housed 6.50 gears that were replaced every dozen or so runs.

Ault left the line at 8,500 rpm and shifted at 10,000. Quality parts kept the small-block alive, including Brooks rods and Duffy pistons that made 13.1 compression.

Ohio-based Jerry Ault's Corvette held class records and wins all the way back to 1971. Many competitors benefited from a visit to the Ault and James Speed Shop in Dayton, Ohio. (Photo Courtesy Bob Martin)

Jerry Ault's de-stroked Chevy featured Brooks rods, Duffy pistons, 13.1 compression, a modified and lightened crankshaft, turbo heads, and a Vertex magneto.

Before he moved onward to a Chevy Monza in 1979, the Corvette ran best ETs in the 10.20s at 132 mph.

Super Stock

Super Stock cars could now weigh 75 pounds over or under the factory ship weight to better suit their class but could not use the variance to change classes. The Stockers enjoyed the same benefit in 1977.

The Camaro of Carl Bennett and Ron Sirianni was powered by a Truppi-Kling-built, 295-hp 350 engine. The Camaro was the first car in the SS/I class to crack the 10s. In November 1975, Bennett and Sirianni set the class record with a 10.72 ET, and that record lasted for two years. (Photo Courtesy Bill Truby)

Lingenfelter

John Lingenfelter had a talent for making small-block Chevys run well. In 1976, he campaigned a 1973 SS/LA Corvette and the former Bosz and Tores Chevy II in IHRA Super Modified. The Corvette was good for many class wins and the class record, which Lingenfelter set in May with a 11.38 ET at 117.18 mph. The record stood for a year.

Lingenfelter's thrashing on the Corvette at Indy and the lead-up to Indy was one for the books. The week prior to the "Big Go," Lingenfelter rented the Muncie Dragway and tested transmissions, headers, camshafts, and a prototype oil pan. Once at Indy, Lingenfelter won class with an 11.21 ET. Then, he proceeded to eclipse that with an 11.08 ET. Few expected Lingenfelter's weekend to end there, but after he blew the side out of his block, he was done.

Quick-thinking Lingenfelter caught a sightseeing helicopter flight back to his home to Decatur, Indiana, to grab a fresh block. With helping hands from many, he rushed to make repairs for the first round, only to fall

Low compression was a hard pill to swallow after experiencing the muscle cars of the 1960s. John Lingenfelter showed that these cars could be made to win when he dominated with his 1973 Corvette. (Photo Courtesy Michael Pottie)

The AHRA: A Different View

AHRA Super Stock rules varied slightly from those of the NHRA, and the category had its own standouts. The Super Stock champion for 1976 was Larry Mitchell and his big-block-powered Chevelle wagon. Mitchell repeated the win in 1979.

Mitchell was one half of the winningest team in AHRA history. His brother Bill won five AHRA Championship titles through 1984 and campaigned cars in the Modified Street category. The total number of wins between the two was only surpassed by the 10 titles that were won by Don Garlits.

Larry Mitchell drove the Two Ton Rat Chevelle wagon, and his brother Bill Mitchell wheeled the X-Rated II Gremlin. Both men were AHRA champions. (Photo Courtesy Rich Carlson/Grant Bittner Collection)

due to a piece of Teflon tape that hampered fuel delivery.

A Steve Griner lock-up converter that was hidden within the Turbo 400 transmission helped the Corvette to its 11.08 ET. Griner and partner Dave Coan designed a torque converter with a built-in clutch pack in 1975 that was trialed in the Nimo and Coan B/ED. Steve said this was the first 7-inch, take-apart torque converter that was built specifically for drag racing. The NHRA banned the use of lock-up convertors in Econo Dragster, Super Stock, and Stock (unless factory equipped) in 1978.

Stock

The NHRA now allowed for cars as old as 1960 to compete. Handicaps were still the name of the game, which saw Tom Reider and his X/S *Horse Sense* Pinto take category wins at the Gatornationals and Sportsnationals. Reider combined good handicap leads with consistent driving to pull off the wins. At Indy, he pulled off

The AHRA had its own version of the Stock category, and the 1976 World Champion was Dave Workman and his 6-cylinder-powered Maverick. Workman had a fantastic career and raced into the 2000s. (Photo Courtesy Rich Carlson/Grant Bittner Collection)

Gary Wood prepared the Tons A Fun *Pontiac wagon that was driven by Charlene Wood. Fans ate up the starting-line antics. The wagon was sold to a man in Quebec, Canada, and its current whereabouts are unknown. (Photo Courtesy Rob Potter)*

The second Tons A Fun*, with its standard 455 engine, never met the expectations of Gary and Charlene Wood. This car was followed by an F/SA 1972 GTO. (Photo Courtesy Bob Boudreau)*

another win in a Y/S Pinto wagon. It appeared that even the lowest-class Stockers appreciated the weight advantage that a wagon could bring.

Tons A Fun

Charlene Wood used a 1972 Pontiac LeMans wagon to win the Grandnationals in 1976. Appropriately named, the H.O. 455-powered *Tons A Fun* fell heavily (as in nearly 4,200 pounds heavy) into I/SA. Rated at 300 hp and 415 ft-lbs of torque, the wagon bodystyle helped tremendously to get the power to the ground. Those 9-inch slicks needed all the help that they could get. The wagon was famous for its chassis-twisting launches with the left front wheel in the air.

Tons A Fun was prepared by Charlene's husband, Gary, who knew his way around Pontiacs. He built the wagon in 1974, and Charlene took the wheel in 1975. She was no novice and began racing three years earlier behind the wheel of a car borrowed from her father's used lot. She seemed to be a natural behind the steering wheel and on the start line, where races are often won or lost.

Charlene won the Division 1 points championship in 1975. Gary, driving a Firebird in D/SA, came a close third in the standings. Charlene came within a few rounds of repeating her division win in 1976, but she fell short to Jerry Stein and his *Teacher's Pet* car at the final points meet of the season.

Charlene's Grandnationals win in 1976 showed consistency. She won the final three rounds with duplicate 12.37 ETs. Her final 12.37 ET came in the final, where she defeated the F/SA Oldsmobile convertible of Paul Mayo.

The wagon was sold in 1978, and a new *Tons A Fun* car was built for the 1979 season. Although the wagon with a standard 455 engine ran well, it never met expectations. Gary and Charlene retired from racing in 1982 after they campaigned a 1972 GTO. Brake-light racing had returned, and it wasn't for them.

Scott Main: World Champion

Scott Main and his 1968 Cobra Jet Mustang coupe fought the odds and won the world championship in 1976. Due to the coupe's stubby rear, which offered no weight to plant the 9-inch slicks, the Mustang wasn't supposed to win races. Barrie Poole drew that theory into question when he won Super Stock with his coupe at the 1970 Winternationals.

Main's 1 of 50 Cobra Jet–powered coupes went together under strict rules in the spring of 1976. Main, who won the Division 5 title in 1974 with a fastback Mustang, said that things changed significantly in 1975 when Winston came on board.

"We went from running for $300 and a trophy to racing for $1,200," Main said. "Things got a lot more serious, and I felt that I needed to build the new car."

Main debuted the C/S coupe in the spring of 1976

Physical education teacher Jerry Stein named his car appropriately. As with most division champions, Stein credited his success to a strong work ethic and attention to detail. It helped that famed racers/builders Jere Stahl and Pete Tritak were his mentors. (Photo Courtesy Rob Potter)

Teacher's Pet

In spite of his success campaigning Plymouths for years, Jerry Stein was not a fan of the people at Chrysler or its backed racers.

This disdain dated back to the beginning of the decade when he debuted his *Tomato Can*, a 1964 Max Wedge Plymouth. It was a no-no to beat the factory-backed cars and drop records.

"They hated anyone dropping the record," Stein said. "It wasn't until I built a car with Jack Werst in the '90s that I got [Chrysler's] support."

Stein won the Division 1 Stock Championship in 1976 and repeated in 1979 with a Max Wedge wagon. Few could piece together a 426 engine better than Stein. The man was dedicated and few worked harder. It wasn't unusual to see Stein at the track swapping cams or converters. He counted on the proven parts (as opposed to the trick-of-the-week parts) and used a B&M "J" converter and Lunati camshafts to win five national events.

at a division race and won it. He built his own engines and counted on Verle Stevens to perform the machine work. Main said that he had no real issues with his combination outside of oiling and bearings, which he finally worked through. It helped that Stock rules limited valve-spring pressure to 90 pounds closed and 290 pounds open.

"With shimmed valves, you could only rev from 5,900 to 6,000 rpm before you floated the intake valves," Main said. "You just couldn't hurt the engine at those RPM."

Peak power came in around 5,500 rpm.

It was a great season for Main, who won his second Division 5 title in three years, which earned an invite to the World Finals. There, the Mustang ran consistent 11.60 ETs as Main battled his way to the final round. In the final, he faced the I/SA Dodge of fellow Denver resident Ron Peters. Ron took the handicap start but lost because he ran too fast, as he attempted to hold off the Mustang's 11.67 ET. For his efforts, Main earned bragging rights and a cool $12,000.

Although Scott Main and his Cobra Jet Mustang won the Division 6 title and Stock world championship, he never received much ink. Main said that this was because his Mustang didn't have a fancy paint job. (Photo Courtesy Steve Goddard)

CHAPTER SEVEN

1977: DRAG RACING IS FAR OUT

Indiana's Pam Sanders (shown here in 1976) entered the 1977 season as the Division 3 Stock points champion. Her 1969 Camaro ragtop was powered by the famed 255-hp 350 engine and was capable of 12.40 ETs and a record top speed of 107.27 mph.

The world of drag racing featured three sanctioning bodies with a combined 27 national events, and total attendance approached half a million. That doesn't count the following independent meets: Bakersfield, the Super Stock Nationals, and the Popular Hot Rodding meet. The PRO race, which Garlits started back in 1972, was still on (minus Garlits) but was dying a slow death. In addition, many Fuelers, Funny Cars, and Pro Stocks competed in weekly match races. There was definitely no shortage to feed the addiction.

Top Fuel

The only significant change in NHRA Top Fuel rules for 1977 pertained to ground clearance. To ensure that the start and finish lamps were not tripped before the tires cleared the beams, the leading-edge ground clearance had to be at least 3 inches. The new rule affected all pro-category cars.

Drag racing a Fuel car was getting no cheaper, as a gallon of nitro was around $7.50. Multiply that by about 8 gallons per run. All in, a single run down the track by a Top Fuel car cost about $300.

Swamp Rat 24

After being pestered by Donovan, Don Garlits swapped in one of Donovan's aluminum Hemis to replace his usual Keith Black engine. The story goes that Garlits felt that Black was stealing his secrets and giving them to the likes of Shirley Muldowney, Don Prudhomme, and Gary Beck. Interestingly, Muldowney had a successful 1976 season and won the world title in 1977. Prudhomme, with wrench man Bob Brandt, was doing fine in Funny Car and won his third of four consecutive

Don Durbin's idea of enclosing the slicks and improve how the car moved through the air wasn't successful. The weight of the covers was the biggest issue. (Photo Courtesy Michael Pottie)

Swamp Rat 24 *was built in 1976 and initially featured a unique two-piece frame and a B&J 3-speed transmission. Both experiments failed, and in short order, the frame was welded and the 3-speed was replaced with a 2-speed. (Photo Courtesy Dan Williams)*

titles. Beck was in a slump and saw his last win come at the Grandnationals in 1976. More than likely, Garlits's switch had more to do with money.

Garlits built the Donovan engine with high compression (7.5 to 8:1) and redesigned the Donovan cylinder heads that featured larger coolant passages. Garlits affixed a water pump to the front of the engine, which pulled coolant from a 2-gallon tank located behind the seat. The increased capacity cured any detonation issues that were caused by the higher compression, and it kept things cool for any starting line antics (burndowns). Garlits said that he ran his engines soft when compared to others. He ran the Bower blower 35 over, ran 52 degrees of ignition lead, and had an 88-percent load of fuel in the tank.

In his book, *Don Garlits and His Cars*, Garlits said that the *24* car was his best car. He campaigned it for three full years, and it helped him earn $600,000. In 1978, Garlits returned to running Keith Black engines, as he felt that they were stronger.

In God We Trust

According to Garlits, toward the end of 1976, he received a call from US Navy recruiters, who offered to sponsor him for two years, beginning with the 1977 season. As part of the deal, the dragster was painted blue and white. As a sign of his Christian faith, Don decided to grace the white cowl with a cross and the words "God Is Love."

When Garlits arrived at Pomona for the Winternationals, the *Los Angeles Times* picked up on the cross and ran a not-so-flattering piece on Garlits and the Navy's apparent lack of neutrality when it came to religion.

"The Navy was unhappy," Garlits said. "They wanted the cross removed at once, or moved into the cockpit, where it couldn't be seen by cameras. I wouldn't comply, and the Navy withdrew the sponsorship. I'm a Christian, and I figured God would work it out, and did God ever!"

Garlits walked away with the 1977 IHRA World Championship. In 1978, the Navy caved to Garlits and the cross. Garlits went on to win the 1978 and 1979 AHRA Championships.

In late 1977, Don Garlits painted* Swamp Rat 24 *after agreeing with the Navy on a sponsorship deal. The car ran 5.70 ETs at 248 mph before the car was replaced. (Photo Courtesy Rob Potter)

Cha-Cha Ching

Shirley Muldowney became the first woman to win a pro category world title when she took NHRA Top Fuel honors in 1977. Her first of three world titles (she also won in 1980 and 1982) came on the strength of regional event wins and national event victories at Columbus, Englishtown, and Montreal.

Muldowney's outfit was first class. Her Ron Attebury 250-inch chassis mounted a 488-ci Keith Black engine that was fitted with the best parts of the day: an Ed Pink 8-71 magnesium blower, Enderle fuel pump with a Lenco overdrive, a Moldex stroker crank, Waterman rods, ForgedTrue pistons, and a Crower camshaft. Power was transmitted through a Hays triple-disk clutch and Lenco 2-speed transmission to a magnesium rear end. Although most of the goods used by Muldowney were pretty much standard fare in Top Fuel and Funny Car, it took a good mechanic to make it click, and she had one of the best in Connie Kalitta. Kalitta oversaw Muldowney's Top Fuel operation from 1975 through the end of the 1977 season.

Shirley Muldowney won her first world championship in 1977. She went on to become one of Top Fuel's most successful drivers. (Photo Courtesy Bob Sitre/Rob Potter Collection)

Ron Attebury competed using "Jungle" Jim Liberman's colors through 1977 in AHRA-series events. Liberman asked Garlits to build him a Fueler 1975 but backed out of the deal. (Photo Courtesy Bob Snyder)

Chevy's Last Stand

By 1977, the world of Top Fuel (and Funny Car for that matter) belonged to the aftermarket Hemi. The last pure Chevy Top Fuel car to win an NHRA national event belonged to Dwayne Lidtke and Ray Zeller. With Stan Shiroma at the helm, the team's Kenny Ellis–chassis dragster took the win at the 1977 NHRA Fallnationals. The feat was accomplished using a tall-deck Chevy block and steel open-chamber heads. Zeller was responsible for building the engine, and he set out from the beginning to prove that a Chevy could live on nitro (despite the rumors).

"When I got into the partnership with Dwayne, Chevy had a very bad reputation for tossing blowers, which I thought was stupid," Zeller said.

Ray believed (and rightly so) that the issue had to do with the tuning and nothing to do with it being a Chevrolet.

Helping the Chevy run high-5-second ETs was a 4.125 stroke and a flat-tappet cam cut by Jack Engle to Zeller's specifications. The engine ran an enormous 84 degrees of ignition timing and all the fuel pump that they could beg, borrow, or steal. Zeller called Keith Black a mentor and followed his lead by running a low 6:1 compression. The engine's one weak link was that it would, on occasion, crack open at the head studs.

At the Fallnationals, Shiroma qualified 10th with a 6.0 ET and defeated Frank Bradley, James Warren, and Ernie Fall before he faced and defeated the Rodeck-powered Valley Fever car of Rance McDaniel. The old saying goes, "You've got to be good to be lucky, and you've got to be lucky to be good. On this day, Shiroma was good and lucky. McDaniel failed to fire and allowed Shiroma to single for the win. With the Rodeck being an aftermarket Chevy block, this can be viewed as the last all-Chevy Top Fuel final.

The Dwayne Lidtke and Ray Zeller Chevy Top Fueler was driven by Stan Shiroma. The team later switched from a Chevy cast block to an aluminum Rodeck. A 2-speed transmission and 4:30 rear-end completed the driveline.

Funny Car

There were very few rule changes for Funny Car in 1977. The three sanctioning bodies let them fly, and fans sat back and enjoyed. Each sanctioning body saw different world champions: Don Prudhomme, Tom Hoover, and Dale Pulde.

This was Mickey Thompson's last drag car (as driven by veteran Bob Pickett). Pickett won the Springnationals by defeating Don Prudhomme. The body mimicked an Oldsmobile Starfire, but it was often mistaken for a Chevy Monza. (Photo Courtesy Bob Snyder)

Hoover

As with Prudhomme, Tom Hoover ran Top Fuel cars through the 1960s and made the move into Funny Car in 1970. Hoover's operation was a literal mom-and-pop show, and the team had its most success at AHRA events. In 1977, Hoover won his second AHRA Funny Car Championship in a row. The same season, he won his first NHRA national event (the Grandnationals) at Sanair in Quebec, Canada.

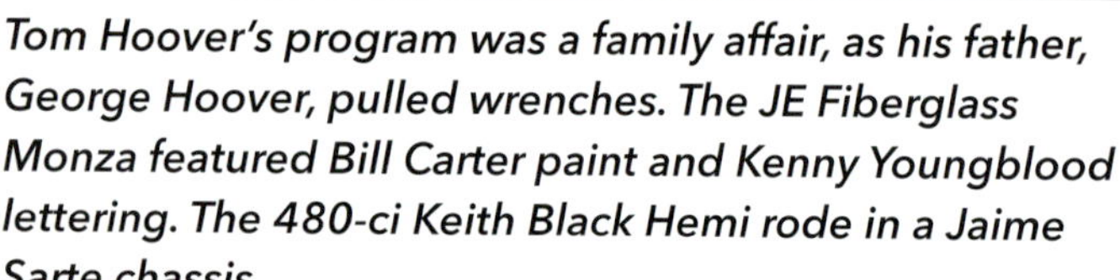

Tom Hoover's program was a family affair, as his father, George Hoover, pulled wrenches. The JE Fiberglass Monza featured Bill Carter paint and Kenny Youngblood lettering. The 480-ci Keith Black Hemi rode in a Jaime Sarte chassis.

Prudhomme

In 1977, the Chinese Year of the Snake, Don "the Snake" Prudhomme added three more NHRA national event victories to his list, and the third of four world titles in a row. Wins weren't as easy for Prudhomme, as the competition was catching up, making clutch and fuel delivery improvements.

In an old Hot Rod *magazine article, Don Prudhomme said that he was able to compete in drag racing due to his sponsors and the approximate 60 match races that he ran each season. The approximate $57,000 he made from national event wins wasn't going to cut it. (Photo Courtesy Michael Pottie)*

The Bubble Up team enjoyed an amazing weekend at the 1977 World Finals, where Gordie Bonin won the Funny Car category. In 1977, Bonin, Graham Light, and car owner Bob Lawrence teamed with Ron Hodgson and Gordon Jenner to add their Top Fuel car to their team. Light was runner-up in Top Fuel at the Finals. (Photo Courtesy Bob Snyder)

Pulde

At times, Dale Pulde has been referred to as the busiest man in drag racing. He piloted at least 64 different cars at the drag strip throughout his career. Nearly all of them were AA/Funny Cars. If success is measured in national event wins, Pulde more than proved himself with 20 IHRA wins; world championships in 1977, 1982, and 1985; a half-dozen NHRA national event wins; and a half-dozen AHRA national event wins.

"Jungle" Jim Liberman's final full season may have been his best. His 1976 Monza became the third Funny Car into the 5s, when he recorded a 5.964 ET at Green Valley in April. (Photo Courtesy Michael Pottie)

The Dale Pulde-driven War Eagle *was painted by Bill Carter. Pulde had a great year. He won the IHRA championship and was sixth in the NHRA's final standings. (Photo Courtesy Ed Aigner)*

RIP "Jungle" Jim

"Jungle" Jim Liberman showed that success isn't always measured in victories. Liberman was a showman; a man born to this sport. He was pure entertainment and aimed to please. It all came to an end on September 9, 1977, when a collision with a transit bus on Pennsylvania's Westchester Pike ended his life.

Liberman first drew attention in 1965 behind the wheel of Lew Arrington's *Brutus*, a Pontiac LeMans match racer that terrorized southern California tracks. In 1968, Liberman campaigned twin Chevy Novas of his own with Clare Sanders as a hired driver.

Liberman had at a half-dozen national event victories under his belt, starting with a win at the AHRA World Championship Drags at Lions Drag Strip in 1966.

Liberman's forte was match racing, which he did up to 100 times a season. With Liberman on the bill, a promoter could nearly guarantee a packed house. Fans ate up his antics—from his 1,000-foot burnouts, back-up burnouts, return-road burnouts, and late arrivals that had him unload the Funny Car right on the track. To Liberman, drag racing was far out!

Prior to his passing, Liberman picked up his first major sponsor in 7-Eleven, the convenient store chain. Things were looking up for him and a bright future was on the horizon. He was taken just three days shy of his 32nd birthday. It's left to our imagination to think what could have been.

Carl Ruth took control of the "Jungle" Jim Liberman Monza for a while after Liberman's passing. (Photo Courtesy Michael Pottie)

Pro Stock

When it came to NHRA Pro Stock, it was more of the same. Those dreaded weight breaks jumped from 19 pounds in 1976 to 22 pounds in 1977. Ford's Cleveland remained in the rule-makers sights again. Any car running the engine was forced to carry more weight than any other combination in the category. In spite of the added weight, "Dyno" Don Nicholson in his Don Hardy–built Mustang II walked away with the world title.

Rules revisions required bodies to be no older than 1973, which was changed from the previous season, when it was 1969 or newer. This brought an end to the 1970 Mustangs. The minimum wheelbase requirement dropped from 94 inches in 1976 to 92 inches in 1977, which opened the door for the newly restyled, shorter-wheelbase Dodge Colt.

"Dyno" Don Nicholson, with partner Jon Kaase, returned the Pro Stock championship to the Ford camp in 1977. Here, at Indy, he faced and defeated Bob Glidden in the final round. A clutchless 5-speed transmission may have helped. (Photo Courtesy Terry Gray)

Wally Booth updated the panels on his Hornet in 1977. After a successful 1976 season, he struggled. Note the fabricated intake. It was one of the first of the period. (Photo Courtesy Bob Snyder)

After a season that Bob Glidden would rather forget in 1976, he bounced back in 1977 and came up just short of winning the championship. An engine with a reported 342 ci helped him set the ET record at 8.50. (Photo Courtesy Terry Gray)

The IHRA Leads the Way

The biggest news in Pro Stock in 1977 came from the IHRA, which ditched those awful weight breaks altogether and went to a straight 2,350-pound minimum weight and any cubic inch format. In a competitionplus.com interview, Ted Jones, vice-president of competition at the IHRA at the time, reflected on how in the fall of 1976, he presented the idea to IHRA President Larry Carrier.

"I told him that we needed to come out with a new version of Pro Stock and call it 'Run Whatcha Brung,' Jones said. "No cubic-inch limits. Bolt in the biggest damn motor you can in the car and bring it on. There will be safety of course, but make them weigh 2,350 pounds, run pump gas, and have two 4-barrel carburetors. We don't even need to know how big the motors are. We'll just tell them to put the big motors in there and come on out and race."

Carrier pondered the idea, looked at Jones, and said, "Make it happen."

Jones did just that.

The General

When the new IHRA format was introduced, Chevy stalwart Lee Edwards was ready. The "General," as he was nicknamed, had been campaigning Pro Stock–legal Camaros and Vegas while match racing the cars at every opportunity that he could. When the new rules were implemented, he hit the ground running with 490 ci of tall-deck Chevy.

Lee's Mountain motor went together with a passenger-car block, a long stroke, and a few extra head gaskets to prevent the valves from destroying the pistons. Lee was the first star of IHRA's Mountain Motor Pro Stock and won the championship in 1977, and again in 1978 with a revised, tall-deck, stroked Chevy nestled in his state-of-the-art Vega. By the late 1970s, the cubic-inch war was in full swing. Aftermarket Rodeck aluminum Chevys were introduced and stretched upward to 570 ci and more. Gapp & Roush built 588-ci Boss Ford engines, and the Hemis followed suit.

Ronnie Sox teamed with Billy Stepp in 1977 to field this Don Hardy-built Plymouth Arrow that housed a big-inch Hemi. IHRA legal times were in the 8.20s. Rumors persisted regarding nitrous use by the team. (Photo Courtesy Mike Dimery)

Lee Edwards was the first star of the IHRA's Mountain Motor Pro Stock category and won championships in 1977 and 1978. He quickly went from Chevy blocks to aftermarket hardware of more than 600 ci. (Photo Courtesy Mike Dimery)

Pushing the Rules

"Dyno" Don Nicholson and his crew chief, Jon Kaase, swapped the Lenco 4-speed in Nicholson's Mustang II to trial a Nash 5-speed. The downside of the Nash was that, unlike the Lenco, it required the clutch to be engaged with each gear change. This ate up precious time. Nicholson and Kaase skirted the rules by rigging up a pressure-sensor button on the shift knob that momentarily cut the ignition and allowed Nicholson to shift without engaging the clutch.

Cutting the power takes the strain off of the synchros to allow full-throttle shifts to be made without fear of damage. A number of critical details had to be hammered out to ensure that the system worked. For instance, if the pressure on the shifter lever was set to low, the lever could be pulled out of gear without enough force to engage the next gear. If the pressure was set to high, the ignition could have come back on before Nicholson had the chance to complete the shift, and it could cause a missed shift.

Just as critical to the setup was the ignition cutout. Too short of a cutout would not allow the gear to free itself from the engine strain. Too long of a cutout costs engine speed, and quarter-mile times suffer.

Fellow racers complained of the setup and tried to mimic it. Pro Stock competitor Frank Iaconio was one.

The 1977 season was an amazing one for "Dyno" Don Nicholson. His car's clutchless 5-speed transmission, which was developed by Jon Kaase, had the competition tearing out its hair. (Photo Courtesy Michael Pottie)

Southern California racer Randy Humphrey proved that a low-buck Chrysler die-hard could still make it in Pro Stock. At one point in the season, the Duster's 8.70 ET made it the nation's quickest Mopar Pro Stocker. Ron Butler helped build the Duster in 1974. Bob Lambeck's engine work kept the Duster in contention through 1978. (Photo Courtesy Terry Gray)

Butch Leal built his Hemi Arrow as a heads-up match racer. In competition, he usually competed in B/Gas, where he held the class record with an 8.80 ET at 156 mph. (Photo Courtesy Michael Pottie)

Seven Seconds to Glory

The squabble goes on. Who was the first to run a 7-second ET in a Pro Stocker?

Many believe that it was "Dyno" Don Nicholson, as he ran a 7.99 ET with his 516-ci Pro Stock Mustang II in the summer of 1978.

However, many disagree and say that it was Butch "the California Flash" Leal in his Ron Butler–built Plymouth Arrow. Leal, with a 454-ci Hemi in a match race against Larry Lombardo in Bill "Grumpy" Jenkins's Monza, recorded a 7.96 ET at Englishtown during the summer of 1977.

Some argue that Leal's Arrow was not a Pro Stocker. Although it occasionally ran in the category, it was built as a match racer and raced legally as a Gasser. For his season-long effort with the Arrow, Leal was presented with the NHRA Modified Driver of the Year award by *Car Craft* magazine.

Shag No More

Speaking volumes to the quality construction of the Pro cars was the Don Hardy–built *Shag* Monza of Andy White.

The Texas-based car was destroyed at the NHRA Winternationals when a tire let loose and sent the car on several high-speed barrel rolls. Driver Shelby Jester walked away from the incident. The *Shag* was the first Pro Stock Monza to debut and appeared at the Gatornationals in 1975. It had previously survived a wreck at Indy in 1976.

Andy White's Shag was pretty while it lasted. After a crash, little survived aside from fan souvenir parts. (Photo Courtesy Bob Snyder)

"[Nicholson] was an innovator," Iaconio said. "He used to beat everyone with that trick 5-speed—a clutchless transmission when they were illegal. Somehow, he made it work and got away with it. We tried to figure it out, buying electronics and all, but found that we were chasing our tails."

The Mustang II was over a tenth of a second faster and more than a 1 mph quicker with the Nash. In the end, the NHRA finally rejected the setup.

Dave Settles, in his Tony Casarez-chassis A/FD, brought the NHRA Pro Comp title to Division 4 in 1977. Settles previously drove the Top Fuel car of Candies and Hughes. (Photo Courtesy Larry Pfister)

Pro Comp

There was never a dull moment in Pro Comp, as the season battles raged between the usual suspects. Dave Settles, in the Settles and (Joe) Barry A/FD, kicked the season off by winning the NHRA Winternationals. There, Settles faced the only other A/FD in the program: the all-but-obsolete, front-engine, injected Hemi car of Adams and Enriquez. Settles took the heads-up final with a 6.67 ET. He followed with wins at the Cajun Nationals and World Finals, where he defeated the Donovan-powered alcohol dragster of Dale Armstrong with a 6.73 ET. Settles's secret was using reworked Hemi heads by Bob Mullen that featured 2.30-inch intakes. Mullen had been working for Chrysler for some time, including working on the dual-plug Hemi and the LA-series W-2 castings.

Armstrong came on strong as the season progressed and won the last three national events of the season leading up to the World Finals. At the Finals, he laid down the low ET with a 6.60. In the final round, Veney and Settles ran matching 6.73 ETs, but Armstrong won the race on the starting line. Not to go home empty handed, Armstrong won the Grace Cup season battle and the $15,000 that went along with it.

Ken Veney returned to the track in mid-1977 after he purchased Cottrell and Speelman's Chicken Chokers AA/DA car. The best run for the blown Cleveland car was a 6.65 ET at 208 mph. (Photo Courtesy Terry Gray)

There's no questioning what propelled Dale Armstrong's Alcoholic or the AA/DA car that brought him the most success in 1977. Both of his cars ran consistent mid-6-second ETs with Donovan power. (Photo Courtesy Michael Pottie)

Comp Eliminator

Comp saw the NHRA reintroduce the old Factory Experimental classes in 1977. Gone since 1966, the category was reborn to deal with a number of Pro Stock and ex–Pro Stock cars that were taking over the Altered classes. Three classes were created: A/FX, which carried a 5.50 to 7.49 pounds to cubic inch break; B/FX with a 7.50 to 9.49 break; and C/FX with 9.50 pounds per cubic inch (minimum). Cars were limited to 1967 or newer to keep them out of the Altered classes.

At the same time, the Altered rules were revised and stated pre-1967 cars only. Roger Denny with his 1977 Plymouth Arrow set the first new A/FX record in June 1978 with an 8.55 ET at 158.74 mph. In 1985, the FX category was once again eliminated.

The 1977 Comp season was a see-saw battle among a few proven veterans. Dennis Ferrara didn't like the speeds of Econo Dragster, so he purchased the Pro Stock Camaro of Richie Zul and raced the car in B/EA. John Lingenfelter moved up from Super Stock and ran in B/EA using the ex–Bob Glidden Pro Stock Monza. Perennial winner Joe Williamson, in his 6-cylinder-powered E/Altered, hung around to be a pain for the competition.

Dennis the Menace: World Champion

Econo Altered (A and B/EA) was a new class in 1976, and Dennis Ferrara chose it in 1977 because he liked the soft index. Rules were similar between the two classes. In A, the weight break was 5 pounds per cubic inch, and you were limited to a maximum 850-cfm carburetor. In B, the break was 6.50 pounds per cubic inch, and the maximum carburetion was 750 cfm.

Ferrara debuted his B/EA Camaro at the Gatornationals with a McBett's 427. Out the gate the car ran 9.60 ETs and won Comp Eliminator. With rules that dictated a maximum carburetor of 750 cfm, Ferrara ran a string of continuously shrinking big-blocks. He knew a large-cubic-inch engine couldn't make as much power with the small carburetor as a small-cubic-inch engine could. By the end of the season, he settled on 373 ci.

Removing weight is like adding horsepower, and Dennis Ferrara's Camaro was stripped to the bare minimum. ETs in the 9.30s were realized from the 373-ci engine. (Photo Courtesy Michael Pottie)

Ronnie Sox competed using the former Don Carlton Hemi Colt at Indy in 1977. Don Hardy built the chassis that housed a Clyde Hodge de-stroked Hemi, a Lenco transmission, and 5.57 gears. The slicks measured 14x32. (Photo Courtesy Dan Williams)

This was no ordinary aluminum-head, big-block Chevy. The rule that limited carburetor size to 750 cfm led to incredible smaller engines. (Photo Courtesy Bob Snyder)

After seeing his Chevy-powered B/EA Monza being recategorized by the NHRA, John Lingenfelter switched to a Gapp and Roush Cleveland engine. The change came prior to the NHRA Summernationals, which was a race that he won. (Photo Courtesy Terry Gray)

Going by the rules, fewer cubic inches meant that the car's weight was reduced, and the Camaro was stripped to an inch of its life. Ferrara said that with him on board, the car weighed 1,900 pounds.

Ferrara ran a turbo 400 transmission in the Camaro and incorporated drag racing's first transbrake. With the help of Roger Lamb, he developed the brake the previous season and perfected it in 1977. Primitive but ingenious, the brake was a drum brake attached to the rear of the transmission in the same fashion as Ford's old Super Duty trucks. The brake that held the car in gear while Ferrara brought the revs up over 8,000 was activated by an air solenoid running off a bottle of compressed air. Ferrara first ran the brake while winning the 1977 Sportsnationals and picked up a tenth of a second in the process. Ferrara said the competition was tough.

"We butted heads with [John] Lingenfelter all season," Ferrara said. "Rumor was that he was running a lock-up convertor, which was illegal in class. At the World Finals, he was running 9.50 ETs. We ran a 9.40 ET, and people screamed, figuring there was no way we could run that quick with an aluminum head." When Ferrara defeated Joe Williamson in the final round, both Williamson and Lingenfelter protested the Camaro.

Ferrara credited his win to the aluminum heads provided by Grumpy Jenkins. The heads, which carried a Chevy part number, were approved by the NHRA. However,

On July 5, less than a month after winning Comp at the Springnationals, Don Carlton died when his Colt crashed during a testing session in Martin, Michigan. (Photo Courtesy Robbie Robertson)

Don Carlton

On July 5, less than a month after winning the Comp Eliminator title at the NHRA Springnationals, Don Carlton lost his life when he crashed his Dodge Colt during a test session at Milan Dragway in Michigan. Carlton had reportedly run an 8.18 ET at 169 mph in the 437-ci powered Colt just weeks before he was killed.

Don's reputation remains intact today due to the lasting impression he made driving for Sox & Martin and Billy Stepp before taking the wheel of the *Motown Missile*, *Mopar Missile* cars, and *Rod Shop* cars.

It wouldn't do Carlton justice if his work off the track wasn't mentioned. He was always looking at ways to improve on-track performance and continually tested new or modified parts. Carlton's likeability contributed immensely to the advancement of the sport.

after the win, Ferrara was told not to come back with them. The same engine but with steel heads was run at the Little Guy Nationals where it set the record running 9.35 ETs. It drove Lingenfelter nuts, as he still couldn't get ETs out of the 9.40s with his Monza, which was now powered by a Gapp & Roush Ford Cleveland.

Ferrara said he eventually sold the Camaro "to some street racers in Brooklyn because the NHRA killed the index. We put a bigger-inch motor in it, and it still ran 9s."

Modified Eliminator

In the door-car ranks, rules made it clear that drooping front ends were not acceptable. Many of the boys in Modified had mimicked the Pro Stocks by dropping the leading edge of the fenders and hood, and the NHRA had no appreciation for it.

In 1977, the short-wheelbase Corvettes were effectively booted from the Modified Production classes when NHRA imposed a 100-inch-wheelbase minimum rule. Consequently, the 1963 and newer Stingrays were only legal in the Gas classes. Larry Kopp countered by building a long-wheelbase 1961 Corvette that scored three national event victories in 1977–1978 in D/MP.

Samurai Warrior

With the majority of drag racers being raised on American V-8 engines, few understood (or cared to understand) the rotary engine. Portland, Oregon's Terry Hoard was one who was intrigued. He left many in the Modified ranks scratching their heads and covering their ears in disbelief of his 11-second RX-3 *Samurai Warrior*.

Without taking a deep dive into the workings of a rotary engine, it differs significantly from a traditional engine. However, it follows the same four strokes (intake, compression, combustion, and exhaust) as a conventional piston-driven engine. But, instead of these cycles all taking place in a cylinder, a rotary engine does each stroke in its own part of an oval-shaped chamber. The rotor itself is triangular and connected to an output shaft that spins at three times the speed of the rotor. The four cycles occur three times for each spin of the rotor. Unlike a piston engine, where duration, lift, and overlap are determined

Jack Trost turned Grumpy Jenkins's old Toy X into a Modified winner. He partnered with the Jesel Brothers and Terry Clark and flew the CMS colors from 1976 to 1977. (Photo Courtesy Michael Pottie)

Terry Hoard gained rotary experience with this showroom-fresh 1970 R-100. By the close of 1981, Hoard had won four national events and two Division 6 titles. (Photo Courtesy Rich Carlson/Grant Bittner Collection)

The best ETs for the RX-3 in legal trim were in the 11.80s, but rumors exist that the car ran ETs as quick as 11.30. Terry never ran anything other than a pre-1973 12A rotary. In conjunction with the block, he used 1974-type rotors because they had a better combustion chamber and better compression. (Photo Courtesy Dave Kommel)

Hoard's Mazda ran at a 16.5-pound weight in 1977, based upon double the advertised cubic inches. Engine modifications included a reworked 600-cfm Holley carburetor on a Denny Aldridge-fabricated intake manifold. Aldridge also fabricated the lone header. (Photo Courtesy Steve Jackson)

by the camshaft, in a rotary engine, these values are all determined by the ports. In performance applications, an additional port, referred to as a bridge port, is added to increase lift and duration at higher RPM.

The upside of a rotary engine was that it had fewer moving parts, operated smoother, and made more power than anyone expected.

Terry Hoard bought his first race-ready rotaries from Dick Haag of Rising Sun Rotary before he built his own. With growing interest in the rotary, Hoard opened his own shop, the Rotary Clinic, in 1973. His father, a millwright by trade, worked behind the scenes and taught Hoard immensely. Business grew as local Mazda dealers moved business his way. Those early rotaries were known to wear out prematurely, and many dealers had no idea what to do with them. The increased workload led Hoard to open a new business in 1975 called Auto World. He remained in business until 2002.

The *Samurai Warrior* was a team effort between Terry and Gary Parham. Gary supplied the new RX-3 in 1977, and Terry built the potent twin-distributor 12A engine. Denny Aldridge performed most of the remaining tasks that it took to turn the Mazda into an 11-second screamer.

Behind the 12A engine was a Doug Nash 5-speed transmission that was adapted by using a Ford Lakewood bellhousing. An 11-inch clutch and

Modified World Champion Buddy Ingersoll's turbocharged Pinto was untouchable. Ingersoll set the class record every year from 1977 through 1980 and hit a best ET in the 9.80s at 137 mph. Using a 2.0 block and an Air Research turbo, the engine made 500 hp at 26 pounds of boost. A Doug Nash 5-speed and 6.50 gears rounded out the drivetrain. (Photo Courtesy Rob Potter)

a heavy Ford flywheel were incorporated. Out back was a narrowed Dana 60 rear end that housed 7.17 gears. A ladder-bar suspension and floating axles helped plant the 10.5x28-inch Firestones.

Terry's biggest issue with the rotary was the apex seals, which served the same purpose as the piston rings in a conventional engine. The seals had a short lifespan, and when they would become worn or broken, power would be lost. Terry discovered that by replacing the existing 6-mm seals with 3-mm two-piece seals, he could get up to 25 runs before rebuilding.

This Camaro of Joe Scott began life as a 396-ci, 4-speed-equipped Indy pace car. With Scott at the wheel and a 350-ci engine under the hood, the Camaro saw more action on the track than it ever did on the street. Scott took S/S honors at Indy in 1977. (Photo Courtesy Michael Pottie)

The rotary loved the high RPM and left the line at about 11,200 rpm. Through the traps, it buzzed at 9,500 rpm. The first time out with the car, Terry ran right on the C/MC record. He broke the class record again and again and eventually ran ETs in the 11.80s.

Terry retired the RX-3 at the end of the 1981 season when Modified Eliminator was dropped by the NHRA. He could have continued if he wanted to because the Modified Compact classes were absorbed by Super Stock and ran at a 15.00 to 16.49 pounds to cubic inch break based on double the engine displacement formula.

Super Stock

Regarding the rules, things became more strange in 1977. Not only could vehicle weight be adjusted to better suit a given class, drivers were now weighed with the car, and a standardized driver weight of 170 pounds was decided upon. This meant that a driver weighing 200 pounds had to subtract 30 pounds from the car's weight, and a 150-pound person could add 20 pounds. Just a few years prior, all you needed to know was the car's ship weight and engine options for a given class. If the combination didn't fall close to the low end of a chosen class weight break, you looked for a car that did.

Other changes were rear frame rails on unibody cars could be replaced with 2x3 members to make room for tires, which could measure up to 14.5 inches wide and 33 inches tall.

Morgan's Mustang

When Division 1's Jim Morgan built himself a Mustang in 1977, he took advantage of the tire rule and showed the extent that Super Stock racers would go to in an effort to win. Morgan converted an original 1970 Boss 302 Mustang into a 1969 model and ran it with a 428 engine in SS/GA. It was an impressive car that made room for the large Firestones and incorporated a 12-bolt Chevy rear end, Mopar Super Stock springs, and a pinion snubber. Why did he use a Chevy rear end? At the time, there was a rumor circulating that due to the angle of

Jim Morgan's Mustang was an original 1970 Boss 302 car that he converted into a 1969 Cobra Jet. It was the 1976 Division 1 champion. He campaigned this car through 1979. (Photo Courtesy Michael Pottie)

the ring and pinion gear, there was better roll resistance. Morgan noticed that fellow Super Stock racer Jim Kinnett ran a 12-bolt under his Hemi Mopar, and he figured that he'd give it a try. Whether it made a difference, Morgan never knew, as it was a whole new car.

Backing Morgan's Cobra Jet was a C-6 transmission with a Marv Ripes convertor. Unlike today's modifications that allow C-6 transmissions to be fitted with Chrysler 727 innards (that are worth 2/10 of a second), there were only stock parts to work with back then. The 12-bolt rear was fitted with upward of 5.57 gears. Morgan raced this car through 1979, ran record 11-teen ETs in 1977, and won class at numerous national events.

High Stall: The Great Equalizer

High-stall torque converters for automatic transmissions have found their way onto the drag strip since the late 1960s. One could call them the great equalizer to make the automatic transmission–equipped cars nearly equal in performance to comparable manual transmission–equipped cars.

Stall is the amount of braking force that is required to hold a car stationary while power is applied. The more stall, the higher the RPM reached before the rear wheels break loose. Obviously, you want those RPMs to be at the engine's power level, as that's where you want to be when the light turns green.

By the mid-1970s, several aftermarket companies produced converters for drag-strip applications, including A-1, B&M, ATI, and Turbo-Action. Terry Earwood, a driver for Steve Bagwell, recalled one test session he had with Chrysler representatives in 1977. They invited him to bring the SS/AA Barracuda that he campaigned for Bagwell up to Michigan to test the new B&M "J" converter in the car.

Earwood had worked with Paul Forte of Turbo-Action for some time. He first met him in Gainesville in 1974, when he was campaigning Bagwell's Hemi 'Cuda convertible. At the time of the test session, Earwood was running a Turbo-Action 8-inch converter that Forte produced using a Ford Cortina part. For the Chrysler representatives, testing didn't go quite as planned. The Barracuda ran a 10-flat ET with the "J" converter at 132 mph. Earwood swapped in the Turbo-Action converter and ran a 9.82 ET. Jaws dropped!

Earwood told the Chrysler representatives what he had installed and let them know that Forte would like his converters added to the Direct Connection catalog. As Earwood recalled, they were shocked and went as far to say that they would even give him the cover for that kind of results. The Turbo-Action converter was added to the catalog, and the rest is history.

Hardy Boys: Pro Super Stock

Regarding the rules, the envelope was pushed in every class and category. If it's not clear that you can't do it, then you can, right? Some racers took it further to stay competitive. Veteran Super Stock racers (and brothers) Terry and Pat Hardy put into practice what they learned when it came to building their 1956 Chevy, a car that was often referred to as a Pro Stock wrapped in a shoebox.

The brothers' 150-series Chevy debuted at the Winternationals in 1977 and incorporated every trick in the book and then some. Running SS/N, SS/O, and SS/P at different times, the 3,300-pounder counted on a 265 engine that was bored 0.058 over to gather wins.

The Hardys' connections within the industry paid off. They worked closely with Chas Knight of Crane Cams, who ground cams to engine builder Pat Hardy's desired specifications. When it came to induction, the brothers had three variances of the Edelbrock Pro Ram manifold from which to choose. Pat was quick to mention the helping hand that he and his brother received from Jim McFarland at Edelbrock. Perched atop the manifold were twin Carter wrought cast 4-barrel (WCFB) carbs. The

Terry Hardy is off to another great run, as the 13x30 Goodyears bite into the pavement. Pressure in the slicks was around 4 to 5 pounds. Those aluminum Cragar Super Trick wheels reduced unsprung weight. (Photo Courtesy Terry Hardy)

It took a lot to run an 11.44 ET at 115 mph with a 265-ci Super Stock Chevy. Everything worked in conjunction with the factory AFB carburetors. (Photo Courtesy Terry Hardy)

brothers' connections at Carter paid off, as the manufacturer supplied countless carburetors and other parts.

Although modifications to the heads were limited by the rules, the Hardys spent a lot of time tweaking the ports. To hide the unruly modifications, they glass-beaded and shot-peened the surface to bring back the stock appearance. Others turned to acid dipping and metal spraying surfaces. By 1979, the NHRA had finally figured out how to test stock-appearing heads for such modifications.

Because the Chevy came with a 3-speed transmission, rules dictated that it remain a 3-speed car. The brothers got by with a Doug Nash 4+1 modified to run the 3 gears. The first-gear ratio was a 2.98. The ladder bar–supported Dana 60 housed 6.50 gears. The shift from first to second gear was quick!

To place greater weight on the rear of the car, the brothers had the front body panels acid dipped, and like a lot of racers, they hid lead weight out back. Cut into the top of the gas tank was a tray that they filled with lead. More lead was hidden in the crossmember the brothers installed to mount the shock absorbers. Since the taillights didn't work anyway, they filled those with lead as well. Those Super Stock guys were sneaky, and they still are, no doubt.

Stock

In Stock, there were not many rule changes for 1977. Some clarity was added regarding manual transmissions. Rules stated that no clutchless transmissions were allowed. A clutch had to be used for each gear change.

The category now allowed any valve spring to be used as long as it had a stock appearance (for example, a single spring with damper or dual spring with damper), and it was required to meet the listed open and closed specifications. The change went hand in hand with the previous allowable use of blueprinted camshafts. Drag racers, being as ingenious as they are, always found ways around some of the rules.

Tony Rainero's Little Secret

Tony Rainero's high-revving Cleveland-powered I/Stock 1971 Mustang convertible left many competitors scratching their head. Limited by rules that dictated a stock valvetrain, Rainero managed to pull an extra 1,500 rpm out of his 351 engine that made power upward of 7,500 rpm.

When Tony built the Cleveland, he took it to the shop of Super Stock racer Don Bowles to tune on his dyno. Once on the dyno, Rainero had Bowles run the engine up in increments to 7,500 rpm before Bowles decided to take a break. Bowles was stunned by the numbers he saw and invited Jack Roush down to see what was going on. Before Roush arrived, Rainero had the engine off the dyno and loaded on his truck.

Rainero's little trick was accomplished by getting shorter pushrods and special shims (0.001s) for under the rocker arms that were not easily visible. He did each valve separately and brought the hydraulic lifter plunger to

Tony Rainero campaigned this 1971 Mustang with great success in I/S from 1977 to 1980 and earned class wins at Indy and the Sportsnationals. A razor-thin slit cut through the seam of the rear plastic glass relieved air at speed. (Photo Courtesy William Bozgan)

Tony Rainero's Mustang was campaigned as a 1972 model. Note the ram air. Oddly, it was only available on the 2-barrel-equipped Cleveland in 1972. As Rainero recalled, Ford's Bruce Sizemore released a technical bulletin on the ram air setup for the 4-barrel-equipped Cobra Jet. He thought that it was funny how the NHRA accepted it without question. (Photo Courtesy William Bozgan)

within 0.005 of fully extended. This basically made the lifter act as a solid lifter.

The modifications allowed Rainero to make better use of the Cleveland's large ports. His reward came in the form of a class record and a win at Indy in 1977, when he defeated the Camaro of Wayne Shaw with a 12.53 ET at 108.56 mph. He set the class record in April 1979 with a 12.11 ET at 110.97 mph and had a best ET of 11.84.

Don McElroy switched to a Barracuda after he won Stock Eliminator at Indy in 1975 with his 1969 Camaro. The 360-ci-equipped Barracuda was a consistent winner and a record holder with a 12.35 ET. (Photo Courtesy Don McElroy)

All-Plymouth World Finals

Jacksonville, Florida's Stan Mizell and Ronnie Robinson's A/SA Hemi 'Cuda (driven by Mizell) were the 1977 Stock Eliminator World Champions. The all-Plymouth final saw Mizell defeat Indy and Fallnationals winner Don McElroy and his J/S, 360-ci-powered 1973 Barracuda. The factory loved this car and had its hands all over it. McElroy recalled the parts deal that he received after he won class at Indy in 1976.

"If I needed another engine, trans or rear end, a head, etc., I'd just call and go pick said part or parts in Hamtramck," McElroy said. "Back my truck up to their loading dock with the tailgate down, and they loaded everything. I think when we switched to the 440, they initially gave me three complete engines."

Chad Langdon drove Joe Threatt's 1972 H/SA Mustang to a Winternationals victory at only 19 years old. Langdon was a popular Southern California racer and part of the famed Wilson Ford Drag Club. (Photo Courtesy Rich Carlson/Grant Bittner Collection).

CHAPTER EIGHT

1978: NOT *STAR WARS*—CAR WARS!

Popular Oregon-based racer Jim Plummer is the only known person to die due to the violence of tire shake. According to dragstripdeaths.com, Plummer lost his life on May 20, 1978, at Orange County International Raceway. He spent nine days in a coma before he passed away due to a brain injury. (Photo Courtesy Lou Hart)

The *Star Wars* movies were all the rage in 1978. Movie theaters were filled, and the related merchandise was popular. I wasn't a fan, but I know that Harrison Ford played a lead role because he also starred in the 1973 hit movie *American Graffiti*.

From Top Fuel to Stock Eliminator, drag racing had its own wars in 1978. Without hesitation, I can recall the highlights and the players. However, I couldn't name more than two actors or actresses who appeared in *Star Wars*.

Top Fuel

A new NHRA rule for 1978 stated that Top Fuel and Funny Car engines could be no larger than 500 ci. This wasn't a big deal, as most competitors ran under this number anyway.

Builders and tuners continuously searched for more power and pumped greater amounts of air and fuel into engines. By 1978, the average Fuel car ran a Hilborn or Enderle fuel pump that delivered 18 to 20 gallons per minute with an overdrive on top of that. This fed the approximate 90-percent load into at least 16 nozzles. Today, some cars have 42 nozzles.

Combinations varied to some degree because each builder had his or her own thoughts regarding what worked best. Compression could be as low as 6:1 and up to 8:1. Spark lead was generally in the mid-50s, and the blowers were usually spun around 40 over crank speed. Was it just my imagination, or were there a greater number of blower explosions?

Pat Foster built this low-slung Fueler for Gary Beck. Note the low engine, adjustable wing, and independent front suspension. A 180-degree crank was also tested. Here, at Indy, Beck fell in the second round. (Photo Courtesy Terry Gray)

The Unsinkable Kelly Brown

It was a season like no other for the team of Jim Brissette, Mike Drake, and driver Kelly Brown. Formed practically overnight at the end of the 1977 season, the team dubbed "the Other Guys" were a low- to no-buck operation that made good by winning the world championship.

No one could have guessed that the snow-delayed NHRA Winternationals in mid-February was the beginning of a season that would be full of surprises. At the winter meet, Brown defeated the relatively unknown Gordon Fabeck in the final round. What's really mind-numbing about the win is the fact that Brown hadn't been near a Fuel car in six years. He had never driven a rear-engine dragster before, and his first full pass in the car came while qualifying at the Winternationals.

The team had one Donovan engine to start the season that ran an old 392 crankshaft and a set of Donovan heads that had been pegged for Don Garlits. The combination allowed Brown to qualify in the second spot with a 5.87 ET, just a tenth of a second behind Garlits. Garlits's weekend ended abruptly as Richard Tharp sent him packing in the first round. Garlits's wish to wrestle the Top Fuel crown from Muldowney wasn't off to a good start. As the season progressed, it didn't get any better. A good consolation for Garlits was winning his first of three consecutive AHRA World Championships. Muldowney's dream of a repeat championship didn't fare any better. At the Winternationals, Brown sent her on her way in the second round.

Don Garlits began the year with a category win at the AHRA Winter Nationals. Powering the Swamp Rat was a 417-ci Donovan engine, which was topped with a Bowers 8-71 blower and the recently developed Crower eight-port injector. Here, at Indy, he defeated Rob Bruins in the final. (Photo Courtesy Terry Gray)

Veteran Kelly Brown, back from a six-year hiatus, showed the world that he hadn't lost a step. The Other Guys were a team that surprised a lot of people. (Photo Courtesy Michael Pottie)

There was no stopping the team of Jim Brissette, Mike Drake, and Kelly Brown in 1978. The team was one of the first to use a fabricated rear end. The design proved to be nearly unbreakable, and the setup helped eliminate wheel hop. (Photo Courtesy Terry Gray)

The Good, Bad, & Ugly of Dick Oswald, Lee Cohen, Dave Uyehara, and Henry Velasco was the 1978 Division 7 champion. The car featured a Woody Gilmore chassis and Keith Black Hemi. Uyehara earned the low ET at Indy with a 5.84. (Photo Courtesy Terry Gray)

The Northwest provided its share of top-notch Fuel racers, including Rob Bruins. Bruins drove Gaines Markley's Fueler to wins at the Fallnationals and the World Finals. (Photo Courtesy Michael Pottie)

Additional wins for the Other Guys came at the Cajun Nationals, Springnationals, and Grandnationals. Bad main bearings had the team playing runner-up to Garlits at the Gatornationals.

Funny Car

The story within Funny Car during 1978 that stands head and shoulders above the rest was the emotional final round of the 24th running of the NHRA US Nationals. The two finalists were long-time track rivals and long-time friends Don "the Snake" Prudhomme and Tom "the Mongoose" McEwen.

We Meet Again

The rivals had faced off earlier in the season at the Springnationals, and Prudhomme earned the win, just as he had in the pair's three previous national-event, final-round meetings. At Indy, the real story centered around McEwen. He had lost his 14-year-old son Jamie to leukemia two weeks prior to Indy. After Jamie's passing, McEwen didn't want to attend the race. Jamie had wanted his dad to go and beat Prudhomme, and with a little coaxing, McEwen had a change of heart. He competed in honor of his son.

Qualifying for the quickest Funny Car field in NHRA history saw Raymond Beadle grab the number-one spot with a 5.98 ET. He was followed by Prudhomme, who ran a 5.99 ET. Both men were previous Indy winners and the odds-on favorites to do it again.

However, McEwen had other ideas. He struggled initially but he finally locked down the number-five spot with a 6.09 ET. It was his best run to date.

McEwen defeated 1976 Indy winner Gary Burgin in the first round before upsetting low-qualifier

Without a major sponsor, Jim "Shady" Glenn worked a regular job to keep his Funny Car in contention. His Duster, driven here by Car Craft magazine publisher Jim Adolph, featured an S&R chassis and a stroked Keith Black Hemi. In 1978, the oldest-model bodies that were accepted in the Funny Car category were from 1973. (Photo Courtesy Terry Gray)

Pat Foster and Jim Hume (H&H Racecraft) built a new car for Don Prudhomme for 1978. It replaced the Jaime Sarte car from 1977. The new Arrow carried a torsion-bar front suspension, which was opposed to the more-common straight axle. (Photo Courtesy Bob Snyder)

Raymond Beadle in the second round with a 6.18 ET at 236.22 mph. Prudhomme, in his march to the final round, disposed of Pat Foster in the first round and set the low ET and the track's top speed record with a 5.97 ET at 245.23 mph before he eliminated John Loper's entry, which was driven by Tripp Shumake.

Ron Colson in Roland Leong's *Hawaiian* singled when his opponent, Kenny Bernstein, bowed. Uncharacteristically, Colson disqualified himself when he crossed the centerline on the run. This gave McEwen a single in the semifinals. Prudhomme recorded a 6.05 ET in the other semifinal race to send John Lombardo home.

Because he ran the semifinals' low ET, Prudhomme was able to choose his lane in the final round. He chose the right lane, which had shown all weekend to have the better surface. Few held out hope for McEwen, being that he was one to two tenths of a second behind Prudhomme all weekend and hadn't won a national event since the 1973 Supernationals. Prudhomme's record spoke for itself. He had already won three national events in 1978 and had the world championship locked up at Indy.

However, this weekend was all about McEwen. His Cinderella run nearly came up short when he went to fire up the Hemi after the semifinal-round thrash and discovered that it was seized. With little time to spare, they tore into the engine and discovered that one of the cylinder sleeves had rotated and hung up a connecting rod. Crew Chief Pay

Both Tom "the Mongoose" McEwen and Don "the Snake" Prudhomme ran Keith Black 480-ci Hemis. McEwen's Corvette rode on a Jaime Sarte chassis. (Bill) Carter Pro Paint laid the color, which made this car and so many others of the era look so good. (Photo Courtesy Michael Pottie)

Tom McEwen was one of the sport's more entertaining racers. Although his track record against Prudhomme wasn't good, this match is the one that most fans remember. Blue Max crewman Waterbed Fred had the best seat in the house. (Photo Courtesy Terry Gray)

Spectators lined the fence for this race, and cheers went up as McEwen took the win, with a 6.05 ET to a 6.33 ET. (Photo Courtesy Michael Pottie)

Galvin fixed the issue and had the engine ready with minutes to spare.

With burnouts completed, the pair staged. This run had everyone's attention. On the green, Prudhomme took the lead but smoked the tires just past the tree. McEwen, in the supposed bad lane, hooked and was gone! Prudhomme fought to catch him, but not on this day. McEwen took the win with a career best 6.05 ET to the Prudhomme's 6.33 ET.

Coming off a gig driving the Chi-Town Hustler, Denny Savage joined forces with John Powers in 1978 to win the IHRA Funny Car world championship. Powers's Camaro featured the best of parts, including a Sid Waterman Hemi in an S&R chassis. ETs between 6.13 to 6.19 were common. (Photo Courtesy Bob Snyder)

The Versatile Denny Savage

Versatility was the name of the game, and few were as versatile as Denny Savage. While Prudhomme was sewing up another NHRA world title and Gene Snow grabbed the AHRA title, Denny Savage (in the Camaro of John Powers) was the reigning champion in IHRA Funny Car.

Savage had been riding Funny Cars since the birth of the category. In these heady days of the 1970s, when crews generally consisted of no more than two or three guys, Savage did it all. Prior to hooking up with John in 1978, which was the most successful year of his career, Savage had driven for some of the biggest names in the sport, including Roland Leong and the team of Coil, Minick, and Farkonas. With Dan Geare pulling wrenches, Savage captured additional wins at Bakersfield and the NHRA Summernationals.

Pro Stock

There were 22 NHRA weights breaks in 1978 (the same as in 1977), and that number remained the same for the rest of the decade. Cleveland-powered Fords continued to carry more weight than any other combination, but somehow, Bob Glidden continued to win big.

Bob Glidden: The Face of Pro Stock

Bob Glidden steamrolled through the category in 1978 on his way to his first of three consecutive Pro Stock world titles.

Glidden began the year with his existing Don Hardy Pinto. He won two of the first four NHRA national events and was runner-up at the other two before he showed at the Summernationals with a fresh Don Hardy–built Fairmont. The new car was all about the weight breaks, allowing the Fairmont (with a longer-than-105-inch wheelbase) to run 0.15 pounds per cubic inch lighter than a Mustang II or Pinto with the same engine.

At the time, Glidden's engines varied in size from 322 to 340 ci, and they made a substantial amount of power. Glidden found hidden power where others seemingly failed—by reworking the intake and heads. He heavily massaged the Edelbrock UR-19 intake by taking volume out of the plenum and straightening the runners.

The heads went through a complete reworking. The intake ports were raised, and the chambers and area below the seats were welded and reshaped. On the exhaust side, port

The Frank Iaconio and Ray Allen Monza was runner-up to Glidden at the 1977 Fallnationals, and again at the same meet in 1978. At one point in 1978, the Monza was the quickest small-block Chevy Pro Stocker in the nation and recorded 8.50 ETs. (Photo Courtesy Michael Pottie)

Bob Glidden began the year running this Pinto but made the switch to the famed Fairmont after he lost to the Camaro of Richie Zul at the Springnationals. (Photo Courtesy Michael Pottie)

The Holley dominators sit atop a significantly-modified Edelbrock intake on Bob Glidden's Cleveland. Note the strategically placed towels, hiding the intake. (Photo Courtesy Michael Pottie)

Drag-racing historian Ariel Cordero documented the undefeated streak of Bob Glidden's Fairmont–from its late-spring regional meet debut at Edgewater Dragway to its retirement at the end of the 1978 season. (Photo Courtesy Michael Pottie)

plates were installed. Secrecy was important in Pro Stock, and few knew the modifications that the next racer was making.

At the Summernationals, Glidden's Fairmont was leading the competition by close to two-tenths of a second. He steamrolled his way to the final round, where he ran an 8.55 ET at 154.37 mph and defeated Larry Lombardo's 8.71 ET at 155.17 mph. Glidden went the remainder of the season without a national event or division loss. He retired the undefeated Fairmont at the end of the season.

Joe Satmary (near lane) gave one of the best showings of his career here at Indy. It was a shame that his 8.77 ET wasn't good enough for Bob Glidden's 8.61 ET. (Photo Courtesy Michael Pottie)

In mid-1977, Andy Mannarino joined Dick Maskin to form the M&M Boys. They earned AMC its final Pro Stock national event win when Mannarino defeated Shelby Jester at the AHRA Grand Nationals with an 8.85 ET to a 9.07 ET. (Photo Courtesy Bob Snyder)

After a year-long absence, Lee Shepherd was back and drove the new RMS Don Ness-built Camaro. A small-block propelled the car to 8.40 ETs. A new Pro Stock rule for 1978 required a driver-side window safety net. (Photo Courtesy Bob Snyder)

Pro Comp

For a class with a 3-pound-per-cubic-inch break, AA/DA was not supposed to be the place for small-block-powered cars. John Samolyk, Dale Hall, and Kenny Cook were some drivers who proved the critics wrong.

Dale Armstrong earned NHRA national event wins in 1978 with his Donovan-powered AA/DA. Off the track, Armstrong was credited with some of the sport's most advanced innovations. (Photo Courtesy Michael Pottie)

Indy Surprise

At Indy, where 24 cars in the 32-car Pro Comp field were alcohol dragsters, Joey Severance (in his Mile High Nationals–winning, Rodeck-powered AA/DA) held the number-one spot with a 6.64 ET. It was the quickest Pro Comp field in drag racing history with only 0.21 seconds separating the winner from 32nd place.

New Jersey's John Samolyk and his 355-ci Chevy held the number-20 spot. Samolyk took holeshot wins in the first three rounds to earn a berth in the final, where he faced Severance. To the surprise of pretty much everyone, Samolyk took the win, running a 6.77 ET at 198.23 mph to Severance's 6.83 ET at 202.70 mph.

Cook and Thorn

Walking away with the world title was Ken Cook, driving the Cook and Thorn blown small-block Chevy-powered AA/DA *Cheap Thrills*. The pair had campaigned the car most of the season in B/FD with an injected small-block but moved up in class late in the year by bolting in the blown, alcohol-fed 355 engine.

Division 6 Champion Joe Severance Sr. seemed to be the low qualifier wherever he competed. At Indy, his Rodeck Chevy had the field covered heading into the final. (Photo Courtesy Terry Gray)

It's amazing what a small-block Chevy can do in the right hands. John Samolyk showed his abilities when he took three consecutive holeshot wins at Indy with his 355-ci Chevy to reach the final round. (Photo Courtesy Michael Pottie)

Cook qualified fourth at the World Finals with a 6.74 ET and ran consistent 6.70 ETs. He knocked off Dale Armstrong and then defeated Severance in the semifinals with a 6.62 ET. In the final round, Cook's ailing Chevy held off the injected Hemi-powered A/FD of the Carroll brothers that was driven by Ben Griffin. This was the team's first national event victory.

Kentucky-based Ken Cook and Dick Thorn, who pulled wrenches, got the most out of their combination. The small-block Chevy, backed by a 3-speed transmission, ran consistent 6.70 ETs at 3 pounds per cubic inch. (Photo Courtesy Michael Pottie)

Comp Eliminator

Unlike 1977, when the door cars seemed to hold Comp hostage, the Econo Dragsters held a grip on Comp in 1978. John Lingenfelter won the Sportsnationals, US Nationals, and Fallnationals in his B/ED, and played runner-up at the Gatornationals, Summernationals, and Grandnationals. Bobby Cross and Bubba Corzine's C/ED won the Summernationals, Mile High/Sportsnationals, and the World Finals.

Wayne Clapp took his Gapp and Roush–powered B/A to wins at the Winternationals and Cajun Nationals. Joe Williamson, in his everlasting E/A, pulled off wins at the Gatornationals and Springnationals.

Dennis Ferrara made the move into the A/EA class with a Vega in 1978. He referred to the car as a total disaster. "The car never worked right," Ferrara said. "I don't know why. We put the 373 engine from the Camaro in it and qualified number one at the Winternationals with an 8.776 ET but lost in the semifinals to Wayne Clapp. I hated the car. It was just rough and never ran 8s again after the Winternationals." (Photo Courtesy Bob Boudreau)

Cross and Corzine: Season Champions

Under everyone's radar at the beginning of the 1978 season was the pairing of Bobby Cross and Bubba Corzine. The two teamed up in 1977 when Corzine received an A/Fuel Dragster in a trade for a boat that he had for sale at the marina that he operated. It was a Hemi car with a 2-speed Powerglide and a Lester Gullory 227-inch chassis. It was a good, solid car, but with no interest in running a Fuel car, the pair set its sights on Econo Dragster.

Cross was tight with the Pro Stock team of Reher and Morrison, having previously teamed with them in campaigning his Modified Maverick, so he had them had been building a 304-ci engine to run C/ED with the former Fuel car. David Reher had been building several small-inch engines for customers using junkyard 307 blocks and 283 cranks. Cross laid out $7,500 for the complete engine, from the intake to pan to dyno tuning. The cost was offset a bit when the Fuel Hemi and related parts were sold to Dave Settles, who at the time campaigned an A/Fuel Dragster in Pro Comp.

The Bobby Cross and Bubba Corzine Econo Dragster counted on Reher-Morrison power to win the World Finals. The pair ran in the A/ED, B/ED, and C/ED classes between 1978 and 1980 and won a total of eight NHRA national events. (Photo Courtesy Dave Kommel)

In went a 304 engine backed by a Marv Ripes A-1 Powerglide and transbrake.

"We never heard of a trans brake before," Corzine said. "Reher explained how it worked and showed us how to wire it up. We were the first in the South to have one."

The first race with the car was in 1978 at the Cajun Nationals, where they lost to the B/Altered of Wayne Clapp in the semifinals. As they sorted out the combination, it got to the point where it ran four tenths of a second under. At the Sportsnationals, they won but lost. After defeating Lingenfelter's B/ED in the final, the 304 was inspected by tech inspector Jim Dale.

"Because we picked up a tenth in the final, he figured that we must have cheated somehow," Corzine said. "Dale decided we had modified the exhaust ports, which was a no-no after he found some silicone residue. Everyone used silicone to seal the port plates that the headers bolted to."

Being robbed of the win, they took their first national event win cleanly at the Summernationals, where Cross once again defeated Lingenfelter. It was the exact same engine and same

Wayne Clapp was a B/A standout in Dean Thompson's 1923 Turtle Deck Model T Roadster. A Charlie Scott chassis housed a Gapp and Roush Cleveland engine. (Photo Courtesy Michael Pottie)

heads they had been disqualified with at the Sportsnationals. They continued to campaign the car through the end of the season and gave it a new coat of paint midseason.

Corzine sold his marina during the season and went to work for Reher-Morrison midyear. There, he overhauled small-inch customer engines and ran the dyno for them. Corzine reflected on what kept them going.

"Although the NHRA never paid Comp well, the big money was paid by sponsors," Corzine said. "Back then, contingency from sponsors would come in at $1,000 to $1,500 each."

Today, it might fall in the $200 to $300 range.

The pair campaigned the car through the beginning of 1979, drew runner-up finishes at both the Winternationals and Gatornationals, competing in B/ED with a Reher-Morrison 352-ci engine. Over the winter, they worked with Don Ness on a new car. Ness pulled out all the stops to make the car as light as possible. It made its debut at Columbus in fine fashion.

Modified Eliminator

Outside of the usual weight-break revisions, which seemed to be an annual occurrence, rules now noted that wheelie bars were acceptable in Modified Production, Modified Compact, and Super Modified. With the advancement in tire technology and concrete starting lines becoming more common, wheelie bars became a necessity.

Rule revisions for both A/SM and B/SM allowed for the use of any original manufactured cylinder head. This was a change from previous rules that called for production installed heads. The new rule favored the small-block Chevy that had to compete against the canted-valve Cleveland Fords. Opening up the rules to any head made by Chevy meant that the angle-plug 492- and the 292-casting turbo heads for Pro Stock and NASCAR could now be used. The new rule also allowed aluminum big-block Chevy heads in A/SM with oval-port exhausts and other performance enhancements over the production BBC castings.

Those Are the Breaks

The NHRA seemed to have a bee in its bonnet when it came to Ford's Cleveland. Pro Stock wasn't the only category where cars using the engine were saddled with additional weight. Comp and Modified Eliminator suffered the same injustice.

Arlen Fadely's Maverick was one of the toughest B/SM cars in the land. His 331-ci engine featured Arias pistons, BME aluminum rods, and a Race Cams roller camshaft. Gapp and Roush provided the fabricated oil pan and single-plane intake manifold. A modified Doug Nash transmission was backed by 5:83 (or steeper) gears.

The Dave Hutchins–driven Wayne County 1927 Model T competed in the B/SR class. The 287-ci Chevy and Nash 5-speed were working overtime, pushing a lot of air to a record run (a 9.18 ET at 144.69 mph). (Photo Courtesy Michael Pottie)

Arlen Fadely, who campaigned a 331-ci Cleveland engine (a 302 that was bored 0.030 over) in his B/SM Maverick said, "I went to Indy for the first Division 3 points meet of the season. Before the race was rained out, I set the record with a 10.17 ET at 133.50 mph, weighing 9.50 pounds per cubic inch. Right after that race, the NHRA added weight. So, at the next points meet at Edgewater, we had to run at 9.80 pounds per cubic inch. I won that race and reset the record. We went back to Indy for the rescheduled points race, and because it had started with a 9.50-pounds-per-cubic-inch weight, we were allowed to drop weight. Again, we lowered the record."

Jay "Cotton" Perry and his H/MP 1967 Chevy II proved that six in a row does go. Perry relied on Jim Headrick, who was his uncle and partner, to build the 301-ci 6-cylinder engine that turned the Modified category on its ear through the mid-1970s. (Photo Courtesy Larry Pfister)

The Maverick eventually ran as quick as a 10.07 ET at 137 mph in NHRA trim and a 9.91 ET in the more-liberal IHRA.

The Maverick dominated in 1978 and was the quickest B/SM car in the nation. Fadely set the low ET at the Gatornationals, Springnationals, Summernationals, Sportsman Nationals, and Grandnationals. Red-lighting at Indy prevented him from repeating his 1977 class win.

Tired of Super Modified and wanting to build a Comp dragster, Fadely sold the Maverick to Mike Edwards at the end of the 1978 season. Edwards won back-to-back Division 4 titles in 1980 and 1981 with the car. In 1981, he used the Maverick to win the last-ever NHRA Modified championship.

A Kay Sissell head topped the Cotton Perry engine, which had 14.5:1 compression, revved to 11,000 rpm off the line, and shifted at 7,200 rpm. (Photo Courtesy Roger Leister/Joe Gripp)

Pocket Rocket

Jay "Cotton" Perry's H/MP 1967 Chevy II, with its 301-ci of inline six, was the scourge of Modified in 1978. Running at 10.50 pounds per cubic inch, up 1 pound from 1977, Perry and his partner Jim Headrick won four national events, as well as the Honest Charley Stars 'n' Stripes Open in Atlanta and the Popular Hot Rodding meet in Michigan. Perry's reign of terror began in 1975, when he won NHRA Division 2 Modified crown. He backed it up in 1976, and won it again in 1978.

The Chevy II's 301 was stuffed with gas-ported Venolia pistons and topped with a Kay Sissell modified cylinder head. Compression was a healthy 14.5:1. Three Holley 550-cfm carburetors were mounted to an aluminum intake fabricated by Headrick. A Cam Dynamics shaft with 0.900 lift actuated the valves. There's no denying that coming off the line at 10,800 rpm and shifting at 7,200 rpm was hard on parts. Perry recalled that they raced up to 60 rounds per month and went through heads and rings frequently. They destroyed blocks and crankshafts at a regular rate before they made a switch to

At one time, Cotton Perry campaigned two Chevy IIs. In this 1976 photo, Perry's white Chevy II carries the competition number 21 for his 1975 division championship. Allan Patterson, a former two-time AHRA world champion, purchased the Chevy II at the end of the 1978 season and won the 1979 NHRA Winternationals with it. Making the move from Modified to S/S, Patterson said that cylinder heads now cost him $200, as opposed to $2,000. (Photo Courtesy Bill Truby)

aluminum rods, which seemed to lessen the shock.

Backing the 301 engine was a 27-pound flywheel and a 3.45-first-gear Nash 5-speed transmission. A Dana third member supported by a 4-link carried either 5.57 or 5.88 gears.

At the World Finals, Perry made the semifinals before falling to Rick Voegelin's Super Modified Camaro driven by Norm Mayersohn. Jeff Leininger defeated Mayersohn in the final. ETs in the 10.60s for the Chevy II were realized before the car's run ended due to the death of Modified in 1981.

Super Stock

Super Stock got off to a rocking start at the NHRA Winternationals in 1978 as fans were treated to a 48-car field. Six rounds of eliminations happened before the final round, which saw Ron Zoelle's SS/MA Chevelle wagon defeat the SS/CA 1965 Plymouth of Dave Wolfe. The low qualifier was Jim Weakland, who bookended the 1978 season when he faced Bobby Warren in the category final at the World Finals.

Bobby Warren

Engine building was big business, and success breeds success. Tobacco farmer Bobby Warren was one of many people building engines for outside customers by 1978. He had a track record of building winning Stockers and Super Stockers, especially 350-powered Camaros.

Warren accumulated a total of 15 career national-event wins. By far, his most successful season was 1978, when he won four national events and his third world championship behind the wheel of Harold Bently's SS/MA 1969 Camaro. Warren pocketed $15,000 for winning the Grace Cup and another $9,000-plus for winning the world title.

The SS/JA *Krunchy Chicken* Camaro defeated Jim Weakland's SS/HA 1967 Camaro in the final round with an 11.34 ET (on an 11.40 dial-in) to a 10.84 ET (on an 11.01 dial-in).

Bobby Warren (far lane) drives Harold Bentley's Krunchy Chicken SS/JA 1969 Camaro. The 350-ci Powerglide combination took Warren to four national event wins and earned him the world title.

Judy Lilly's Volare was built for SS/MA but was bumped up a class by the NHRA, which made wins a little more difficult to earn. A Turbo Action-prepped TorqueFlite transmission and a 5.57-gear Dana rear end were behind the 360-ci engine. (Photo Courtesy Mike Cochran)

July Lilly: Miss Mighty Mopar

"Miss Mighty Mopar" Judy Lilly was the winningest woman in drag racing's Sportsman categories. She earned event wins at the 1972 NHRA Winternationals, 1973 Springnationals, 1975 Gatornationals, and 1975 Fallnationals.

A multi-time Division 5 champion, Lilly retired from Super Stock racing at the end of 1978 after campaigning an SS/LA Plymouth Volare. The 360-ci engine, which was re-factored by the NHRA to have 275 hp, recorded 11.80 ETs. Lilly briefly returned to drag racing in 1982 and drove Pro Stock for Mike Musso before she retired for good in 1984.

Stock

When it came to the Stock rules in 1978, the NHRA gave some leeway. It now allowed for solid rear control-arm bushings and the option for rear coil-spring suspension cars to reposition their upper control arms. Engine modifications now allowed the use of the windage tray and baffles.

AHRA Stock Classes

The AHRA Stock category varied greatly from what the NHRA presented. Dating back to 1964, the AHRA broke its Stock classes down by carburetion and camshaft. This doubled the number of classes and offered everyone a greater chance of winning.

By 1978, the AHRA had four levels of the Stock category that were based on various degrees of modifications: Showroom Stock, Formula Stock, Hot Stock, and Factory Stock. This excludes specific classes for Corvettes, mini cars, pickups and vans, and Volkswagens.

The overall Stock World Champion in 1978 was Bob Bowe, who campaigned a Formula Stock 1957 Chevy wagon. Formula Stock allowed Bob to run a 283 engine that was bored 0.060 over, and his combination included 12.5:1 compression, a Comp Cams roller cam, Turbo 400 (or sometimes a Powerglide) with any converter, and a Dana 60 rear end with 6.17 gears. The book *Drag Racing's Rebels: How The AHRA Changed Quarter-Mile Competition*, which I wrote for CarTech, describes the AHRA Stock Eliminator program.

Maryland's Kenny Koonce terrorized the East Coast for years with his Stockers. In 1978, it was with a 427-equipped A/SA 1969 Camaro. The Camaro was an 11.21 ET record holder during the 1977-1978 season. (Photo Courtesy Michael Pottie)

Bob Bowe's Chevy wagon held the AHRA ET and top speed record in three classes. To do so, he ran a Holley 750-cfm double-pumper carburetor atop the 283-ci engine in F-2, a Holley 650-cfm 2-barrel carburetor in F-3, and two Holley 500-cfm 2-barrel carburetors on a custom adapter in F-1. (Photo Courtesy Bob Bowe)

Jim Waldo got many miles and wins out of his 1967 427-equipped Fairlane. Waldo opened the 1979 season by winning Stock at the Winternationals. (Photo Courtesy Rich Carlson/Grant Bittner Collection)

The First 10-Second Stocker

Taking into consideration the strict rules that those in Stock Eliminator were forced to follow made Jim Waldo's 10.95 ET at Seattle, Washington, in May even more amazing.

To record the NHRA's first 10-second Stocker pass, Waldo counted on a twin 4-barrel-equipped 427 Fairlane to accomplish the feat. Rated at 425 hp and 480 ft-lbs of torque, Waldo and the Fairlane reset class records 30 times and won the world title in 1987. The following year, Waldo sold the Fairlane to a gentleman in Finland.

CHAPTER NINE

1979: GROWING PAINS

AMC relabeled the Hornet as the "Concord" in 1979. Wally Booth only wished that his Concord flew like the Corcorde airplane. AMC support had dried up by 1979, as did the wins. Booth retired at the end of the season. (Photo Courtesy Hilak Bros. Photography)

Things were looking up for the nation as a whole as the 1970s wound down. The cringe-worthy disco craze that grabbed hold of the airwaves around 1974 was fading out, and automotive performance, which had been dormant in Detroit, was making a comeback. Drag racing continued to grow in participation due partially to the exploding popularity of bracket racing. Bracket racing is an affordable form of racing that originated in Southern California in the early 1960s. It consisted of several classes that ran off a given ET.

A few tragic incidents in 1979 led to changes regarding safety. Freelance cameraman Joe Rook lost his life at Indy when he was hit with a blower that was tossed from the Top Fuel car of Frank Ruppert. Shortly after the incident, blower-restraint straps became mandatory. Along with Rook, Indy saw the loss of Ernie Rife, whose Fuel bike crashed into the guardrail after it lost the front wheel. In 1986, the Armco guard railing that runs parallel to each side of the track was replaced with concrete retaining walls.

In a horrific incident at the Olympics of Drag Racing in May, three spectators lost their lives when they were hit by shrapnel from the exploding clutch in the Clayton Harris–driven Peek Brothers Top Fuel car. The incident led to the development of the titanium bellhousing produced by Trick Titanium in Michigan.

Top Fuel

A rule regarding driver safety (arm restraints) was implemented in 1979. Arm restraints kept the driver's arms and hands from flailing outside of the roll cage in the case of a wreck. Some said that the restraints were long overdue.

Lou Patane's Fueler incorporated several unique features: a shorter-than-usual Jaime Sarte chassis, short front tires, Funny Car–style headers, and a low wing. A Milodon Hemi made the car competitive despite it all. (Photo Courtesy Hilak Bros. Photography)

In 1979, Top Fuel had its surprises and upsets. Rule revisions were minimal, which left the door open to new ideas. Although not all new ideas were good ideas, each paved the path forward. On the track, familiar names were the highlight.

The More Things Change

Pomona, California, home of the NHRA Winternationals, received a new concrete starting pad that took some adjusting to get used to. ETs were off pace to start the event but improved. Bob Noice came out of retirement to drive the Brissette and Drake Fueler after Kelly Brown vacated the seat at the end of 1978.

Noice made the program with a 5.95 ET in the Donovan-powered ride, which was good enough to bump Garlits from the show. In the second round of competition, Noice put a smile on the faces of Brissette and Drake when he met and defeated Brown with a 6.09 ET to a 6.15 ET. In the final round, Noice soloed for the title as his opponent Rob Brown, driving for R. Gaines Markley, developed a fuel leak and had to shut off.

Bob Noice, the 1968 Top Gas World Champion, showed that he still had it. Noice earned Top Fuel honors at the Winternationals. (Photo Courtesy Michael Pottie)

Swamp Rat 24 ***won a combined total of more than $600,000 when Garlits campaigned the car. Garlits was in the midst of three AHRA World Championships. (Photo Courtesy Bob Snyder)***

This is the Aussie-built, 4-camshaft McGee engine. Rather than using a chain to run the four cams, the McGee engine used 13 gears. The initial engine measured 511 ci (prior to the NHRA implementing the 500-ci limit in 1978). Aside from the Hemi crank that mounted in the two-piece iron block, almost everything else was fabricated. (Photo Courtesy Bob Snyder)

Engine of a Different Stroke

When it came to aftermarket blocks, by the late 1970s, Keith Black and Mondello had the market cornered.

Before the NHRA dictated what could be used by the Fuel cars, there were a number of manufacturers who took a kick at the can. One that first made the scene back in 1975 was the McGee, a four-cam, four-valves-per-cylinder engine developed by Phil and Chris McGee out of Australia.

At the 1979 World Finals, the McGee engine was campaigned into the 1990s with Gary Beck and Kenny Bernstein (among others) giving it a whirl. A lack of funds and a change in NHRA rules regarding allowable engines (Hemi design only) spelled the end for the McGee.

At its NHRA World Finals debut, the car earned the Best Engineered award.

Rob Bruins, who drove Gaines Markley's Fueler, won the NHRA championship without winning a single national event. Crew chief Christian "Butch" Horn made it seems easy. (Photo Courtesy Michael Pottie)

In a season that held 10 national events, Kelly Brown won 4 of them for the Over The Hill Gang. He closed the season second in points to Rob Bruins. Bruins, who entered the World Finals with a slight lead, clinched the title when Brown uncharacteristically failed to qualify. Bruins held the distinction of being the only

Foster Yancey and Brad Camp, with Dave Settles at the wheel, flew the Blue Max *colors for Raymond Beadle in 1979. Beadle hoped to cash in by running two cars, but it never panned out financially. The Fueler's one big win was at the IHRA Spring Nationals. Robert McNeil pulled the wrenches on the Keith Black Hemi, which was nestled in a Tony Casarez chassis. (Photo Courtesy Michael Pottie).*

The Over the Hill Gang, which consisted of Bill Schultz, Kelly Brown, and Steve Montrelli, strapped in a Nick Aria 8.3L Chevy Hemi for the March Meet and proceeded to make a run with a 5.88 ET. That earned the number-two qualifying position behind Garlits's 5.86 ET. At national events, the team ran a Milodon Hemi. (Photo Courtesy Dave Kommel)

The Arias Chevy Hemi

Nick Arias's whole idea behind his Chevy Hemi was to build a better Hemi head to beat the Chryslers.

Arias first got into the aftermarket business when he, Harry Warner, and Bob Toros bought Frank Venolia's piston business. It was all uphill from there, as Arias struck out on his own in 1969 after he purchased Louie Senter's Ansen Piston business. Arias Pistons was born. It was a quick step to the Hemi heads that were under development by 1972.

Arias theorized that the Chevy had a stronger bottom end, and all that it needed was the Hemi heads, so he went to work. His engines were killer in drag-boat competition but never really caught on at the drag strip. By the mid-1970s, aftermarket Hemis, based on the Chrysler design, had proven themselves and left Arias on the outside.

By 1979, slicks used in Top Fuel and Funny Cars measured 34 to 35 inches tall and up to 17 inches in width. Rims varied from 12 to 17 inches wide. (Photo Courtesy Roger Leister/Joe Grippo)

person to win a world title without having won a single national event.

Funny Car

Although spoilers were permitted front and rear, rules had us wave goodbye to those beloved side-mounted canards. While Funny Cars looked more radical with each passing year, they still resembled manufactured cars to the delight of brand loyalists. Funny Car champions included Tom McEwen, who took the AHRA title. McEwen had been racing Fuel since the 1950s, and his win seemed long overdue. Kenny Bernstein was on his way after he won the IHRA title, and Raymond Beadle, one of Funny Car's most popular faces, won the NHRA title.

Everyone Loves a Winner

By 1979, Raymond Beadle and the *Blue Max* were one of drag racing's biggest draws. In Funny Car, his popularity was possibly second only to Don Prudhomme. A person couldn't go anywhere without seeing the *Blue Max* crest. Beadle was a great promoter and sold a large number of T-shirts. Halter tops were given away to the girls at the drags, who were often fitted with them on the spot.

Roland Leong's* Hawaiian *featured the popular Corvette skin in 1979. Veteran driver Ron Colson finished the season fifth in NHRA points. (Photo Courtesy Terry Gray)

Having already won the IHRA Funny Car title in 1975 and 1976, Beadle won his first of three consecutive NHRA world championships in 1979, when he barely beat Don Prudhomme, who was aiming for his fifth title. How close was the battle between the two? Beadle held a slight lead in points heading to Ontario but could have lost it if he bowed out early. For Prudhomme to win, he had to set both ends of the national record and beat Beadle in the final. A slippery track that slowed everyone down pretty much guaranteed that no records were going to be set.

The title was decided early, as Prudhomme smoked the tires against McEwen in the first round and brought a quick end to Prudhomme's hopes. Beadle fell in the second round, but it made no difference; the title was his.

Beadle and the Blue Max had won IHRA world titles and national events, and they were in such demand through the mid-1970s that Beadle had to turn away track promoters who wanted to book him for match races. (Photo Courtesy Rich Carlson/Grant Bittner Collection)

The first name in Funny Car, Don Prudhomme, looked to capture an unprecedented fifth world title in 1979. Here, smoking the tires got the best of the Prudhomme. (Photo Courtesy Hilak Bros. Photography)

Sonde Lombardo wears her Blue Max *halter shirt with bellbottom jeans. The combination was fashionable in the 1970s. (Photo Courtesy Dan Williams)*

Don Prudhomme's Plymouth Arrow featured a Keith Black Hemi that was running a 90-percent load through Enderle injection. The headers were twin-wall Cragars. The H&H Racecraft 120-inch wheelbase chassis mounted a J&E fiberglass body. (Photo Courtesy Hilak Bros. Photography)

Gary Burgin completed an upset when he defeated World Champion Raymond Beadle at the Springnationals. Burgin's Jaime Sarte-chassis Mustang was new for 1979. His key sponsor was Pete Rose's energy bar. (Photo Courtesy Hilak Bros. Photography)

240 Gordie

Gordie Bonin had the best year of his career in 1979 and finished third in the NHRA points standings. Driving the *Bubble-Up Pacemaker*-sponsored Firebird, Bonin won the Gatornationals, Indy, and the World Finals. At Indy, he qualified second behind Prudhomme and joined the Cragar Five-Second Club with a 5.97 ET. In the process, he set the top speed record at 245.90 mph. In the final round, he singled to defeat Kosty Ivanof's ailing Corvette.

Gordie Bonin had a great year in 1979. He wasn't only a star on the track. Bonin and his Firebird, with an alternate body, appeared in the 1979 movie Fast Company. *(Photo Courtesy Keith Hudak)*

Bonin's deal with soda drink Bubble Up ended in 1979. In 1980, he went solo with Crew Chief Jerry Verheul along to pull wrenches. The pair gave twin turbochargers a try, not so much to add power but to lower costs. The experiment never panned out. Shortly afterward, Bonin took a brief hiatus from the sport.

Pro Stock

It seemed that by the close of the decade, Pro Stock had come full circle, as once again, Chrysler was back on top. The factory no longer counted on the Hemi as its go-to engine, although a number of non-factory supported Hemi cars were in contention. One of them was the Bobby Yowell–driven Plymouth Arrow of Billy Stepp. The pair came close to seeing a year suspension by the IHRA for running nitrous oxide. Nitrous oxide was frowned upon in legal competition by all sanctioning bodies.

Gordie Bonin's turbo car reportedly ran 6.20 ETs, which were a few tenths of a second off the pace of a competitive Roots-blown F/C from the period. The effort ran into the same issue as early turbo efforts had (syncing fuel and boost). (Photo Courtesy Larry Pfister)

"Dandy" Dick Landy was back. This time, he competed in a Dodge Omni with a Chrysler small-block that measured 340 ci. Brad Yuill and Ken Dondero each drove the Don Hardy car for Landy and recorded ETs in the 8.50s. (Photo Courtesy Hilak Bros. Photography)

Sox & Martin were part of Chrysler's renewed Pro Stock effort. This time around, they got it done with a 337-ci small-block. A 3.10-first-gear Lenco was backed by a 5.57-gear Dana. (Photo Courtesy Hilak Bros. Photography)

Bob Glidden never missed a step when he made the move to Mopar in 1979. He didn't lose an NHRA national event until the Mile High Nationals in June. (Photo Courtesy Hilak Bros. Photography)

Chrysler entered the small-block wars in 1979 with a refurbished 340 block and well-designed W2 heads. Dick Landy, Sox & Martin, and Bob Glidden, who was lured from Ford, each ran small-block-powered subcompact cars.

Glidden's Plymouth

This sentence still sounds strange: Bob Glidden competed in a Plymouth. The switch to campaigning a Plymouth Arrow came when Chrysler Staff Engineer Dave Koffel approached Glidden at the IHRA Northern Nationals in July 1978.

Koffel knew that Glidden had no support from Ford, so he flat-out asked him if he'd like to race for Chrysler. The company offered an enticing deal that included a car, trailer, and parts. Glidden took some time to consider the offer before he signed on at the NHRA Fallnationals, a race that he won by defeating the SRD-built Chevy Monza of Frank Iaconio. Iaconio returned the favor by defeating Glidden at the same race in 1979 with a new Don Ness Camaro.

Things happened fast, as "Mad Dog" Bob Glidden set his sights on debuting the Don Hardy–built Plymouth at the season-opening Winternationals. Somehow, the fact that Glidden had signed with Chrysler was kept under wraps until the new year. You can imagine the reaction

Bob Glidden spent an extensive amount of timing reworking the Holley carburetors, Edelbrock intake, and W-2 heads of his small-block Mopar. His first runs with the Plymouth came at Orange County International Raceway a week before the Winternationals. (Photo Courtesy Daniel Levesque)

of Glidden's peers when he showed up in Southern California driving a Plymouth. At the Winternationals, Glidden defeated the Camaro of Joe Satmary in the final round for his seventh consecutive national event win and gave Chrysler its first NHRA Pro Stock victory since 1973. Of the 10 NHRA national events in 1979, Glidden lost only 3, and two of those were due to red-lighting.

Glidden set the class record with an 8.48 ET at the Gatornationals, and soon after, the NHRA hit the short-wheelbase, small-block cars with more weight. After seeing the beating that the Hemi took from the NHRA, the Chrysler fraternity must have felt that it would never catch a break from the sanctioning body. Initially, the small cars ran at 6.70 pounds per cubic inch, which was bumped to 6.80 pounds per cubic inch. Most other combinations saw a drop in weight. It didn't matter, as Glidden kept marching forward.

Powering the Arrow was a 339-ci engine, although various engines were trialed, including a 342 ci. The power was transferred through a 3.10-first-gear Lenco transmission to a 5.83 Eaton-geared Dana rear end.

Here, at Ontario for the World Finals, Bob Glidden closed the season by defeating Frank Iaconio in the final round with an 8.65 ET. The pair finished one and two in the points standings. (Photo Courtesy Hilak Bros. Photography)

Randy Humphrey's finest moment came at the Mile High Nationals, where he defeated Sonny Bryant in the final round after he defeated a red-lighting Bob Glidden in the semifinals. A Bob Lambeck 394-ci Hemi helped set the class record in April with an 8.46 ET at 159.01 mph. (Photo Courtesy Dan Williams)

A Battle for Second Best

After winning the seven national events, Glidden left little room for others when it came to NHRA competition. Over in the AHRA, Bobby Marriott and Lee Shepherd tied for the Pro Stock title. In IHRA competition, Warren Johnson won the title with his Chevy-powered Oldsmobile Starfire. Johnson teamed with Oldsmobile in 1979 and began a partnership that lasted well into the 2000s. This led to the development of GM's series of Drag Racing Competition Engines (DRCE).

Jenkins's Lotus Camaro

Jenkins's Lotus Camaro, aptly named due to its unique frame that was similar in design to a Lotus race car, used the drivetrain as a main torsional support. The total weight of the bare frame was a light 135 pounds. The Camaro failed tech inspection at the Winternationals upon its debut for several infractions. One was the empty casing placed between the engine and transmission that moved the weight of the Lenco 4-speed farther to the rear of the car. Once corrections were made, Lom-

Tom Chelbana rang in a new era when he debuted Dave and Karen Smith's 349-ci Oldsmobile-powered Starfire at the NHRA Winternationals. Their efforts garnered the Best Engineered Car award. Chelbana qualified with an 8.73 ET at 155 mph, but an engine failure ended his weekend. (Photo Courtesy Hilak Bros. Photography)

Jenkins built his Grumpy's Toy XV Camaro in 1979 to take advantage of breaks that favored the small-inch, long-wheelbase cars. His 331-ci engine produced 700 hp and propelled the Toy to ETs in the 8.60s. (Photo Courtesy Rob Potter)

With Bob Glidden competing for Chrysler, it was a quiet year for Ford and Mercury. The Cleveland remained the go-to powerplant for racers such as Don Nicholson, Tom Chase, and Lee Hunter, who is seen here with his Willie Rells-built, 366-ci Mercury Zephyr. (Photo Courtesy Bob Snyder)

This was the last Grumpy's Toy *that was built by SRD. Don Ness would build the next one. Bill Jenkins gave up his patented 3-link for a ladder-bar setup. In hindsight, Jenkins felt that the ladder-bar suspension was a mistake. "You had to stand the car up about 3 feet to make it run, and you'd be pulling second gear in mid-air," Jenkins said.*

bardo fell in the second round to Glidden with an 8.70 ET to an 8.50 ET. A runner-up finish to Glidden at Indy was Lombardo's final ride with Jenkins.

Pro Comp

In Pro Comp, no season was a walk in the park. However, on paper, Billy Williams made it seem that way. He closed the 1979 season by winning six national events, which was a record number for the Sportsman categories. Powering the AA/DA car was a Donovan Hemi, which was nestled into a Britting chassis. The versatile Williams drove and tuned the car as well. His ongoing success led to him opening his own business in 1979. His specialty was building blown alcohol engines.

Williams's weekend at the World Finals netted him close to $25,000 in payouts. He collected $15,000 in Grace Cup winnings, and then collected his winnings for defeating the AA/DA of Brian Raymer in the final round on Sunday. Williams qualified number one with a 6.54 ET, which also counted for the low ET of the meet, which went hand in hand with his top speed of the meet (211.76 mph). Williams's time on the final run was a 6.75 ET at 209 mph to a 6.82 at 205.

Billy Williams carried the number 1 here in 1980 in recognition of his 1979 Pro Comp championship win. Williams and Art "Cookie" Kazanjian called Torrance, California, home. (Photo Courtesy Terry Gray)

It was a relief to those in Pro Comp when Billy Williams moved up into Top Fuel in 1981. Williams was a great driver and knew what worked. Several competitors made use of his engines. (Photo Courtesy Steve Jackson)

The Wayne Clapp-driven, Dean Thompson-owned AA/DA was powered by a Ken Veney-built 366-ci Cleveland engine. It had ETs in the 6.60s at 205 mph. The low wing (used here) would be replaced by a taller unit placed high in the clean air. (Photo Courtesy Michael Pottie)

Larry Tores built this Econo Altered Opel using a Mark Williams chassis kit. The Opel held the class record through most of 1979 with a 9.48 ET at 141.50 mph. Tores had three runner-up finishes with the car before he won the 1980 NHRA Winternationals. (Photo Courtesy Dave Kommel)

Comp Eliminator

Many may best remember Bob Newberry from his success with Alcohol Funny Cars. However, in 1979, he won his first world championship behind the wheel of the Bill DeJohn–sponsored B/EA 1925 Ford Model T. Newberry prevailed at the World Finals and used his Ron Scott–built car to defeat the equally tough Larry Tores at the final round.

Bob Newberry, shown here in 1978, was the Comp World Champion with this E/Altered in 1979. Ron Scott built the 1923 Model T. Bill DeJohn's race engines took care of the Chevy engine. (Photo Courtesy Terry Gray)

Tores and Shenberg

Unlike Newberry, Larry Tores was new to Comp. He made the leap from Super Stock in 1978 when he and his partner Jim Shenberg debuted a C/EA Opel GT.

"Comp was a fun place to race," Tores said. "In 1975 in Super Stock, you could run as hard as you could. There was no breakout. In 1976, they stayed no breakout at national events but the WCS races had a breakout. So, a lot of guys switched from Super Stock to Comp."

The Opel went together in 1977 and made use of a Mark Williams chassis kit. Chassis kits were a booming business by 1979. A number of shops, such as Williams, Alston, and

Hardy, now offered ready-to-assemble chassis, which allowed racers to do it their way and save some money in the process.

Encasing the 100-inch wheelbase chassis was a significantly modified Fiberglass Trends body. Initial power came by way of a Rick Voegelin 292-inch Chevy engine. This was replaced with a 317-ci (3.25 stroke) engine that took Tores to a runner-up finish in Division 7 in 1978 and won him the title in 1979. A win at the NHRA Winternationals came in 1980.

Cross and Corzine: Part II

Bobby Cross and Bubba Corzine were back and debuted a new 227-inch Ness car at the Springnationals. How did they decide on a 227-inch chassis? It was because their trailer couldn't hold anything larger. Such was the science.

Ness threw every trick in the book at the new car to make it as light as possible. The car had 0.024-inch-thick body panels that were anodized, as Ness didn't want the added weight of paint. The 9-inch Ford rear end was welded to the chassis, as opposed to being bolted to it because welding it reduced weight. Corzine remembered weighing about 50 rear ends to find the lightest one.

"Ness didn't miss a trick," he said. "Everything was aluminum or titanium, and the bolts were rifle drilled."

With the new chassis came a new 362-ci Reher-Morrison small-block. This was the first single 4-barrel small-block Chevy to make more than 700 hp, as it produced 705 hp on the Reher-Morrison dyno. The larger engine bumped the car to A/ED, which generally was considered a big-block class.

Two of the period's toughest competitors were Bobby Cross, and Larry Tores. Tores took the handicap start here in the Indy final, but his 9.69 ET couldn't hold off Cross's 7.61 ET. (Photo Courtesy Rob Potter)

At the Springnationals, Cross qualified number one and covered the field by 0.15 of a second. A red-light in the Comp final to the front-engine A/Dragster of Dan Parker ruined an otherwise-flawless debut. The pair never lost another race that they entered, until the World Finals. There, they fell in the semifinals to Bob Newberry.

The A/ED rule changes for 1980 specified that only big-block cars were allowed and forced the guys to move on. They briefly ran in the B/ED class while a big-block went together at Reher-Morrison. The new engine measured 381 ci by using a 409 crank to put them back into A/ED. The wins came but not as consistently, as Corzine found that the heads were "just junk."

Accomplishing more than they expected, the pair sold the dragster at the end of the 1980 season. They half-heartedly carried on with a new Ness car before Corzine moved into Pro Stock in 1982. Corzine said that he and Cross "got lucky considering the competition. We had a good three years."

Modified Eliminator

The caliber of cars in the Modified category was astounding. National event winners varied widely and included Garley Daniels, who pulled his 1967 Chevy II out of Super Stock to run C/SM. The move won him the Modified world title in 1979. Cotton Perry and his H/MP *Pocket Rocket* continued its dominance, while Bill Mansell in his H/G 1967 Corvette earned a few national event wins. Terry Hoard was back to fray the nerves of

Ed Sigmon from Canoga Park, California, ran a string of great looking and performing cars during the 1970s. His A/SR 1927 Model T was one of the best. The short-stroke, big-block Chevy, backed by a Clutch-Turbo transmission, was a record holder in 1979 with an 8.80 ET at 154.90 mph. (Photo Courtesy Roger Rodgers)

Here, Garley Daniels wins the C/SM class at Indy with a 10.40 ET. He battled to the Modified final but lost with a red-light against the C/Gas Monza of Don Coonce. (Photo Courtesy Terry Gray)

his competition with his *Samurai Warrior*. For the little screamer, wins came at the Springnationals and Mile High Nationals.

Bowles Bowls Them Over

Not to be left out of the winner's circle, Ford was well represented by Don Bowles, who took his Don Hardy–prepped A/SM Fairmont to a class win at its debut in Indy, where it also won Best Engineered honors. At the Fallnationals, Bowles defeated Terry Hoard to win Modified.

Powering the Fairmont was a Jack Roush 394-ci Cleveland that was derived from the use of a Molodex 3.64-stroke crankshaft and had a bore of 4.135 inches. Brooks rods and pistons filled the cylinders, and the Roush heads were fitted with TRW titanium valves and springs by Cam Dynamics, which also supplied the camshaft. Rounding out the top was a Roush intake and a Holley 850-cfm carburetor. As with a true Modified car, the Fairmont came off the line at 10,000 rpm.

Wayne County Opel GT

There is a reason Chevy small-block-powered cars were so dominant in the door-car categories. It's simple mathematics. With classes determined by a weight-to-cubic-inch factor, the smaller the engine, the less weight one needs to carry and move. As the small-block Chevy combustion chamber limits valve size to a 2.05-inch intake, one needs to build a smaller-cubic-inch engine to compensate. Theory tells us that this is akin to increasing the valve size. The thing about the small-block Chevy is that it will make big power with small cubic inches. Add a heavyweight flywheel, a low first gear, and a final axle ratio of around 6, few will be able to beat that combination.

The guys at Wayne County knew this when they built their 278-ci B/Gas Opel GT. The class weight break fell at a minimum of 6.50 pounds per cubic inch, which meant that they could run the Opel at just over 1,800 pounds. With driver Dave Hutchins on board, the weight came in at approximately 1,800 pounds, saving little room for ballast.

Wayne County had great success running a Street Roadster prior to the Opel but got tired of fighting the wind with the old car. The Opel body was chosen for the obvious reason that it was smaller and aerodynamically superior to probably any car that was permissible in Modified.

A 2x3 rectangle chassis was constructed and carried Pro Stock–style components, including a Lamb strut front suspension. Out back, a 4-link, which was standard Modified fair by 1979, supported the 5.89-geared Ford 9-inch rear end. A Nash 5-speed transmission transmitted the estimated 580 hp. Rumors flew that the guys had rigged the transmission to go clutchless for the first-to-second gear shift. However, these rumors were not confirmed. The NHRA took notice and revised its rule book for 1980 to clarify that no clutchless transmissions or devices were allowed.

The Opel's debut at the Gatornationals didn't go as planned due to handling issues, but by midseason, things had clicked. Hutchens won the Sportsnationals at Bowling Green and defeated the 1962 Corvette of Paul Smith. He closed the season as the Division 3 Modified champion.

Don Bowles and his Cleveland-powered Fairmont overcame the 1979 Modified rule that stated 0.20 pounds would be added to all cars that used the Ford Cleveland. (Photo Courtesy Dave Kommel)

The Wayne County Opel won the Best Engineered Car award at its Gatornationals debut. The car was built with speed, comfort, and ease of maintenance in mind. (Photo Courtesy Dave Kommel)

The Wayne County Opel is pictured here in 1980 as maintenance is performed on it. Note the removable floor pan and the Thrush muffler that is barely visible through the roll cage. (Photo Courtesy Steve Jackson)

In 1980, the Opel was fitted with a 331 engine, basically a Pro Stock mill, and battled the big-blocks for class supremacy. For his efforts, Hutchins won the Summernationals, Grandnationals, and World Finals. There, Hutchins ran an 8.29 ET on an 8.65 index to defeat the E/MP 1961 Corvette of Steve Taylor.

The Opel was sold to Larry Kopp at the end of the season as Wayne County moved into Pro Stock. Kopp did the team proud and helped make the Opel one of the Sportsman category's most memorable cars.

Super Stock

"Once a winner, always a winner" goes the old saying. It holds doubly true in the case of Tennessee's Amy Faulk. Faulk purchased Bobby Warren's 1978 World Championship–winning Super Stock 1967 Camaro and used the car to win the same world title in 1979. In doing so, Faulk became the first woman to win an NHRA Sportsman category world title.

At the Finals, she met the irrepressible Division 3 Champion Bob Marshall in his 439-ci SS/BA *Dodge Material* car. Marshall won the Gatornationals earlier in the season but fell to Faulk's SS/IA car in the final round when he broke out trying to chase her down. Faulk's 11.03 ET was right on her dial-in.

Car Craft magazine recognized Faulk's efforts by awarding her with the Super Stock Driver of the Year honor. She had an amazing career, as she won national events in three different categories: Super Stock, Comp, and T/AD. As of this writing, she is still going strong in Super Stock.

Powering the Opel was a high-winding 278-ci Chevy engine, which was backed by a Doug Nash 5-speed transmission. The Mike Sullivan chassis incorporated a 4-link rear and a Lamb strut-equipped front suspension. (Photo Courtesy Steve Jackson)

Amy Faulk performed well while driving Bobby Warren's old world champion car. Amy's husband, Kenny Faulk, prepped and tuned the Camaro. Note the big number 1, which is worn proudly. (Photo Courtesy Bill Truby)

Wheelie bars were welcomed in Super Stock in 1979. There's no denying that Bob Marshall and his Dodge Material needed them. The car made consistent 9.90-ET runs and was prepped by Ron Butler. Behind the Hemi rode an ATI TorqueFlite and a 5.38-gear Dana rear end. (Photo Courtesy Bill Truby)

Showing that there was plenty of life in the old Tri-Five Chevys, Nebraska's Gene Bichlmeier and his Bick's Beater '55 won class at the NHRA Winternationals in 1979. Bichlmeier is legendary. (Photo Courtesy John Eichinger)

Stock

No rules changes were made in NHRA Stock eliminator for the new season, which saw a variety of category winners. The season opened with Jim Waldo winning the eliminator at the Winternationals with his A/S Fairlane. At the opposite end of the spectrum, George Williams in his Z/S Vega panel won the Fallnationals.

In between was Ray "Tex" Cook and Art Leong, whose B/SA Dodge Challenger took wins at the Summernationals, Grandnationals, and World Finals, where he defeated the C/SA 1969 Mustang of Jeff Powers. Powers, who was from Southern California, was a consistent class winner with his Norm Nevin–prepped Cobra Jet.

Cobra Jet-powered Mustangs were consistent winners in the Stock and Super Stock categories. John Presing's 1969 Mustang coupe was one of many standouts. (Photo Courtesy Michael Pottie)

Cookin'

The Ray Cook and Art Leong Challenger began life as a 383-powered R/T. To that, they fitted the Hemi from their previously campaigned Challenger and Charger. Things got off to a great start when Cook won class at Indy in 1977.

At the World Finals, Cook took a bye run in the semifinals. Then, he chose the bad right lane in the final round.

"Nobody was winning in that lane, but I took a close look at it and knew if Tex [Cook] lined up right, we could do good in it," Leong said.

Cook won the coin toss, and to Powers's disbelief, he chose the right lane. At this point, Powers must have figured the win was all but his. The Mustang, being the slower car, received a slight handicap start. Powers made the mistake of waiting on the solid green before leaving. That was not a good idea! Cook beat him off the line and never looked back.

The Ray Cook and Art Leong Challenger proved to be an unbeatable combination. The pair originally came together to campaign a 1971 Charger. (Photo Courtesy Yoland Cormier)

In this 1980 photo, Ray Cook's Challenger carries the number 1 due to his 1979 World Championship win. Cook also won the 1980 Grace Cup. (Photo Courtesy Rob Potter)

Support from Chrysler helped keep the world championship–winning Challenger on top through 1980. Mopar was deep in Stock and Super Stock and invested to ensure that its racers won. Cook and Leong received help from the factory in the form of parts: pistons, rods, low-gear transmissions, a spool for the Dana, and even a Hemi block that was picked up at Richard Petty's shop, as Chrysler had no more left. Acid ported heads came in 1980 that were good for a couple tenths of a second.

As per the strict rules, modifications were limited, and it included the suspension that ran loose shocks up front, 6-cylinder torsion bars, and clamped rear springs out back to support the 5.38 gear rear.

The guys found a way around the rule that prohibited the unibody chassis from being tied together by running steel tubing through the rocker panels to tie the car together. Another trick was to bring the car up to legal weight. A 383 Challenger convertible weighs less than the same car equipped with a Hemi, so Chrysler sent them a spare floor pan that they would weld the back half of onto the top of the existing floor.

Leong recalled that the factory Super Stock racers hated to pit beside them.

"We could run to the junkyard to get replacement parts," he said. "They couldn't because nothing fit."

They dreaded anyone doing a side-by-side comparison.

The Challenger ran a best ET of 10.99 at Fremont, topping its own 11.11 ET record. The two retired as a team after busting a crankshaft at the Gatornationals in 1981. Leong wanted to step up to Pro Comp with an Alcohol Funny Car, but Cook wasn't interested.

Long-time Oldsmobile proponent, Michigan's Don Holben, won the 1979 Division 3 Points Championship. Here, at Indy, he won class–as he had every year between 1976 and 1988. The 350-powered Oldsmobile 88 was good for mid-12-second ETs. (Photo Courtesy Terry Gray)

CHAPTER TEN

1980: COMING UP

After John Force paid his dues, he landed a Wendy's sponsorship in 1978. Larry Frazier pulled wrenches and helped keep everything together. (Photo Courtesy Bob Snyder)

The 1980 drag racing season was phenomenal. Fans saw season-long battles that weren't decided until the World Finals. They saw major upsets and genuine Cinderella stories. Records were set, thanks in part to the advent of the concrete starting pad. Many new names adorned the winner's circle, while others were busy reinforcing their status as category leaders.

This was the final season where the NHRA Sportsman world champions were crowned based on a win at the World Finals. In 1981, all world champions were determined by a season-long points chase.

Top Fuel

In Top Fuel, the ETs slowly crept lower. Marvin Graham recorded a 5.68 ET at the US Nationals. Although it was still behind Garlits's 5.63 ET that was recorded during the ideal conditions of the 1975 World Finals, the Fuelers were getting closer.

Reversers, first introduced in the late 1960s by the team of John Riley and Dave Powers (the same gentlemen who brought us the self-starter), were mandated in Top Fuel, Funny Car, and Pro Comp starting in 1980.

Jeb Allen had a great 1980 racing season. Aside from Garlits, Allen was the only one to win world titles with all three sanctioning bodies: the AHRA (1977), the IHRA (1980), and the NHRA (1981). (Photo Courtesy Terry Gray)

Campaigning a car wasn't getting any cheaper for anyone. For the Fuel racer, a single run cost about $500. Nitro was $23 per gallon, and it took 6 to 7 gallons to make a pass. An 8-71 blower approached $1,000, and a set of slicks that cost more than $400 were good for a half-dozen-or-so runs. Sponsorships played an ever-increasing role because without them, any pro class venture was a lost cause. National event money and contingency payouts weren't paying the bills.

Garlits's New Bag of Tricks

Don Garlits, long established as the "King of the Dragsters," missed the mark in 1980 when he debuted *Swamp Rat 25*. The car was a bust, and by midseason, he stopped running NHRA events.

According to Garlits, Lester Gilroy began the build for him in mid-1979. Gilroy had some fresh ideas, but ill health sidelined him. Garlits, along with his crew chief, Herb Parks, took over. Features of the car included an A-arm suspension and a 10-gallon fuel tank that was mounted on the leading edge of the chassis. This eliminated the need for extra ballast up front. The tank was hidden by a wide, flat nose, and this contributed to keeping the wheels on the ground.

Built with safety and durability in mind, the weight and girth were too much for the 480-ci Keith Black engine to overcome. Garlits removed some tubing to lighten the car and make it more flexible, which helped some. However, Garlits had the sense to realize that the car wasn't going to cut it. By midseason, a new car was under construction. The best run recorded for *Swamp Rat 25* was a 5.75 ET at 251.39 mph.

Top Fuel Story of The Year

No story in Top Fuel was greater than the one that unfolded at the season-ending World Finals. Heading into the race, the world title was still up for grabs, and four racers had a chance at it: Gary Beck, Jeb Allen, Shirley Muldowney, and Marvin Graham.

Muldowney found herself in the hunt when she won the Fallnationals. The win moved her into striking position after she defeated Beck and then Graham in the final round. Graham's only hope of winning the world title was if Beck and Allen bowed out early in the Finals. Heading to Ontario, Beck's lead had shrunk to 83 points. He picked a bad time to tail off. His last final-round appearance came

Garlits's Swamp Rat 25 was longer than most at 265 inches. The 1980 season was an end of an era of sorts, as it was the last of the 32-car Top Fuel field. (Photo Courtesy Hilak Bros. Photography)

Top Fuel Evolution

Isaac Newton's Third Law of Motion states that for every action, there is an equal and opposite reaction. That law played out when Jerry Ruth was knocked unconscious at Indy in 1979, as his helmet banged into the roll cage due to excessive tire shake.

Ruth received a concussion and sustained serious injuries to his arm and hand when his car hit the guardrail before it ran off the end of the track.

Ruth's reaction to the incident was to design a chassis featuring a Funny Car-style roll cage to prevent the same issue from happening again. The design forever changed how Top Fuel chassis were built.

Jerry Ruth campaigned this Al Swindahl-constructed car for three seasons. The design included an A-arm suspension and a flexible chassis. In 1980, Ruth earned wins at the Mile High Nationals and the AHRA World Finals. (Photo Courtesy Ruth Tice)

Shirley Muldowney had four world titles under her belt by the time that she retired in 2003. A bad crash at the Grandnationals in 1984 curtailed her racing activity. (Photo Courtesy Terry Gray)

In 1980, Gary Beck joined forces with Larry Minor and took over driving chores from Larry Dixon. Beck had a commanding midseason points lead but failed to hang onto it. (Photo Courtesy Jack Muller)

At Ontario, Muldowney surprised low-qualifier Marvin Graham with a 5.86 ET in the first round. Muldowney's pink car featured a Ron Attebury chassis. (Photo Courtesy Keith Hudak)

midseason at the Mile High Nationals, where he lost to Jerry Ruth.

At the Finals, Allen's hope disappeared when he failed to qualify and ran a 6.056 ET on a 6.03 bump. In round action, ninth-place qualifier Muldowney (5.98) faced number-one qualifier Graham (5.86) in the first round. Graham led Muldowney early but lightly hazed the tires at mid-track, which allowed Muldowney to gain ground and power around him. Across the line, it was Muldowney with a 6.07 ET to a 6.09 ET.

Suddenly, things looked really good for Muldowney, as Beck in the slippery right lane lost to Gary Cornwall in the quarterfinals. All Muldowney had to do was beat Cornwall in the semifinals, and the title was hers. She did just that and ran away from a tire-smoking Cornwall with a 5.93 ET. Muldowney took the title from Beck by fewer than 100 points. This was her second world title, which made her the first Top Fuel driver to win two world championships. Beck, a real class act, was waiting at the finish line for Muldowney and presented her with a bottle of champagne.

Funny Car

New NHRA rules required all Funny Cars to be a 1975-or-newer bodystyle. The rule that stipulated all bodies must resemble an American-manufactured car was dropped. John Collins and Gary Densham were quick to capitalize on the change and debuted new Datsun 280/Z-bodied cars.

On the Track

Ron Colson closed his drag racing career in style at the World Finals driving Roland Leong's *King's Hawaiian Bread* Corvette. Colson's long career spanned from Gassers of the early 1960s to Top Gas later in the decade and finally to nitro cars. At the World Finals in 1980, he qualified number one before advancing through the field, where he met the *Blue Max* of Raymond Beadle in the final.

In the first round, Colson took a bye when opponent Dale Armstrong, in Mike Kase's *Speed Racer*, was shut off by the starting-line crew after oiling down the already-poor right lane. Armstrong's brief AA/FC career failed to equal the success he saw in Pro Comp. He retired from driving in 1981, having earned three final-round losses before calling it a day.

Colson moved on to the final round after taking wins from Kenny Bernstein and Roy Harris. Bernstein, having sold his chain of Chelsea House restaurants, now enjoyed racing on Budweiser (Anheuser-Busch) money. The sponsorship lasted 30 years. Roy Harris enjoyed his own

John Collins was the first to capitalize on the new NHRA rule that allowed foreign bodies in the Funny Car category. He debuted his Datsun (Nissan) 280Z at the Winternationals. The 120-inch S&R Race Cars chassis housed a stroked Keith Black engine. (Photo Courtesy Rich Carlson/Grant Bittner Collection)

Budweiser deal put together by car owner Tom Ryan. His deal through a local New Jersey distributor ran during the 1979 and 1980 seasons.

Beadle, who was Colson's final-round opponent, repeated his 1979 World Championship in 1980 and locked up the title at the Fallnationals when he defeated Billy Meyer in the semifinals.

All the same, Beadle came to Ontario to win the race. He had the good lane but smoked the tires on a wild ride and watched as Colson sailed through for the easy win. Colson couldn't ask for a better ending to a driving career that saw him behind the wheel of some of the nation's most successful cars.

Ron Colson and Roland Leong began the year in a Dodge Omni and earned a runner-up finish at the Winternationals. The Jaime Sarte chassis housed a Keith Black Hemi, which produced 2,400 hp by 1980. (Photo Courtesy Lou Hart)

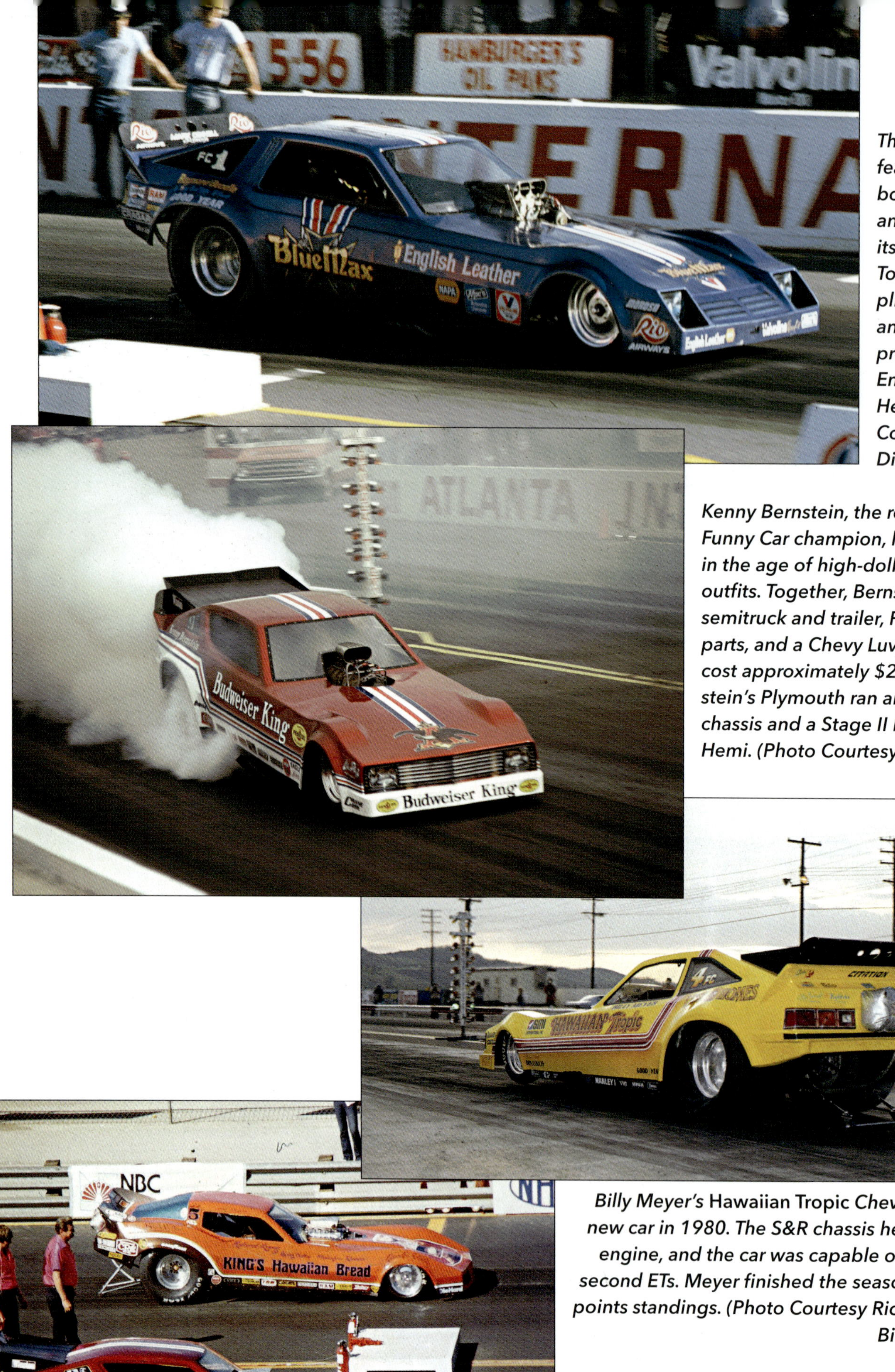

The Blue Max featured a new body in 1980, and it continued its winning ways. Tony Casarez supplied the chassis and Keith Black provided the Dale Emery-tuned Hemi. (Photo Courtesy Mike Dimery)

Kenny Bernstein, the reigning IHRA Funny Car champion, helped usher in the age of high-dollar drag racing outfits. Together, Bernstein's loaded semitruck and trailer, Funny Car, spare parts, and a Chevy Luv parts chaser cost approximately $250,000. Bernstein's Plymouth ran an H-H Racecraft chassis and a Stage II Keith Black Hemi. (Photo Courtesy Mike Dimery)

Billy Meyer's Hawaiian Tropic *Chevy Citation was a new car in 1980. The S&R chassis held a Keith Black engine, and the car was capable of running low-6-second ETs. Meyer finished the season second in the points standings. (Photo Courtesy Rich Carlson/Grant Bittner Collection)*

In round two at Ontario, Bernstein lost to Ron Colson, running a 6.30 ET at 227.84 mph to Colson's 6.21 ET at 233 mph. Bernstein's star burned brightly in the coming years. (Photo Courtesy Keith Hudak)

Pro Stock

In NHRA competition, the body of choice had to be no older than a 1975 model. Minimum weights were adjusted downward slightly to 2,230 pounds for small-block-equipped cars and 2,415 pounds for big-block-powered cars.

The 1980 NHRA season belonged to Bob Glidden and the team of Reher, Morrison, and Shepherd. Of the 10 national events of the season, the two teams won 8, and at least one of the teams appeared in the final round of the remaining two races.

Roy Hill's Plymouth Omni was powered by a twin-plug Hemi in a Willie Rells chassis. Unsatisfied with the NHRA's weight breaks, Hill spent a significant amount of time running match races and competing at IHRA events. (Photo Courtesy Hilak Bros. Photography)

Choose Your Weapons

Glidden began the year still running the Plymouth Arrow at a 6.65-pounds-per-cubic-inch break. The Chrysler deal was dead, but it took until the Cajun Nationals before Glidden was back in a Ford. His Don Hardy–built Fairmont ran a 343-ci Cleveland for most of the season at 7.05 pounds per cubic inch, versus the Lee Shepherd–driven Don Ness Camaro of RMS. The team began its year running a small-block at 6.80 pounds per cubic inch. However, by the summer, it had perfected a de-stroked big-block that measured 362 ci, which allowed the Camaro to run at a 6.60-pounds-per-cubic-inch break.

Reher, Morrison, and Shepherd were off to a phenomenal start and won the AHRA Winter Nationals,

Dave and Karen Smith as well as driver Tom Chelbana had AHRA competition up in arms with their nitrous-induced 410-ci Oldsmobile engine that was based on a 350-ci Oldsmobile diesel block. Many considered the large-bore, short-stroke engine to be a big-block and felt that it shouldn't have been allowed to run with nitrous.

The AHRA Drops the Breaks

With AHRA Pro Stock struggling to field an eight-car program at some series events, it was time to change things up.

Beginning with the Grand Nationals at Dragway 42 in July 1980, the AHRA dropped the weight breaks and adopted similar rules to what the IHRA had gone to in 1977: a 2,350-pound minimum weight and an engine of any displacement. Unlike the IHRA, the AHRA allowed small-block-equipped cars to run nitrous oxide as a way to level the playing field.

At the following series event, the Summer Nationals in Kansas City, Sam Carroll won Pro Stock with an 8.27 ET, which was a half second quicker than Lee Shepherd's winning time at the same event in 1979.

The 1980 NHRA Pro Stock season belonged to Bob Glidden (far lane) and Lee Shepherd (near lane). Glidden lost this U.S. Nationals final-round battle to a red-light.

Bob Glidden proudly flies the number 1 after winning the NHRA Pro Stock title in 1979 for Plymouth. In 1997, he finished his career with 10 NHRA world titles. (Photo Courtesy James Morgan)

NHRA Winternationals, Gatornationals, and the Cajun Nationals. Glidden warned them that the new Fairmont would be a lot faster than the Arrow, and he would prove it. At the Cajun Nationals, Glidden qualified the Fairmont number one with an 8.41 ET at 160.71 mph. Shepherd qualified fifth in the eight-car field with an 8.54 ET, which meant that the two would meet in the first round. It took a mighty holeshot for Shepherd to stave off Glidden, who ran a losing 8.49 ET at 160.71 mph to an 8.54 at 158. Glidden won the following Springnationals and defeated Shepherd in the final with an 8.53 ET. That's how the season went: back and forth. Shepherd won a total of six national events and defeated Glidden in four of those, with three on a holeshot.

The World Finals

With an upset win at the Fallnationals, Glidden moved within striking distance of Shepherd. Shepherd had the season all but locked up heading into the World Finals. He only had to win two rounds, and the championship was his. At Ontario, all eyes were on Glidden and Shepherd. Shepherd qualified number one with an 8.43 ET. Glidden was right behind with an 8.46. Glidden had pretty much lost hope of taking the title, as he had to win the race and set at least one end of the record and Shepherd had to bow out within the first couple of rounds.

As round action opened up, Shepherd put away the Volare of Bob Lambeck with an 8.53 ET. Glidden followed

Frank Iaconio red-lighted in this NHRA Fallnationals semifinal match against Lee Shepherd. Iaconio's small-block Camaro managed two runner-up finishes in 1980. (Joe Webber Photo Courtesy Todd Webber)

by dismissing the Camaro of Brad Yuill who ran an 8.77 ET to Glidden's 8.52 ET. Second-round action saw Shepherd face the Firebird of Maskin and Mannarino driven by Andy Mannarino. It should have been a good match, with Shepherd the favorite as Mannarino had run a best ET of 8.66. However, Shepherd's destiny had been written. On the green, the Camaro stumbled. The Reher, Morrison, and Shepherd team was defeated by a failing transmission.

Glidden marched unabated to the final round and defeated Gordie

No matter your brand preference, Lee Shepherd is regarded as one of Pro Stock's best. The RMS Camaro was built on a Don Ness chassis and began the 1980 season with a 331-ci engine. (Joe Webber Photo Courtesy Todd Webber)

When Rickie Smith debuted his Mustang II in 1978, he was relatively unknown. That changed in a hurry. His Oak Ridge Boys–sponsored Mustang II featured a big-inch Gapp and Roush Boss engine that was nestled in a Don Hardy chassis. (Photo Courtesy Mike Dimery)

Rickie Smith

Rickie Smith can take credit for having run the first legal 7-second Pro Stock elapsed time.

Smith's big-inch Jack Roush Boss Mustang II did the deed in April when Smith recorded a 7.99 ET at the IHRA Pro-Am Nationals at Rockingham, North Carolina. IHRA President Larry Carrier found the feat so astounding that he made an event out of it by stopping the race to honor Smith. Smith qualified number one at the race with an 8.08 ET at 171 mph but slowed in the semifinals to an 8.17 ET and lost to the eventual winner Ronnie Sox. Needless to say, the 7.99 ET was all that's remembered.

Glidden's 343-ci Cleveland held many secrets. The fabricated intake is a work of art. NHRA rules now allowed hood scoops to have a height of 9 inches. (Joe Webber Photo Courtesy Todd Webber)

Rivera and Jim Kinnett on his way. Glidden defeated Frank Iaconio in the final to set the low ET of the meet and the class record with an 8.42 ET at 159.85 mph for his fifth world championship title.

Pro Comp

This was the final season for NHRA Pro Comp. In 1981, the NHRA divided the category to create the Top Alcohol Dragster and Top Alcohol Funny Car categories. The category had become Top Gas 2.0, with the dragsters taking over. The AHRA made the same move back in 1977.

Although the 1980 season all but belonged to Billy Williams, it would be Ken Veney going home with the championship after defeating Williams at the World Finals. Williams had taken ownership of the category by 1980, winning 10 national events over the past three seasons, which was more national event wins than any other Sportsman racer.

Ace Manzo

Frank "Ace" Manzo kept the memories of the Altered fans alive by winning the Sportsnationals. The chassis under his fiberglass 1923 Ford Model T shell was previously under Frank's Alcohol Funny Car. His Sportsnationals win was the first

Qualifiers in the extremely competitive Pro Comp category often fell within tenths of a second from one end of the field to the other. Billy Williams often led the way. (Photo Courtesy James Morgan)

A Keith Black Hemi propelled Ace Manzo's AA/A 1923 Model T to a 6.68 ET at Indy. Class rules called for a minimum of 3.90 pounds per cubic inch. (Photo Courtesy Terry Gray)

in the line of 105 career national event victories. Tim Richards, who later pulled wrenches for Joe Amato, worked hand in hand with Manzo to help the blown/on alcohol Hemi car record mid-6-second ETs.

Comp Eliminator

The Econo Dragster classes A through D held favor in the Comp category through the 1980 season and stole away 6 of 10 national events wins and 7 runner-up finishes. Rules that kept the category affordable made the classes popular. At most national events, Econo Dragster was able to run a 32-car field.

Those who ran hybrid heads continued to be hammered with more weight. Joe Williamson and others had to carry an extra pound per inch over cars with production heads. However, Williamson found ways to win and claimed the Sportsnationals crown. (Photo Courtesy Michael Pottie)

A popular category from its inception, by 1980, the basic rules were as follows. Carburetion remained the only option in all categories. There was no cubic-inch limit in A/ED, while the B and C classes had a limit of 366 ci, with C limited to a maximum 750-cfm carburetion. Minimum weight per cubic inch in each were 3.40, 4.00, and 5.00, respectively. The D class was limited to 4-cylinder, 6-cylinder, and rotary-engine cars, with weight breaks coming in at 6.60 for inline 4-cylinders with a maximum 155 ci, 7.40 for rotary-powered cars, 7.00 for 4- or 6-cylinder cars (with a maximum 245 ci), and 8.30 for opposed 4-cylinder-equipped cars. For the "opposed 4-cylinders," you can read that as "the Volkswagen engine." Years of development made them killers.

The Unusual

When it came to the unusual, Norwin Palmer had the market cornered. Based out of Manhattan, Kansas, Palmer ran his 4-cylinder Datsun-powered rail down in class D with a minimum weight of 700 pounds. His combination clocked well under his class index with 9.70 ETs. Palmer used the home-fabricated car to defeat Dick Hickernell's C/ED to win the world championship. Palmer repeated his world championship win in 1982, campaigning a 6-cylinder Datsun in E/ED.

Norwin Palmer's Datsun-powered rail carried him to the world title. Check out the lack of chassis cross bracing. Palmer knew what worked. (Photo Courtesy Buddy Houts/Wayne Tonia Holland Collection)

Modified Eliminator

NHRA Modified remained a popular and healthy category heading into the 1980s, with only Super Stock and Stock seeing greater participation. No one could have predicted the category would be eliminated at the end of the 1981 season. In the meantime, action was hot and heavy in the category that held 31 classes of cars.

Back For More

David Hutchins took the Wayne County Opel to a world title finish when he defeated the E/MP, 1961 Corvette of J. R. Webb driven by Steve Taylor. Hutchins racked up four national event wins with the Opel before it was passed to Larry Kopp in 1981. Kopp took the car to another five national event wins to make it the winningest car in the category's history. With four previous Modified Eliminator wins, Kopp went in the books as the category's winningest driver.

New Wave

"New wave" wasn't just the music genre that was heard on the airwaves in 1980. The term was also used to reference the increasing number of newer-model cars on the racetrack. It wasn't the death knell for the Corvettes

Division 4's Pete Smith wheeled the Smith and (Curtis) Keene 1962 Corvette to a runner-up finish at the Cajun Nationals. The Chevy Corvette gathered Modified's most wins, with 5 going to the 1961–1962 models and another 15 going to the 1963-1967 models. (Photo Courtesy Bill Truby)

Steve Taylor racked up class wins and had a reputation for building killer engines. Today, his son operates Precision Racing Components, whose carburetors are a staple in all forms of motorsports. (Photo Courtesy Steve Jackson)

It's old versus new in the Super Modified category, as F. J. Smith faces Don Bowles. Smith used his Camaro to compete from 1976 to 1981. He won the B/SM class many times and set class records over and over again. Powering the Camaro were small-blocks built by Smith that measured from 316 to 323 ci. In the late 1970s, Smith began building chassis components and engines for customers. By 1980, he had a full-time staff, and Smith Performance Specialties was in full swing. In 1983, he became involved with Oldsmobile. (Photo Courtesy Rob Potter)

Ed Racis campaigned this 1978 Malibu in the C/SM class through 1981. The SRD-prepped car featured a 290-ci engine and a 2.98-first-gear Doug Nash transmission. The Ford 9-inch rear end was fitted with 6.20 gears. (Photo Courtesy Bill Truby)

and Camaros, nor was it for drag racing. However, racers were seeing the advantage and adapting.

Don Bowles was one of the first out with a newer model when he traded in his aging *Coal Miner* Mustang for a Fox Body Ford Fairmont in 1978. Those who were getting noticed in 1980 were Larry Kopp, who debuted a 1980 Malibu in B/MP, and Ed Racis, who competed in C/SM. Both men liked the advantage that the Malibu offered. This included its superior aerodynamics, lighter weight, greater rear overhang (when compared to a first-generation Camaro), and the superior front suspension (when compared to the primitive design of the early Chevy II).

Although Kopp's Malibu didn't work out as planned in B/MP, Racis found his to be an ideal fit for C/SM. Racis's Malibu (like Kopp's) went together at SRD Race Cars in Pennsylvania. Racis found his combination of a 290-ci engine and a 2.98-first-gear Nash transmission was perfect for class. A 9-inch Ford rear 4-link housed 6.20 gears and helped move the Malibu to 10.30 ETs.

The Ohio-based team of Baker and Kovacs debuted its Fairmont in 1979 and had success with it through the early 1980s. Jon Kaase built the Boss 318 engine, which was backed by a Nash transmission. The newer body and older engine combination would have been a good fit in the NHRA's SS/GT classes that were introduced in the 1980s. (Photo Courtesy Steve Jackson)

Racis parted with the Malibu when the NHRA decided to do away with Modified Eliminator.

"That, and I was 28 years old," Racis said. "I needed to focus on making money, not burning it."

Super Stock

When comparing the category rules of 1980 to the rules at the start of the 1970s, Super Stock looked a lot different. With all of the changes, the same cars remained dominant: the Hemi Mopars, Cobra Jet Mustangs, and small-block Chevys. It was still the same great racing. Only the names on the doors and the readings on the clocks had changed.

On the Track

Joe Scott took the world title with his SS/KA 1969 Camaro ragtop. The factory Indy Pace Car defeated the Chevy II of Clark Davis at the Finals. Amy Faulk proved to

Handicap racing levels the playing field, as Bobby Warren waits for the green light. Note the tremendous crowd. The stands were always full of fans at Indy. (Photo Courtesy Rob Potter)

Tom Kasch campaigned a string of Camaros before he built this SS/NA Road Runner. The 318 showed its abilities with low-12-second ETs. (Photo Courtesy Tom Kasch)

Dean Nicopolis, in the last Ramchargers-sponsored car, campaigned this Hemi 'Cuda from 1974 through 1986. In 1980, Dean won the Division 3 title. The 'Cuda survives and was restored to its as-raced appearance. (Photo Courtesy Steve Jackson)

I don't think there is anything that Al and Bev Provost didn't win. In 1980, Since You was the latest threat from the pair. Al's preference for Oldsmobiles came honestly. He worked as an Oldsmobile engineer before he retired. (Photo Courtesy Terry Gray)

be no flash in the pan and was back with her 1979 World Championship–winning Camaro to win the Springnationals and runner-up at Gatornationals.

No car racked up class wins like Dean Nicopolis's SS/DA Hemi 'Cuda. Sponsored by the Ramchargers, this was the last of the team's cars. The first, the *High and Mighty*, a 1949 Plymouth, dated back to 1959. Nicopolis debuted the 'Cuda in 1974, and retired it in 1986 after a total of 37 class wins and the Division 3 title in 1980.

Stock

Stock was still considered to be the first step into the world of sanctioned drag racing. Where the AHRA had numerous entry-level classes—from the affordable Factory Stock to the less-affordable Modified Stock—the NHRA had but one Stock Eliminator program, and you had to spend to be competitive on a national level.

Nebraska's Finest

Nebraska's Marlin Bogner spent wisely on his H/SA 340-ci-equipped Dodge Demon. He entered two NHRA national events in 1980 with the car (his first two national events ever) and won them both. The Mile High Nationals was his first national event win, and he defeated the Oldsmobile of Don Holben. The second was the World Finals, where he defeated fellow Division 5 racer John Dusenbery.

Marlin won the Division 5 title in 1978, lost it to John Dusenbery in 1979, and got his just reward at the

finals in 1980. Marlin took the handicap start over the Cobra Jet–powered F/S Fairlane of Dusenbery and hung on for the win.

They were practically neighbors coming all the way from Colorado to battle it out in the Stock final at Ontario. Marlin Bogner, with the handicap start, hung on for the win. (Photo Courtesy Dave Kommel)

The Fat Rat III, driven by Bruce Williams, took runner-up honors at the inaugural NHRA Pro Gas event. Williams entered the final round with the 427-powered Corvette nursing a bad converter and hoped that his competition would red-light. (Photo Courtesy Dave Kommel)

Super Gas

We all should have seen the Super Gas train coming. Impressions were that both the AHRA and NHRA were growing tired of the current structure of racing.

Fluctuating weight breaks, continuously changing records, and rule revisions were a time-consuming chore to stay on top of. With Super Gas, and bracket racing in general, they did away with record keeping and weight breaks. Each bracket ran off an index (in this case, a 9.90). If you ran quicker, you lost, unless your competition in the other lane ran farther under.

The NHRA made a trial run of the Super Gas category at the season-opening Winternationals. Bob Tietz, in his 1923 Ford Model T roadster, was the big winner in a 32-car field that was made up of a rag-tag bunch of runners with ETs ranging from the 9.80s to the mid-10s. This was probably part of the reason why Super Gas wasn't added to the regular schedule until 1982.

EPILOGUE:

DRAG RACING IS ALIVE AND WELL

As of this writing, the 1970s are about 55 years in the rearview mirror. A lot has changed. We have become our parents, telling our children and grandchildren how great life was when we were younger.

It is a different world today—as my own children often remind me. Drag racing isn't what it used to be—not when it takes a crew of 8 to 10 men and women to maintain a Fuel car, that now transverses the quarter mile (oops, a thousand feet) in 3.5 seconds. It isn't what it used to be when a brand of Funny Car is unrecognizable or when it's not obvious what brand of engine is under the hood of any given Pro Stocker.

Sure, we miss the days of "Big Daddy" Don Garlits, Don "the Snake" Prudhomme, and Bill "Grumpy" Jenkins, but we have adapted. We have no problem with change and have proven the naysayers wrong.

Drag racing is alive and well, and it's great to see that there are just as many young racers playing along with the old timers. Computers, electronics, and fuel injection—bring it on!

No, drag racing isn't like it used to be; its evolving, just as it always has and always will.

As a wrench man and driver, some don't think that Jake Johnston ever received the recognition he deserved. Shown here driving for Gene Snow in 1972, some bad luck resulted in Johnston falling short of winning the season's NHRA Funny Car title. (Photo Courtesy J.R. Bloom)

APPENDIX:

1970s DRAG RACING CHAMPIONS

NHRA World Champions 1970–1980		
Year	***Class***	***Driver***
1970	Top Fuel	Ronnie Martin
	Top Gas	Ray Motes
	Funny Car	Gene Snow
	Pro Stock	Ronnie Sox
	Comp	Ben Griffin
	Modified	Carroll Caudle
	Super Stock	Ray Allen
	Stock	Bobby Warren
1971	Top Fuel	Gerry Glenn
	Top Gas	Austin Myers
	Funny Car	Ed McCulloch
	Pro Stock	Mike Fons
	Comp	Tom Trisch
	Modified	Jim Stevens
	Super Stock	Ken McLellan
	Stock	Dave Boertman
1972	Top Fuel	Jim Walther
	Funny Car	Larry Fullerton
	Pro Stock	Bill Jenkins
	Comp	Wayne McMurtry
	Modified	Paul Blevins
	Super Stock	Dave Boertman
	Stock	Dave Benisek
1973	Top Fuel	Jerry Ruth
	Funny Car	Frank Hall
	Pro Stock	Wayne Gapp
	Comp	Paul Smith
	Modified	Chris Lawrence
	Super Stock	Bill Hanes
	Stock	Jerry McClanahan

NHRA World Champions 1970–1980 *continued*		
Year	***Class***	***Driver***
1974	Top Fuel	Gary Beck
	Funny Car	Shirl Greer
	Pro Stock	Bob Glidden
	Pro Comp	Don Gerardot
	Comp	David Majors
	Modified	Doc Dixon
	Super Stock	Bobby Warren
	Stock	Jerry McClanahan
1975	Top Fuel	Don Garlits
	Funny Car	Don Prudhomme
	Pro Stock	Bob Glidden
	Pro Comp	Don Gerardot
	Comp	David Majors
	Modified	Doc Dixon
	Super Stock	Bobby Warren
	Stock	Jerry McClanahan
1976	Top Fuel	Richard Tharp
	Funny Car	Don Prudhomme
	Pro Stock	Larry Lombardo
	Pro Comp	Brent Bramley
	Comp	Wayne Clapp
	Modified	Larry Kopp
	Super Stock	Robert Hutchison
	Stock	Scott Main

NHRA World Champions 1970–1980 *continued*

Year	Class	Driver
1977	Top Fuel	Shirley Muldowney
	Funny Car	Don Prudhomme
	Pro Stock	Don Nicholson
	Pro Comp	Dave Settles
	Comp	Dennis Ferrara
	Modified	Buddy Ingersoll
	Super Stock	Dave Boertman
	Stock	Stan Mizell
1978	Top Fuel	Kelly Brown
	Funny Car	Don Prudhomme
	Pro Stock	Bob Glidden
	Pro Comp	Bobby Cross
	Comp	Dennis Ferrara
	Modified	Jeff Leininger
	Super Stock	Bobby Warren
	Stock	Jerry McClanahan
1979	Top Fuel	Rob Bruins
	Funny Car	Raymond Beadle
	Pro Stock	Bob Glidden
	Pro Comp	Billy Williams
	Comp	Bob Newberry
	Modified	Garley Daniels
	Super Stock	Amy Faulk
	Stock	Ray Cook
1980	Top Fuel	Shirley Muldowney
	Funny Car	Raymond Beadle
	Pro Stock	Bob Glidden
	Pro Comp	Ken Veney
	Comp	Norwin Palmer
	Modified	David Hutchens
	Super Stock	Joe Scott
	Stock	Marlen Bogner

AHRA World Champions 1970–1980

Year	Class	Driver
1970	Top Fuel	John Wiebe
	Funny Car	Gene Snow
	Super Stock	Ronnie Sox
	GT 1	Kimball Bros.-Hill
	GT 2	Hielscher-Jones
	GT 3	Hiner-Miller
	Competition	Hahn-Turner
	Street	Hielscher-Atkins
	Top Stock	Tom Akin

AHRA World Champions 1970–1980 *continued*

Year	Class	Driver
1971	Top Fuel	Don Garlits
	Funny Car	Gene Snow
	Pro Super Stock	Jim Hayter
	GT 1	Tomlinson-Topletz
	GT 2	Gary Kimball
	Competition	Joe Williamson
	Street	Joe Williams
	Top Stock	Allen Patterson
1972	Top Fuel	Don Garlits
	Funny Car	Leroy Goldstein
	Pro Stock	Don Nicholson
	GT 1	Tomlinson-Topletz
	GT 2	Scott Shafiroff
	Competition	Don Toia
	Street	Joe Rundle
	Super Stock	John Greenwood
	Stock	Dennis Kucera
1973	Top Fuel	Don Garlits
	Funny Car	Don Schumacher
	Pro Stock	Dick Landy
	Competition	Walt Niesen
	Street	Pete Peery
	Super Stock	Allen Patterson
	Stock	Glenn Pittman
1974	Top Fuel	Don Garlits
	Funny Car	Don Prudhomme
	Pro Stock	Larry Huff
	Pro Comp	Dale Armstrong
	Modified	Walt Niesen
	Street	Whatley Bros.
	Super Stock	Gary Grame (Marlat & Grame)
	Stock	Glenn Erlandson
1975	Top Fuel	John Wiebe
	Funny Car	Tom McEwen
	Pro Stock	Ken Dondero
	Pro Comp	Wayne Stoeckel
	Modified	Walt Niesen
	Street	Ed Ponder
	Super Stock	Billy Ray
	Stock	Glenn Erlandson

AHRA World Champions 1970–1980 *continued*

1976	Top Fuel	John Wiebe
	Funny Car	Tom Hoover
	Pro Stock	Ken Dondero
	Pro Comp	Dion Stewart
	Top Comp	Mike McCloskey
	Modified Street	Jim Ruble
	Super Street	Bill Mitchell
	Super Stock	Larry Mitchell
	Stock	Dave Workman
1977	Top Fuel	Jeb Allen
	Funny Car	Tom Hoover
	Pro Stock	Larry Lombardo
	Pro Comp Dragster	Richard Ogg
	Pro Comp F/C	Mike Savage
	Top Comp	Mike McCloskey
	Modified Street	Donnie Anderson
	Super Street	Jim Williams
	Super Stock	Noel Zweigler
	Stock	Don Spencer
1978	Top Fuel	Don Garlits
	Funny Car	Gene Snow
	Pro Stock	Shelby Jester
	Pro Comp Dragster	Brian Raymer
	Pro Comp F/C	Simon Menzies
	Top Comp	Terry Green
	Modified Street	Larry Smith
	Super Street	Richard Wegner
	Super Stock	Roy Kempe
	Stock	Bob Bowe
1979	Top Fuel	Don Garlits
	Funny Car	Tom McEwen
	Pro Stock	Bobby Marriott/Lee Shepherd (tie)
	Pro Comp Dragster	Porter Donn
	Pro Comp F/C	Mike Savage
	Top Comp	Joe Williams
	Modified Street	Roy Kempe
	Super Street	Barry Shirley
	Super Stock	Larry Mitchell
	Stock	Rick Ducusin
	ET Stock	Jerry Stephens

AHRA World Champions 1970–1980 *continued*

1980	Top Fuel	Don Garlits
	Funny Car	Don Prudhomme
	Pro Stock	Shelby Jester
	Pro Comp Dragster	Porter Donn
	Pro Comp F/C	Richard Day
	Top Comp	Larry Smith
	Modified Street	Bill Mitchell
	Super Street	Wayne Smith
	Super Stock	Billy Ray
	Stock	Rick Ducusin
	ET Stock	Jerry Stephens

IHRA Pro Class World Champions 1974–1980

Year	*Class*	*Driver*
1974	Top Fuel	Dale Funk
	Funny Car	Ron Colson
	Pro Stock	Wayne Gapp
1975	Top Fuel	Don Garlits
	Funny Car	Raymond Beadle
	Pro Stock	Don Nicholson
1976	Top Fuel	Don Garlits
	Funny Car	Raymond Beadle
	Pro Stock	Bob Glidden
1977	Top Fuel	Don Garlits
	Funny Car	Dale Pulde
	Pro Stock	Lee Edwards
1978	Top Fuel	Clayton Harris
	Funny Car	Denny Savage
	Pro Stock	Lee Edwards
1979	Top Fuel	Connie Kalitta
	Funny Car	Kenny Bernstein
	Pro Stock	Warren Johnson
1980	Top Fuel	Jeb Allen
	Funny Car	Billy Meyer
	Pro Stock	Warren Johnson

KEITH BLACK
RACING ENGINES
PRE-STAGED
STAGED
GO NAVY

Additional books that may interest you...

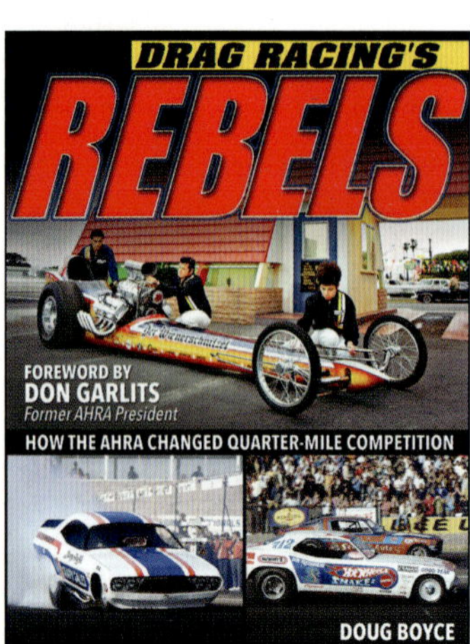

DRAG RACING'S REBELS: How the AHRA Changed Quarter-Mile Competition *by Doug Boyce*
In this first book ever published on the AHRA, get previously unrevealed stories about how the drivers, tracks, and sanctioning bodies operated in the golden era (and, as some argue, the most interesting era) of drag racing. 8.5 x 11", 160 pgs, 450 b/w & color photos, Sftbd. ISBN 9781613257661 Part # CT691

PONTIAC PERFORMANCE 1960-1974: The Era of the Super Duty, H.O., & Ram Air Drag & Muscle Cars *by Don Keefe*
Pontiac drag cars ushered in the creation of the muscle car, creating the most exciting era of American automotive history! 8.5 x 11", 160 pgs, 329 color photos, Sftbd. ISBN 9781613257777 Part # CT694

DRAG RACING'S WARREN "THE PROFESSOR" JOHNSON: The Cars, People, & Wins Behind His Pro Stock Success *by Kelly Wade*
Go behind the scenes for a look at Warren Johnson's path to becoming The Professor of Pro Stock. This book illuminates the life and career of one of the most prolific engine builders and racers ever to compete. 8.5 x 11", 176 pgs, 350 photos, Sftbd. ISBN 9781613255704 Part # CT672

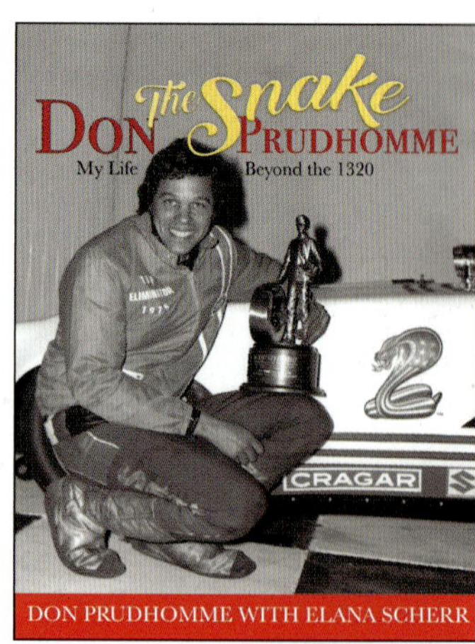

DON "THE SNAKE" PRUDHOMME: My Life Beyond the 1320 *by Don Prudhomme & Elana Scherr*
Don "The Snake" Prudhomme reveals for the first time ever his incredible life and career on and off of the drag strip. He shares lessons about business, life, and the importance of family. 8.5 x 11", 176 pgs, 400 photos, Hdbd. ISBN 9781613255186 Part # CT662

www.cartechbooks.com or 1-800-551-4754